IMAGES
of America

GRIDLEY

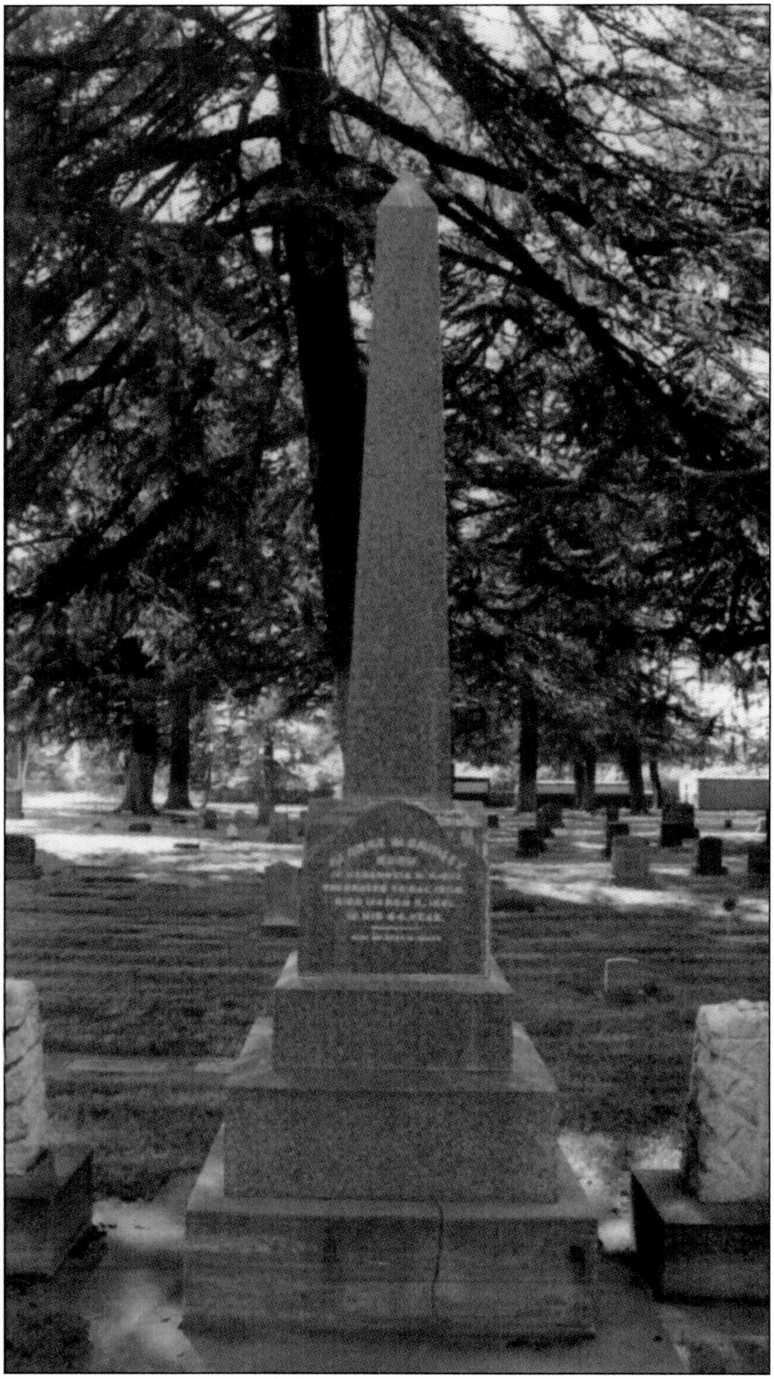

Interest in California pioneers is not just curiosity, but also an expression of gratitude to these forerunners of civilization in the far West. One representative pioneer is George Washington Gridley, in honor of whom the town of Gridley in Butte County was named. In 1850, Gridley undertook to drive some sheep and cattle across the plains to California, and although he lost every head, he made a safe arrival and settled on the land where the town of Gridley now stands.

ON THE COVER: Simpson & Sons were blacksmiths, wagon makers, and horseshoers. Later, the business became a garage when the automobile became popular.

IMAGES
of America

GRIDLEY

RuthAnn King and Lisa Van De Hey
with the Gridley Museum

ARCADIA
PUBLISHING

ISBN 978-1-4671-3359-3

Published by Arcadia Publishing
Charleston, South Carolina

Printed in the United States of America

Library of Congress Control Number: 2015930547

For all general information, please contact Arcadia Publishing:
Telephone 843-853-2070
Fax 843-853-0044
E-mail sales@arcadiapublishing.com
For customer service and orders:
Toll-Free 1-888-313-2665

Visit us on the Internet at www.arcadiapublishing.com

Contents

Acknowledgments

This book is about the time from when Gridley was young until it reached middle age. Choosing photographs was an education. How do you choose? Which ones are the most important, and which ones will capture the viewer's interest? What if we couldn't get enough photos to make this worthwhile? Once we decided which images we wanted to use, did we have enough information to write interesting captions? As we began to collect, we became more excited to get it done. Then, life got in the way and we had to ask for an extension. The next deadline came, and we lost power and data in a freak thunderstorm. Starting again, we ended up with this, the finished product of eclectic photographs we thought were interesting.

RuthAnn and Lisa wish to express gratefulness to the Gridley Museum for allowing us to make our headquarters at the museum office and for putting up with our frustrations. Special thanks go to Marie Wheeler and Julie Ricci; without you, this book would still be stuck in cyberspace somewhere.

We are happy to share our findings of history almost forgotten. The photographs used in this book are from the Gridley Museum, the *Gridley Herald*, the Butte County Historical Society, the William David Burleson collection, and several private collections with the owners' consent. This has been a challenging endeavor. Thank you, Arcadia Publishing, for your patience and guidance along the way.

Introduction

Among the many thousands of gold-hungry men who came to California during the years of the Gold Rush, there were men of vision who strode into the Sacramento Valley and saw a future every bit as golden as the Mother Lode Country promised. Such a man was George Washington Gridley. His thoughts may have been diverted from the gold that lay hidden in the mountains to the riches that could be brought forth from the earth that lay before him.

With courage and that vision, he set the stage for the stream of agricultural wealth that has come forth from the valley ever since. Having left his family comfortable in Illinois, Gridley arrived in Sacramento during a cholera epidemic. Many people contracted the disease, but Gridley, one of the lucky ones, headed north and found the upper valley and his future home.

He returned to Illinois to visit his family in 1852. Not being able to shake the dream of California, he purchased a band of sheep and set out again for the land he would claim as his own. He settled north of the buttes and established the agriculture empire that was to become his monument.

Within a few years, Gridley became one of the wealthiest and largest landowners in the northern part of the state. With the coming of the California and Oregon Railroad, Gridley had 116,000 head of sheep and 25,000 acres of land. He talked the railroad officials into building a station on the site that was to become Gridley. As added encouragement to the railroad, Gridley erected a huge warehouse nearby in which to store his wool for future shipment.

When the railroad surveyor laid out the future town, it became apparent that Gridley should have the opportunity to name the new community. This new town became Gridley Station. Late in the 1870s, Gridley's health began to fail, and by early 1881, he was physically and mentally drained. He passed away on March 7, 1881.

After the many fires that Gridley suffered, the subject of becoming incorporated was discussed. The need to improve fire protection and establish a municipal water distribution system was the principal reason. These discussions started as early as 1891. The only water available came from the fire wells at major intersections, and the equipment was a steam pumper and a hand pumper. These were not effective.

It was William Davis Burleson, the *Gridley Herald*'s editor, who championed the cause for incorporation. A proposal for a water-distribution system made by Burleson was discussed and approved by many of the property owners and citizens of the community. Edward Biggs, manager of the Rideout Bank's Gridley branch, had contended that "sooner or later a bonded indebtedness would be fastened upon the town" if it were to incorporate.

Biggs asserted that if a municipal tax were added to the present levies, it would "discourage investment" in the community. Also against incorporation were Dr. Lewis Quentin Thompson and George Wickman. Burleson, Biggs, and livery stable owner Charles Henry Block were appointed to a committee to draft bylaws.

The fire that finally convinced Gridley it should become an incorporated city was discovered about 11:30 p.m. on July 9, 1905, in some outhouses on the alley between Stone's block of commercial buildings on Virginia Street and Henry Block's livery stable on Kentucky Street. When the pumps were started, it was discovered the valves did not work, and there was not a drop of water to be had. This allowed the flames to spread. The old 1887 hand pumper was brought out, but its single stream of water was no match for the flames. The steamer was first taken to the corner of Hazel and Virginia Streets where there was a fire well. In a few minutes, steam was up and the engine started, but it would not pump water.

It was reported that the fire could have been extinguished without serious loss had the steamer been in working order. It took 45 minutes to repair it, but by then $100,000 in damage had already been done by the flames. Of this, it was estimated that only $55,350 was covered by insurance. It was then that Burleson urged the residents be allowed to vote on incorporation. "It is a fact," he said, "that there are a large number of the people of the community who desire to see the town incorporated, and they should be allowed to have an opportunity to express themselves." Encouraged no doubt by the economic benefit anticipated from completion of the Butte County Canal to Gridley that summer and the coincident subdivision of large land holdings into small farms, the town's property owners lost no time in preparing to rebuild the burnt-out district.

"Gridley is rising from her ashes," the *Herald* proclaimed in headlining a story in its August 25, 1901, issue recounting progress being made. So the town was soon ready to take up the incorporation issue in earnest. A petition asking the board of supervisors to call a special election for a vote on the question of incorporation was being circulated and liberally signed.

The names of the signers and the proposed boundaries of the city were published in the *Gridley Herald* on September 29, 1905, as part of the notice of the hearing on the petition that was to be held before the board of supervisors at the courthouse in Oroville. A delay was caused by the reticence of two supervisors, William Rutherford of the third district and Edgar Wilson of the fifth district, who objected to the loss of the $3,000 in license fees then being paid to the county by Gridley saloons.

After much discussion, the board of supervisors finally agreed to call a special election on November 16, 1905. Firemen's Hall was designated as the polling place. At the election, voters approved incorporation of their town as a city by a vote of 83-58.

The first board of trustees elected were William Brown, president; Thomas Benning Channon, Henry Block, Edward Fagan, and Joseph Hollis, trustees; Edward Ernest Biggs (manager of the Rideout Bank where the first meeting was held), treasurer; Charles Miller, city marshal; and Fred Moesch, city clerk.

Incorporation did not discourage investment. Buildings added after incorporation include the Gridley State Bank in 1909, the new Rideout Bank in 1910, the Carnegie Library in 1916, city hall in 1925, and any number of stores and shops that filled in the spaces in the business center of town. Many of the nicer homes had been built on Hazel Street, and others soon followed. The residential areas fanned out and filled the open spaces rather rapidly.

One

Gridley in the Beginning

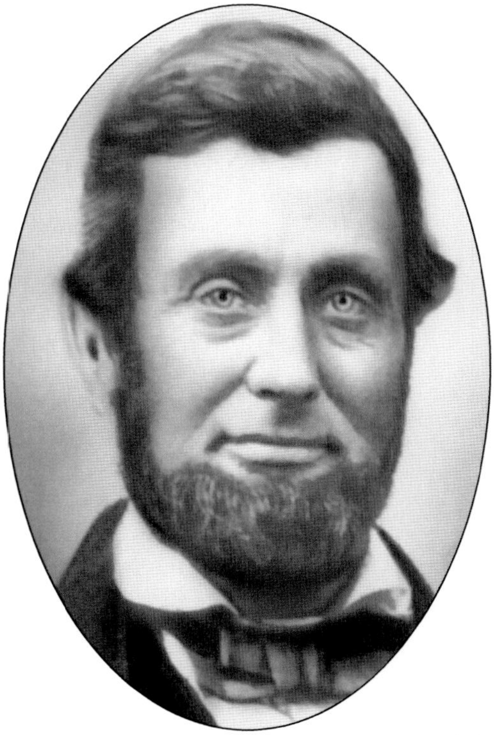

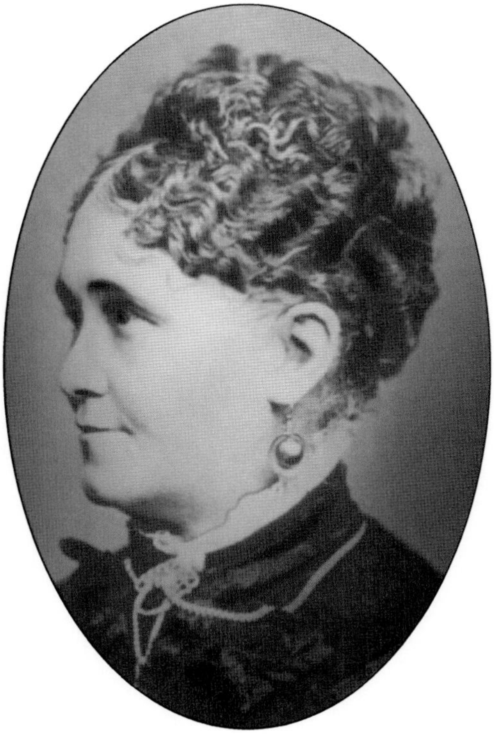

George Washington Gridley (1817–1881) left Galena, Illinois, to cross the plains and come to California. He returned to Illinois in 1852, and in the spring began the trip again, bringing a band of sheep and engaging in sheep ranching. He settled four miles north of the buttes, sending for his wife, Helen, and son Charles. The railroad company laid out the town and asked Gridley to name it. (Both, courtesy of Gridley Museum.)

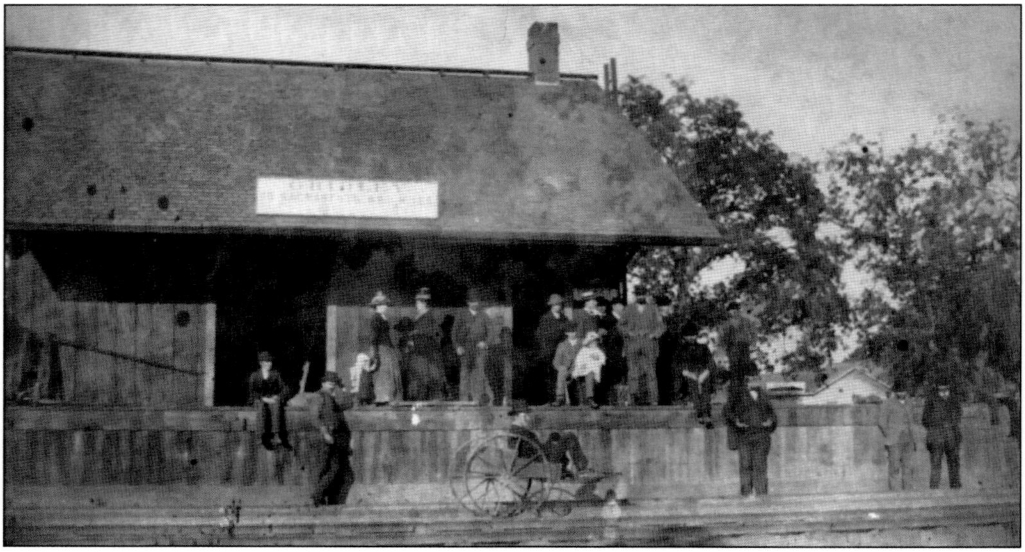

Although the community of Gridley was first laid out in 1870, its origin goes back to 20 years before, in 1850, when George Washington Gridley first settled on the site of the present community. With the completion of the Central Pacific Railroad line to Gridley, the community was established and laid out by a surveyor working for the railroad. (Courtesy of Gridley Museum.)

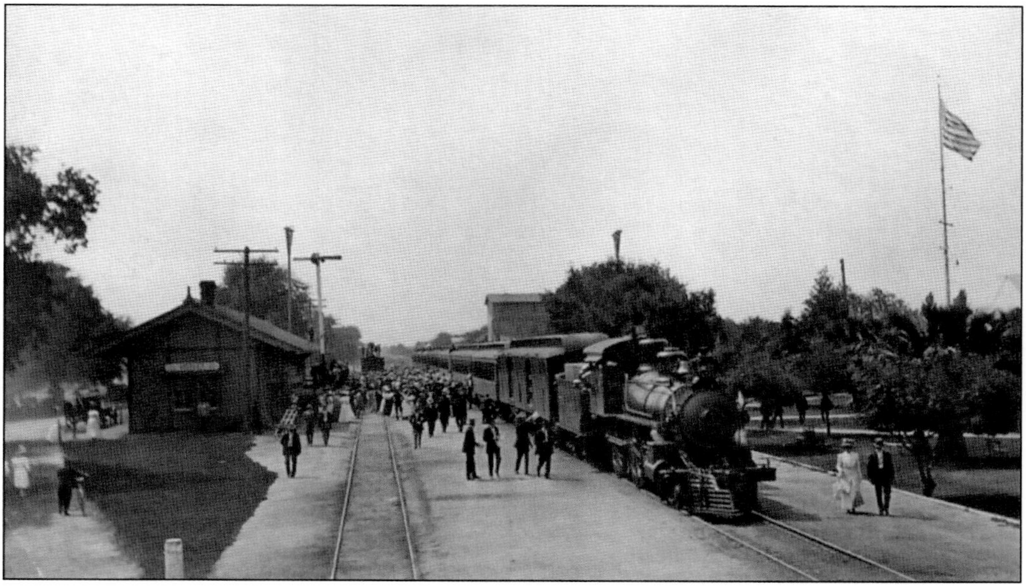

In 1893, the Southern Pacific Railroad depot replaced the diminutive station building that was erected here after the California and Oregon branch of the Central Pacific Railroad, a predecessor, was completed through Gridley in the spring of 1870. This building included a passenger waiting room, a baggage room, and space for storing freight. There was an office for the station agent and his assistant, who sold tickets. (Courtesy of Gridley Museum.)

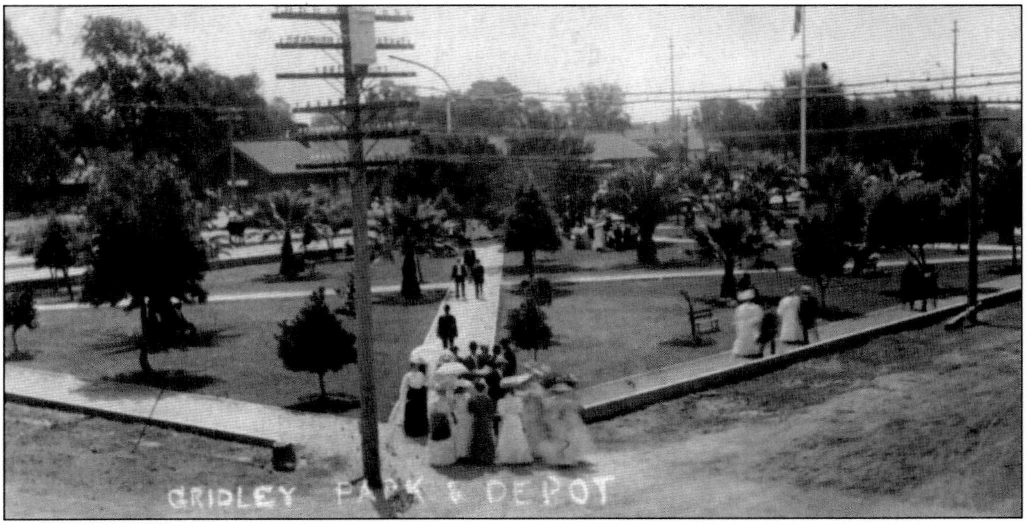

The city plaza, located just west of the depot, was to be owned and maintained by the railroad company. It was a shady block of trees and lawn where a tired wayfarer might stop and rest. (Both, courtesy of Gridley Museum.)

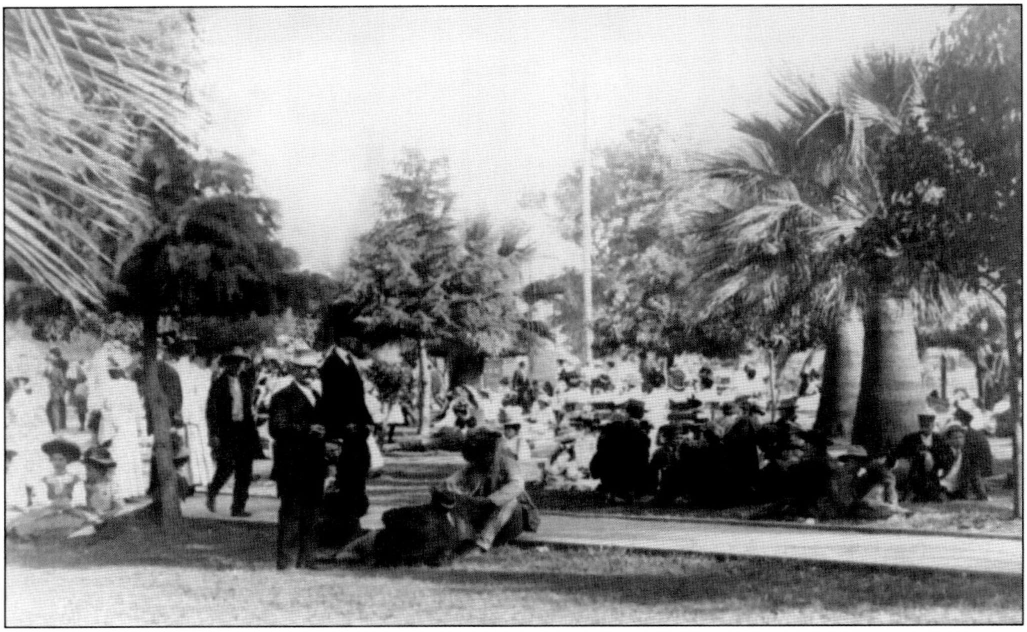

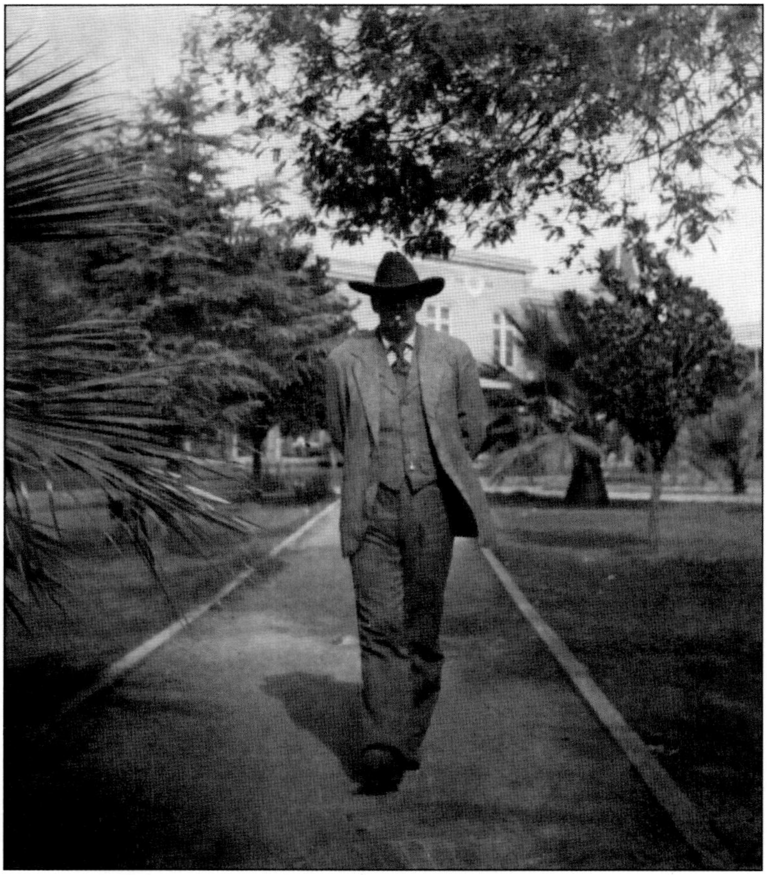

The city plaza in downtown Gridley was set aside and laid out by the railroad in 1870. This shady spot of trees, lawns, and graveled paths was a popular place for all ages both at lunchtime, in the late afternoon, and after school. This area was convenient for travelers to rest while waiting for the next train. On cannery picnic day, this area was always crowded with people meeting family and friends. (Both, courtesy of Gridley Museum.)

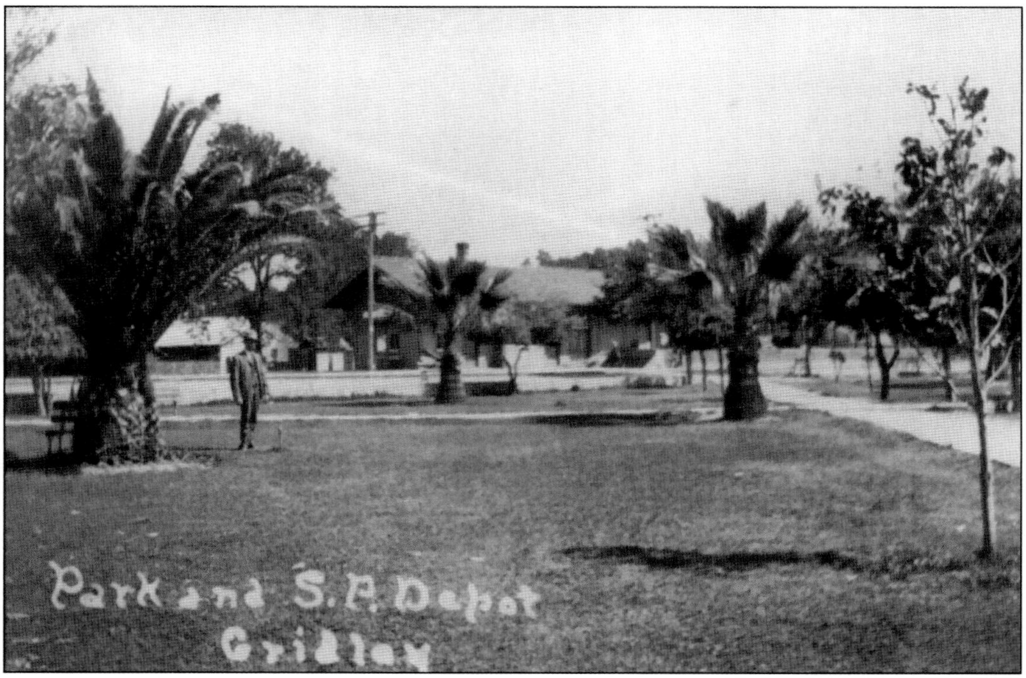

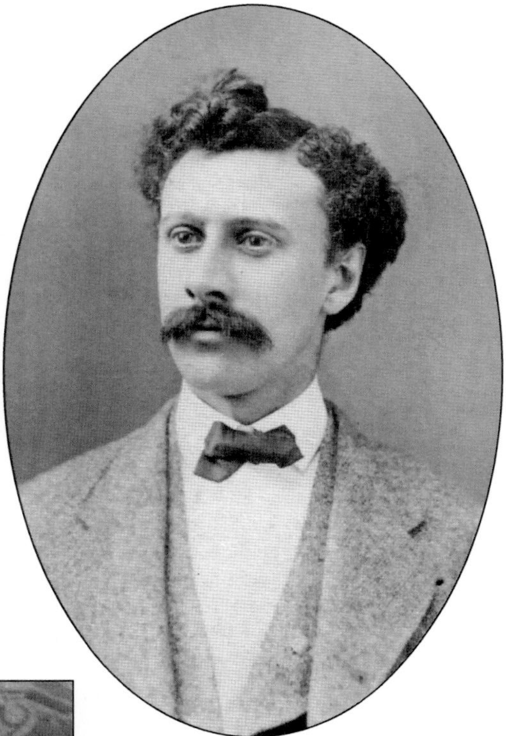

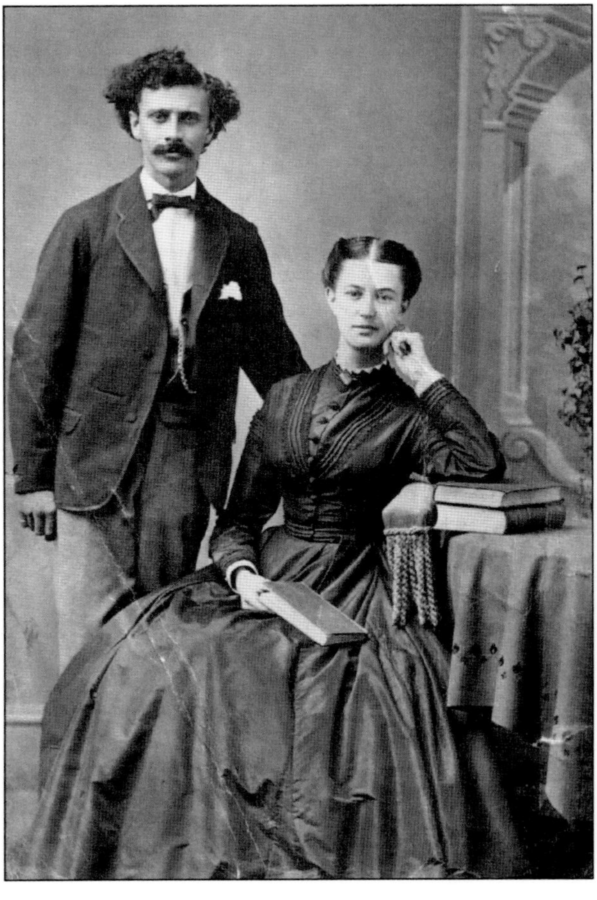

Robert Martin Beebee was a hardware merchant and dealt in stoves, ranges, and tinware as well as pumps and other machinery. A city directory also states that crockery and agricultural implements were part of his wares for sale. His wife, Gussie, was a music teacher. Beebee was also involved in bringing electricity to Gridley and stated at the regular city meeting of October 1, 1906, that he would charge for 32 candlepower at $1 per month for temporary time and 50 candlepower at $1.50 per month. The board voted that Beebee put in 10 or 12 lights temporarily at $1.50 per month as designated and the city furnish the lamps. He also owned the opera house on Ohio Street. (Both, courtesy of Butte County Historical Society)

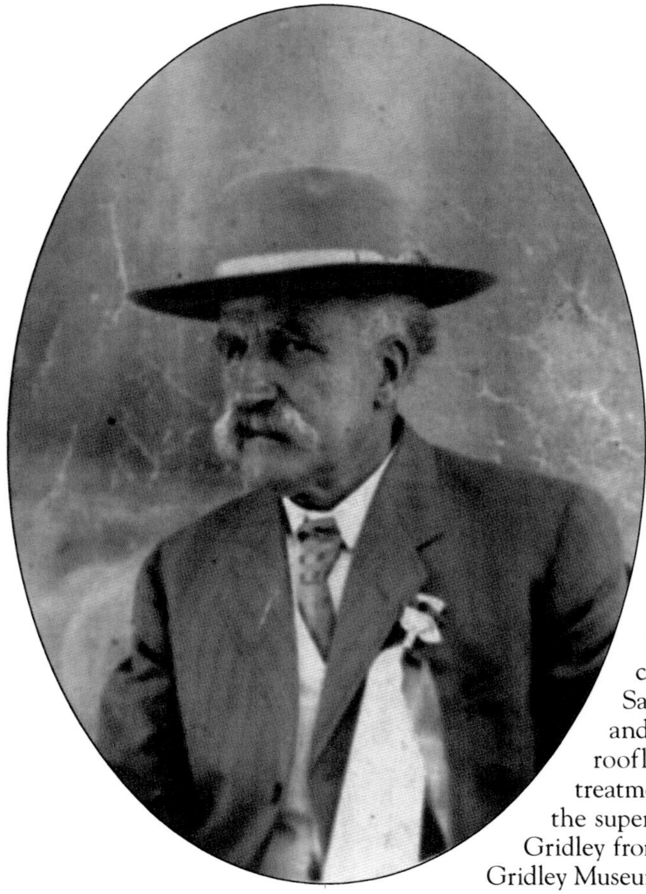

The home below was built around 1910 by John Palmer, who was a carpenter/contractor. He and his wife, Sarah, and children, George, Josephine, and Jodie, lived there. The interesting roofline, pillared porch, and window treatments are charming. Palmer served as the superintendent of streets for the city of Gridley from 1909 to 1916. (Both, courtesy of Gridley Museum.)

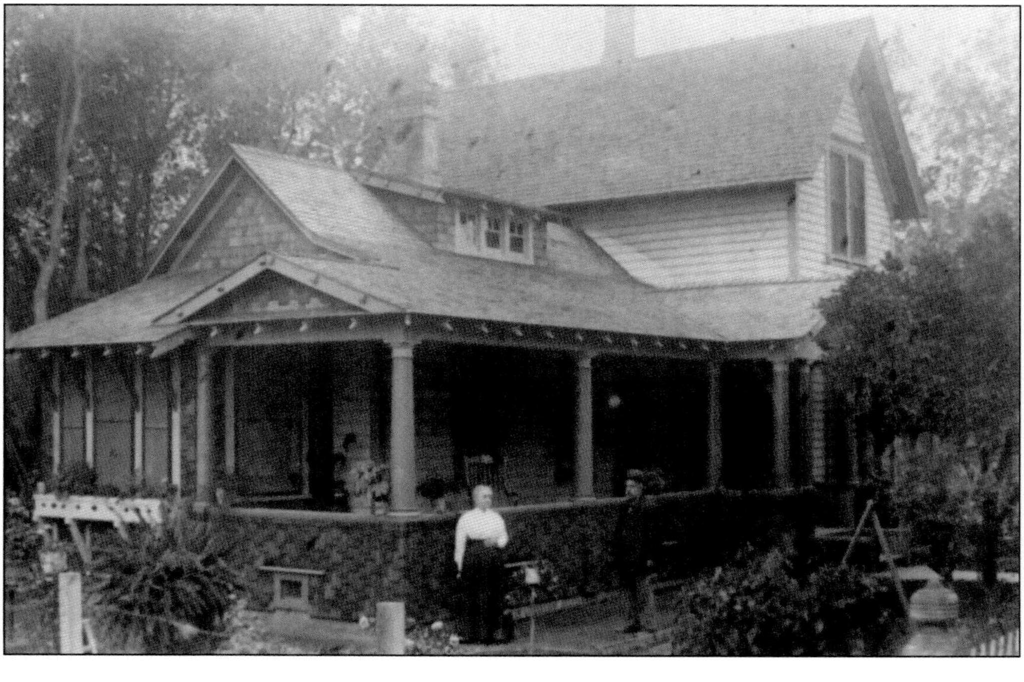

Michael Jason King, born in County Westmeath, Ireland, came to America via Faribault, Minnesota, where he married Alice Ryan. After arriving, King settled 10 miles northwest of Gridley, where he took up a government claim of 160 acres. This he farmed to grain until 1900, when he settled in Gridley on account of his wife's health. His children included six sons and five daughters. (Courtesy of Evelyn King Briggs.)

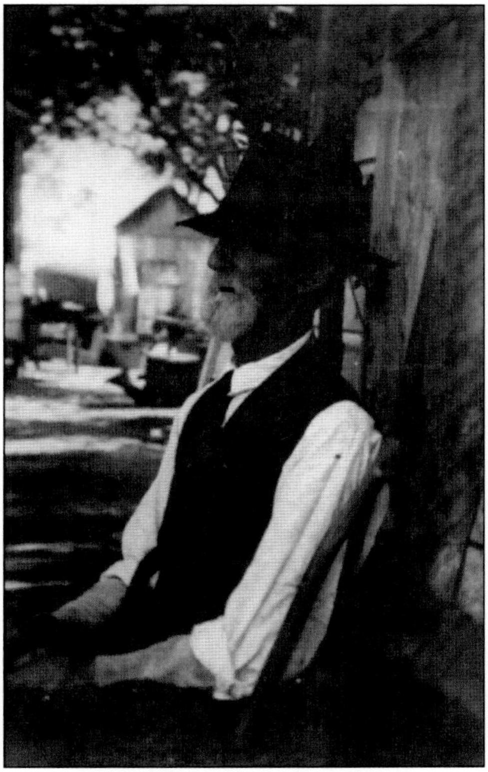

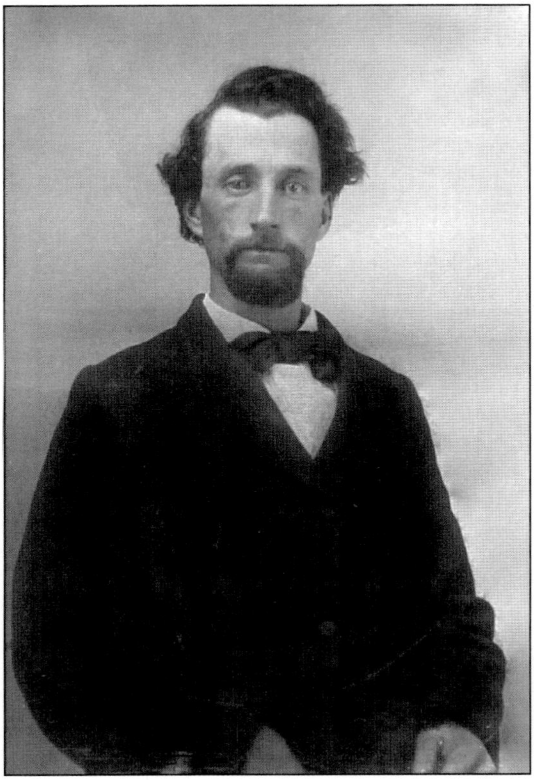

John Francis King, educated in Minnesota and Biggs schools, worked with his father and brothers. At age 22, he bought 160 acres seven miles west of Gridley. He sold it at a good price and then invested in 20 acres five miles west of Gridley, which he devoted to wheat, barley, and rice. With his profits, he started a store, King's Grocery, next to his home in Gridley. (Courtesy of Evelyn King Briggs.)

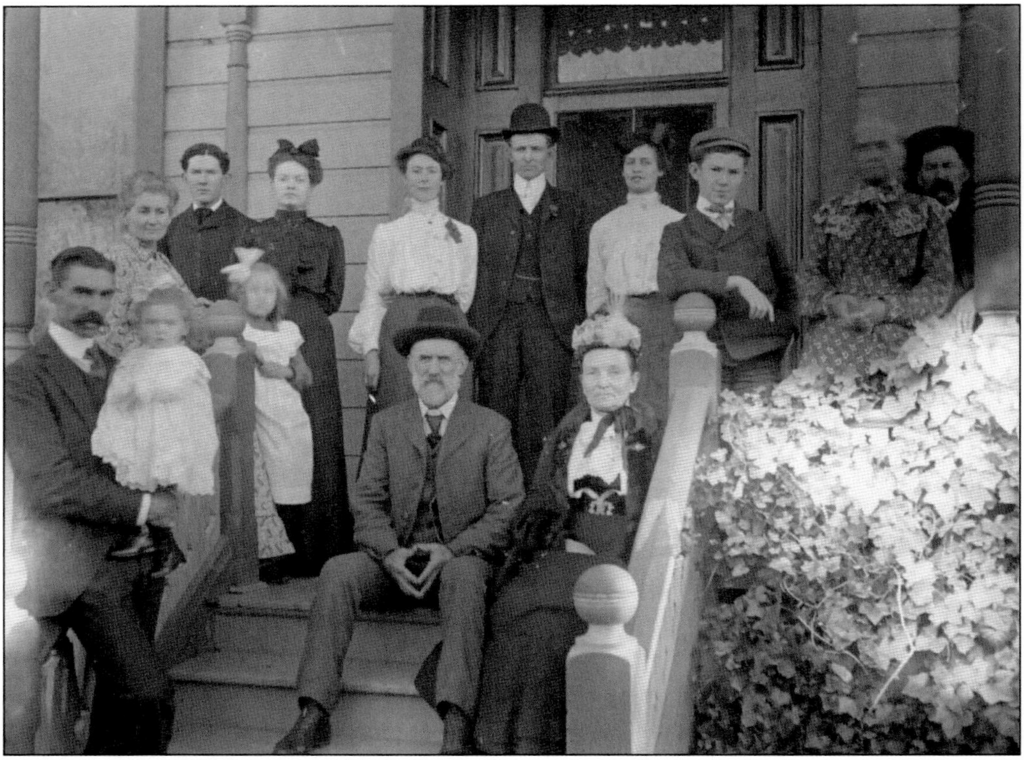

When the William Brown family went to church on Sunday, they practically were the congregation. Brown, the first mayor of Gridley, had his home on Sycamore Street. This photograph was taken shortly after the turn of the 20th century and represents four generations. Brown (seated on steps) was a butcher by trade and owned the Gridley Meat Market on Virginia Street, and was also the proprietor of the Leland Hotel. (Courtesy of Butte County Historical Society.)

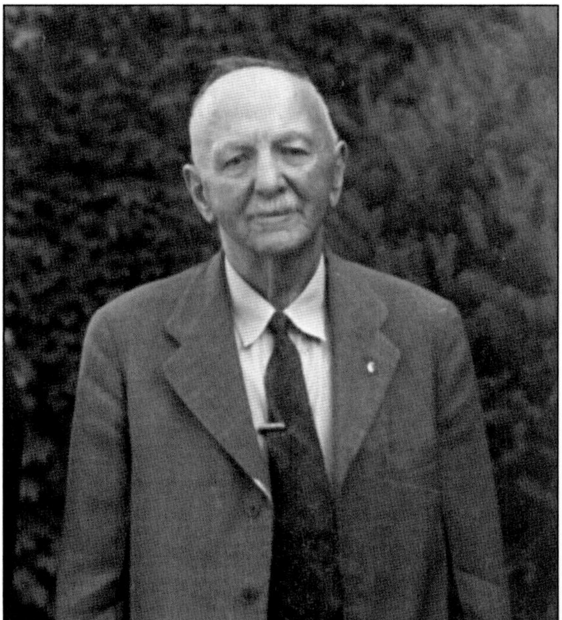

Thomas Benning Channon served as a trustee of the newly incorporated city of Gridley for 16 years. "Uncle Tommy," as he was affectionately known in Gridley, began dry farming exclusively and grew grain on more than 5,000 acres in Butte and Sutter Counties. In 1906, with a partner, he purchased the Gridley Warehouse. He sold his interest in 1938 and retired. He died eight days short of his 100th birthday. (Courtesy of Jean Channon.)

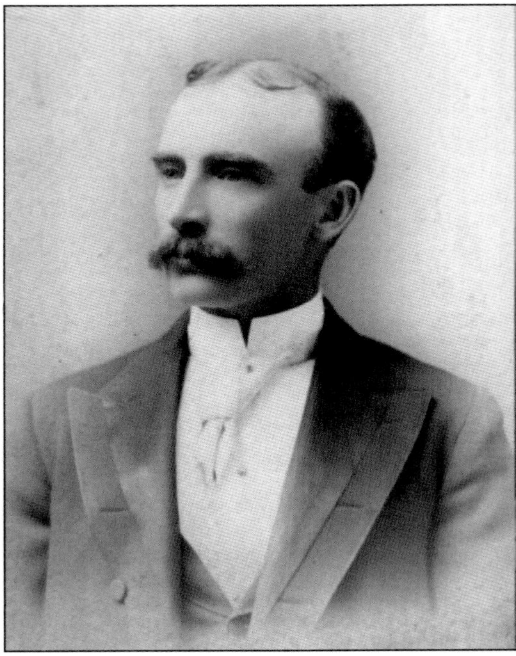

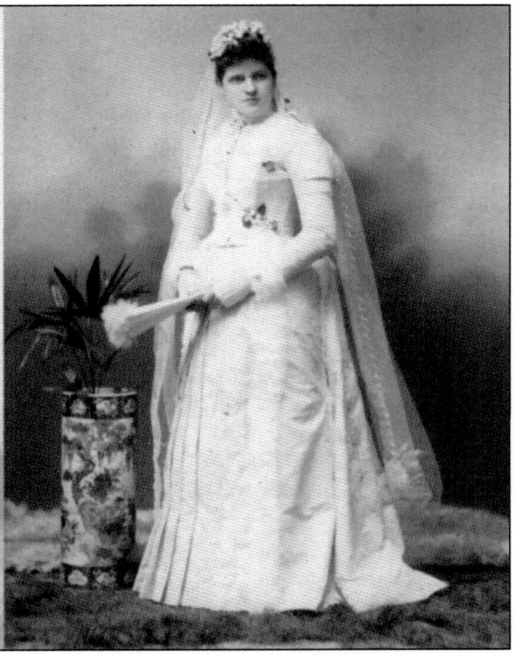

John Franklin Shaeffer was born in 1858 on his family's ranch on West Biggs-Gridley Road. His schooling consisted of West Liberty School, Chico High School, and the Business College in Oakland. After his marriage to Malinda Amelia Aulman in 1899, they lived on the ranch and leased 2,000 acres, raising cattle and grain. Shaeffer loved baseball and managed the Norman baseball team. All his hired hands had to be good ball players. After moving into town, the Shaeffers established and operated the Ford dealership and garage, later selling to Jack Frazier. Malinda built two houses on Hazel Street with money she earned from selling eggs. Both were active in civic, social, political, and fraternal organizations. They were the parents of five children: Irma, John, George, Lawrence, and Enola. Below is the Shaeffer home on Hazel Street. (Both, courtesy of Tyrone Shaeffer.)

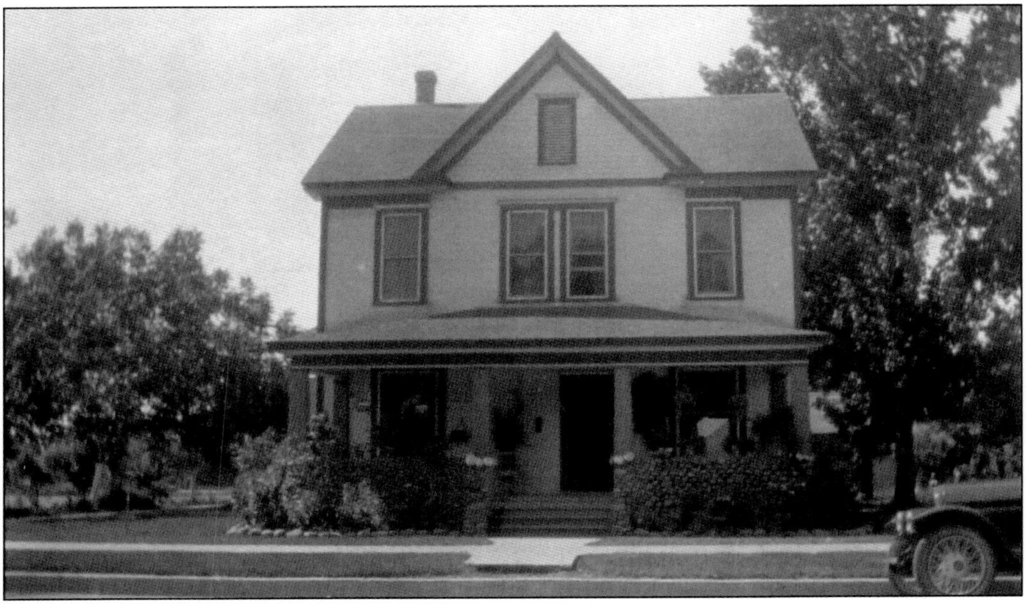

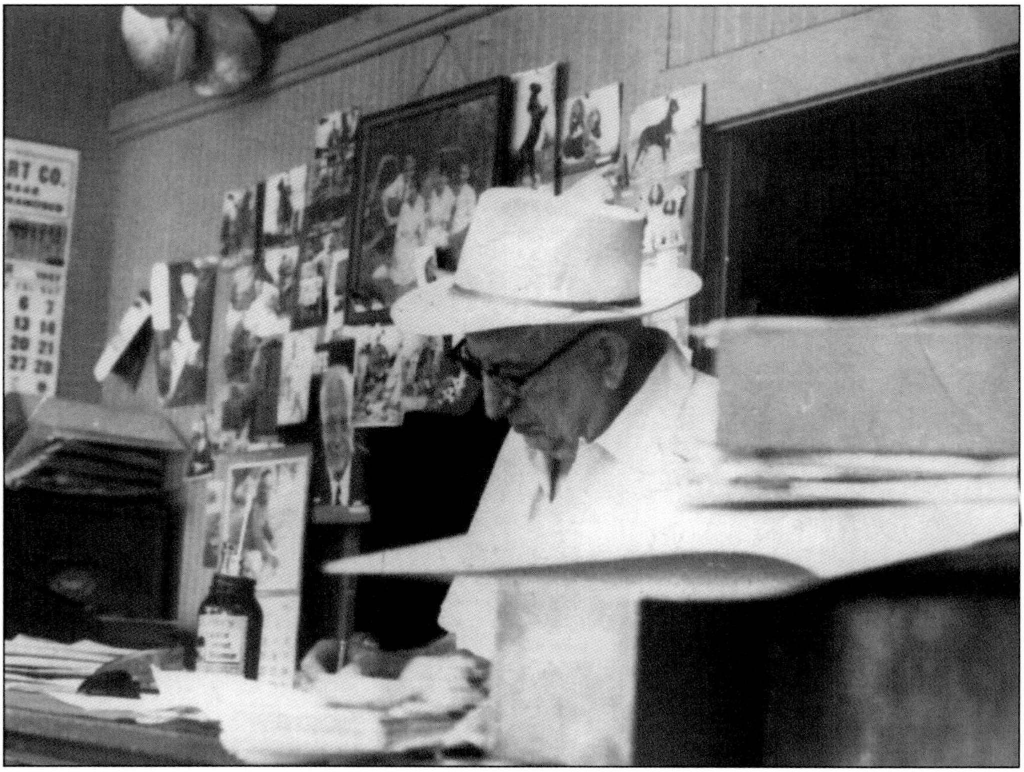

William Davis Burleson arrived in Gridley in October 1897 and was hired as the *Gridley Herald*'s editor and manager just two months after the newspaper plant had been completely destroyed by fire. Burleson rebuilt the newspaper at just 27 years of age, after being in the business only 10 years. He purchased the newspaper in 1908 and when he died in 1936, had gained a wide reputation as an editorial writer. Burleson was instrumental in promoting the Gridley Colonies, which surrounded the town. The very first Burleson home (below) was on Kentucky Street. Pictured above is Charles Burleson, the son of William Davis Burleson. (Both, courtesy of the *Gridley Herald*.)

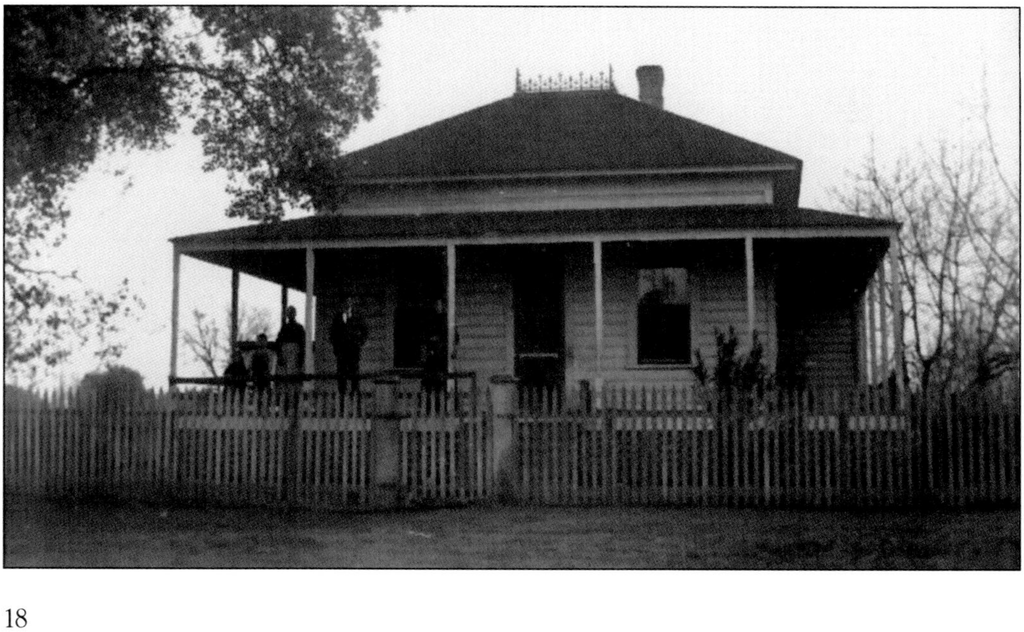

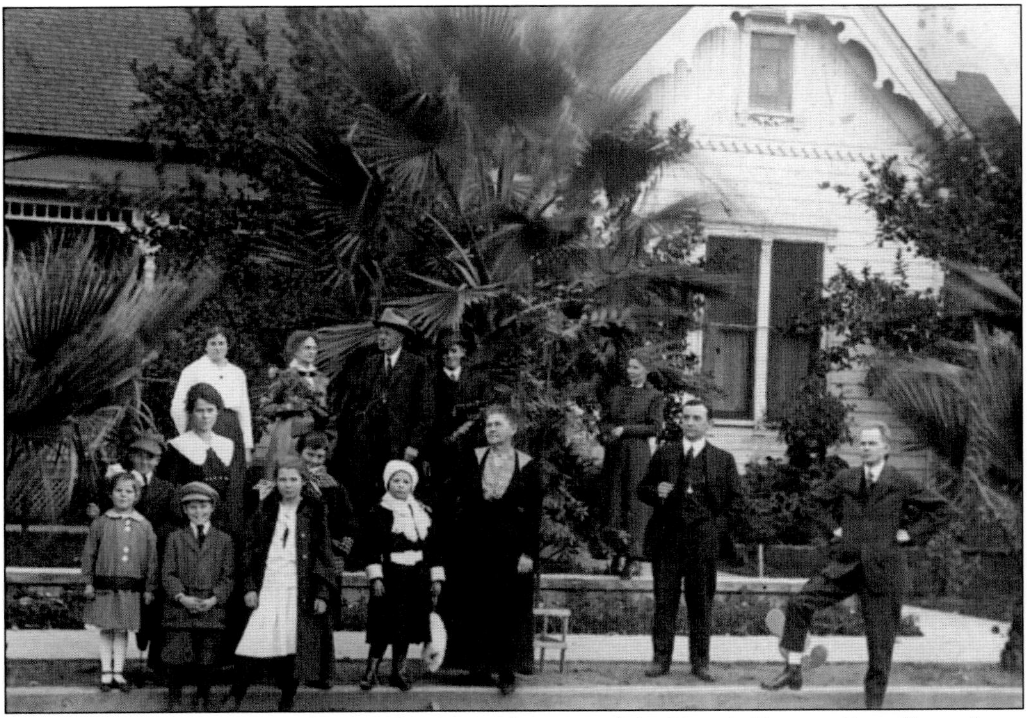

Henry Clay Veatch was a real estate developer who opened the Veatch Tract in Oroville, and was subsequently honored by having a street named for him. He bought property in Gridley about 1905–1908, including a house at 676 Vermont Street. He moved his family after considerable remodeling. Veatch is pictured here with his home, immediate family, and granddaughter Dorothy Crum Cassady (third from left in the front row). (Courtesy of Troy Mendenhall.)

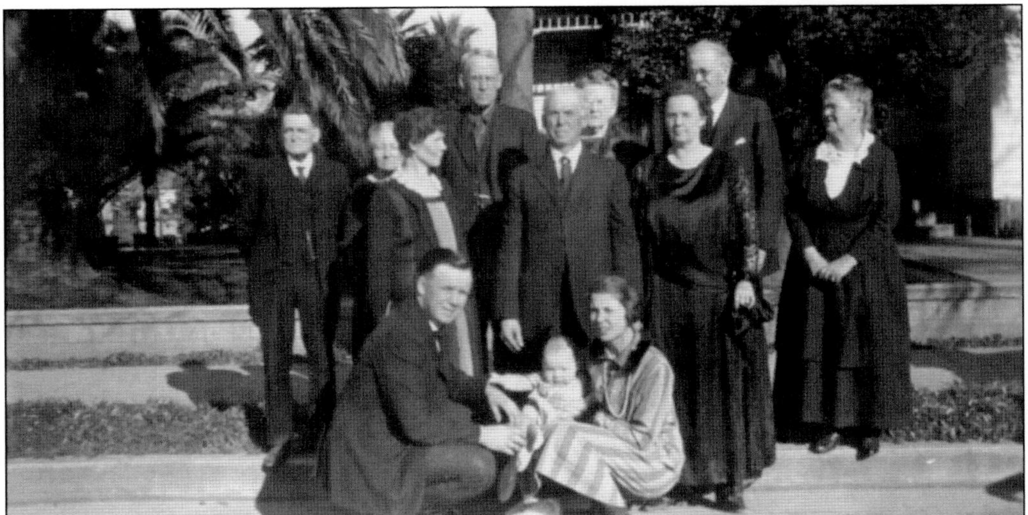

The Veatch family is again gathered at home with the first great-grandchild, Marvin Joseph Cassady Jr. His parents, Marvin Joseph and Dorothy May Cassady, are in front kneeling. The great-grandparents are Arthur and Ella Crum, James and Helen Barker, and Mary and Henry Veatch. The grandparents are Mary Crum and Alexander and Mable Cassady. (Courtesy of RuthAnn Cassady King.)

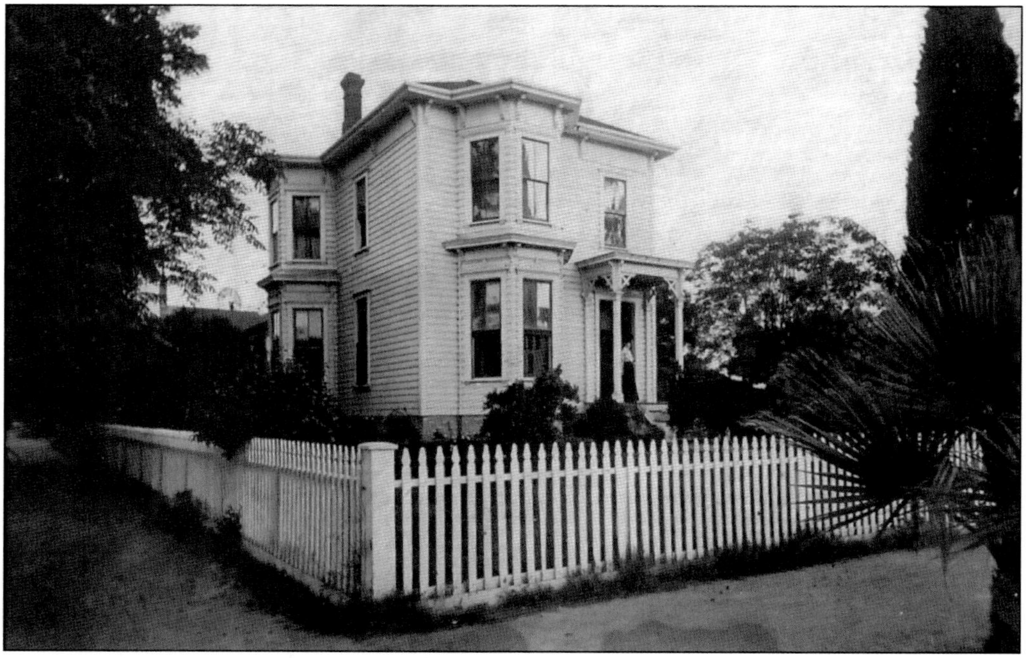

In 1877, John Boyles built what is often referred to as the Block Home at the corner of Hazel and Maine Streets. Henry Block owned and operated the Gridley Livery Stable and worked as an undertaker. Block served on the board of trustees from 1905 to 1908. He and his wife, Nora, had three sons, two of whom became dentists. The third took over the Block Funeral Home. (Courtesy of Gridley Museum.)

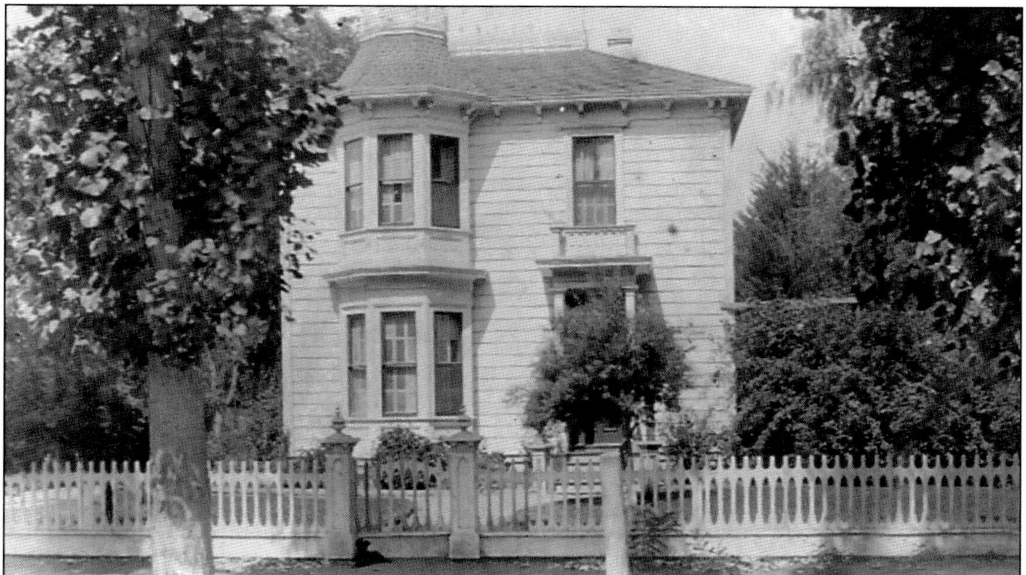

Elwood Victor and Norma DeRuchie lived in this beautiful home at 1015 Hazel Street on the corner of Ohio Street. Victor was born in Gridley on January 25, 1895. He attended Gridley schools, graduating from high school in 1913. He was an electrician by trade and was appointed superintendent of the Gridley Municipal Plant in June 1918, where he had full charge of the Gridley electrical plant and water works. (Courtesy of Gridley Museum.)

This Queen Anne Victorian is reported to have been built by a Mr. Sperry for his wife. In 1919, Frank William Enos bought the home and raised his family there. Enos's daughter Alverde lived there until she married Spencer Robinson. It is believed to be the first home in town with an upstairs bathroom. (Courtesy of Spencer Robinson.)

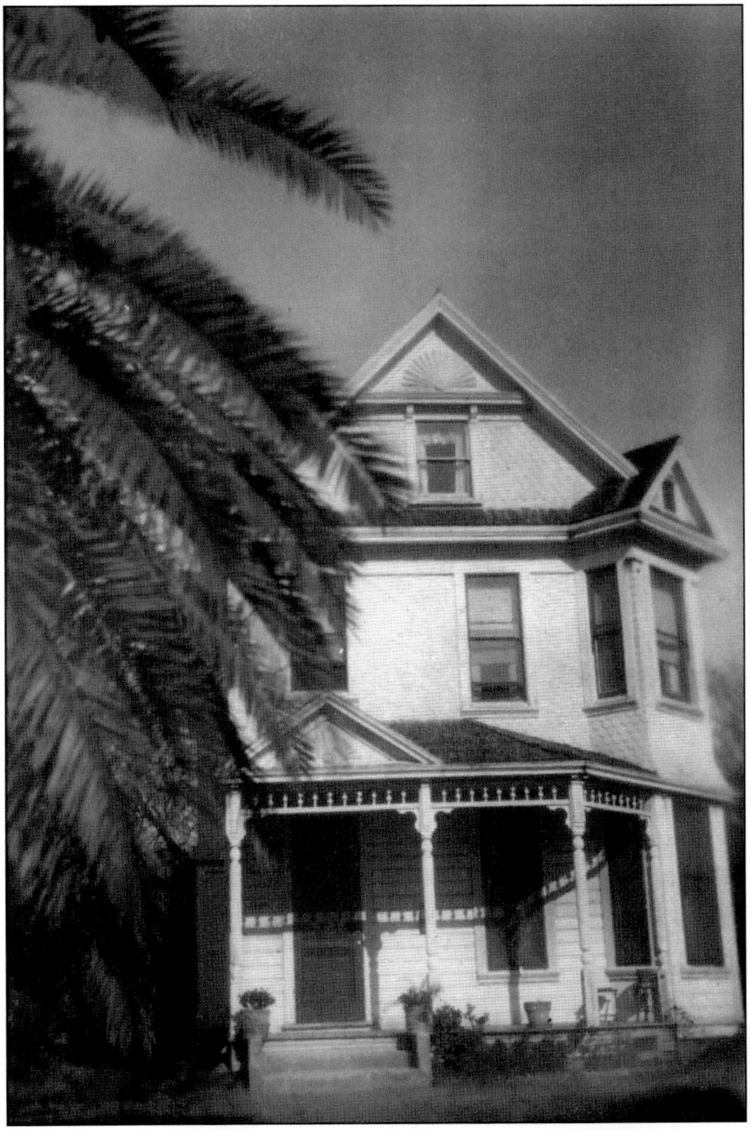

This property was acquired on March 5, 1872, from the Central Pacific Railroad by John Boyles and James Trayner for a sum of $4,000. The house was built in the 1890s and sold to Ida (Cable) and Edward Schirmer, early pioneers in the area. Their daughter Esther married Frank Jefferson Moore. She would not leave her aging parents, so she and Frank lived in their home and cared for them. (Courtesy of Frank Stenzel.)

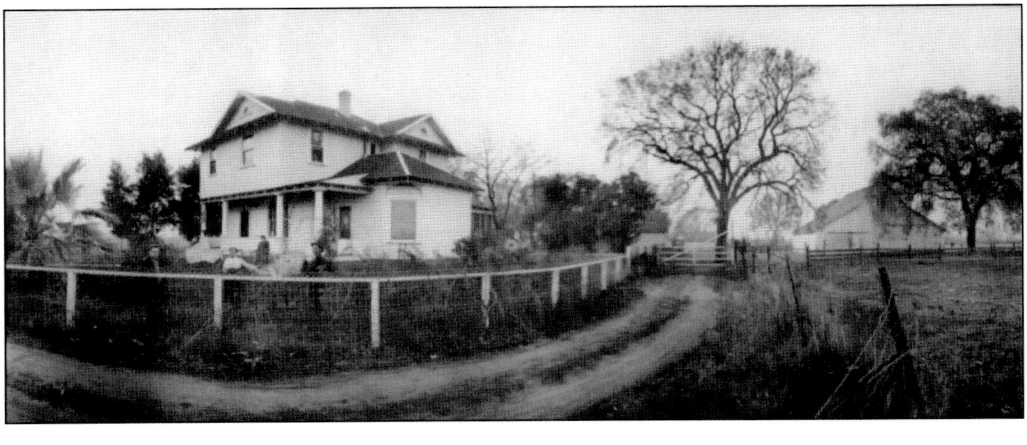

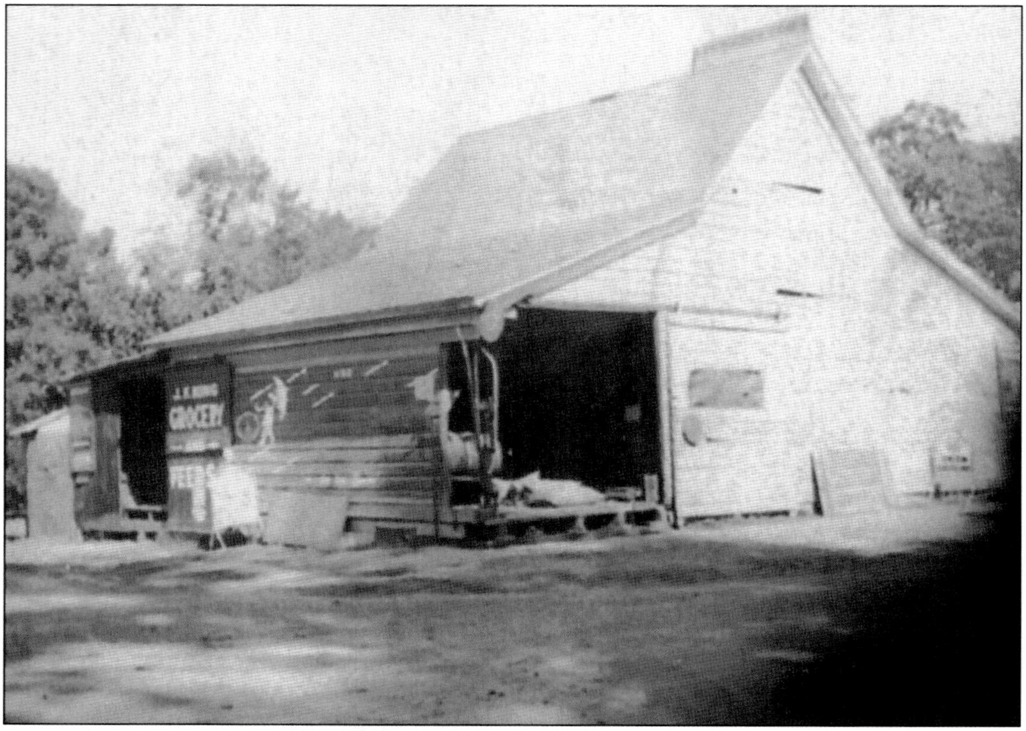

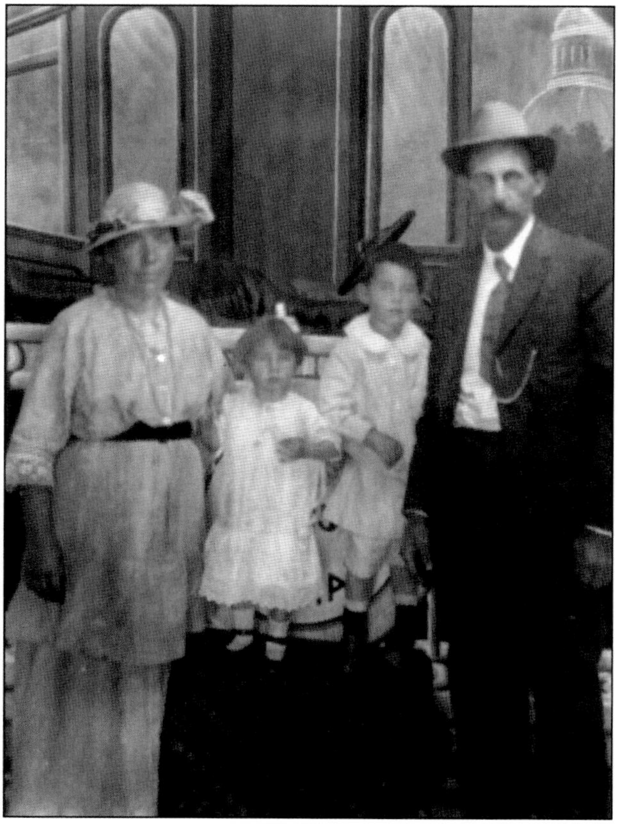

Romance happened when John Francis King began to correspond with Catherine O'Rourke, the daughter of his cook Michael O'Rourke in Belfast, Ireland. After a time, he sent for her to come to the United States to marry him. When she arrived in 1909, he met her in Sacramento, and they were married there in the cathedral. Catherine and John are pictured at left with two of their children, Alice Elizabeth and Leo Emmett. The barn pictured above was next to their home and advertised King's Grocery. (Both, courtesy of Evelyn King Briggs.)

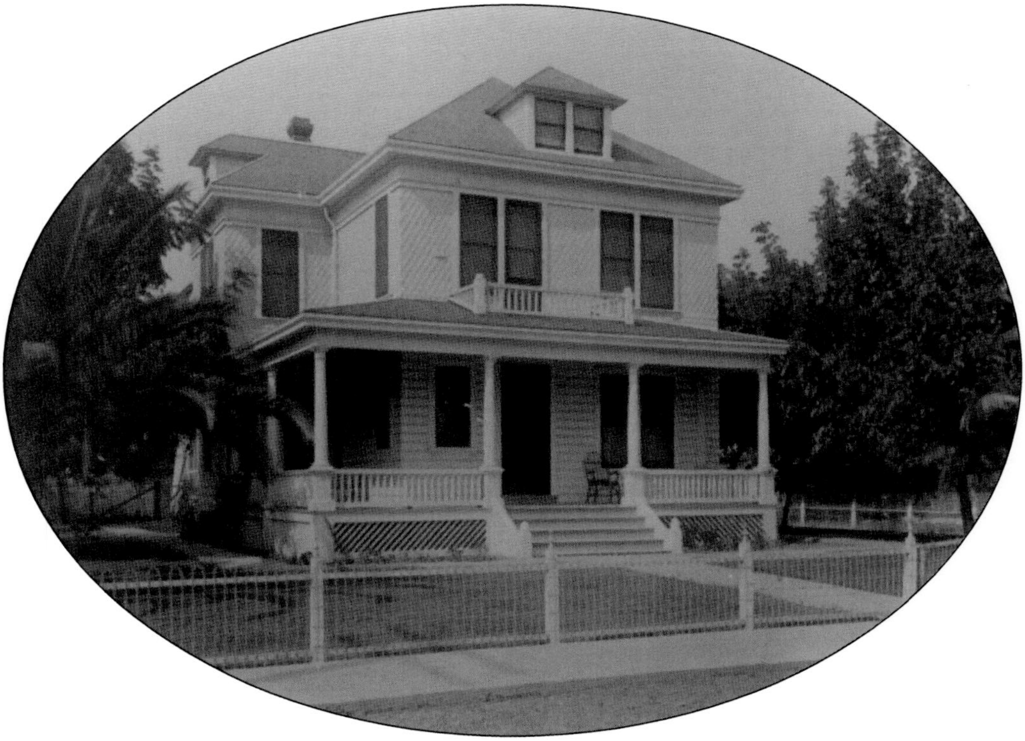

This home is believed to have been built in 1902 by Dr. G.L. Evans and his wife. Dr. Evans passed away in 1913, and Mrs. Evans sold the property to Loreto Antonio "Tony" and Nellie Golden Panecaldo for $4,500 on easy terms because she liked Tony. He was newly immigrated from Italy and just getting his bakery business started in Gridley. The original grounds took up half of the block from Hazel Street to Spruce Street between Lincoln Street and the ally on the east. Originally, there was a carriage house, and between it and the big house stood a tank house, an aviary, and the stable. The sidewalk is stamped with the date 1917, which indicates when it was poured. The original wrought-iron fence is still standing but has been entirely encompassed by a hedge. (Both, courtesy of Colleen Banes.)

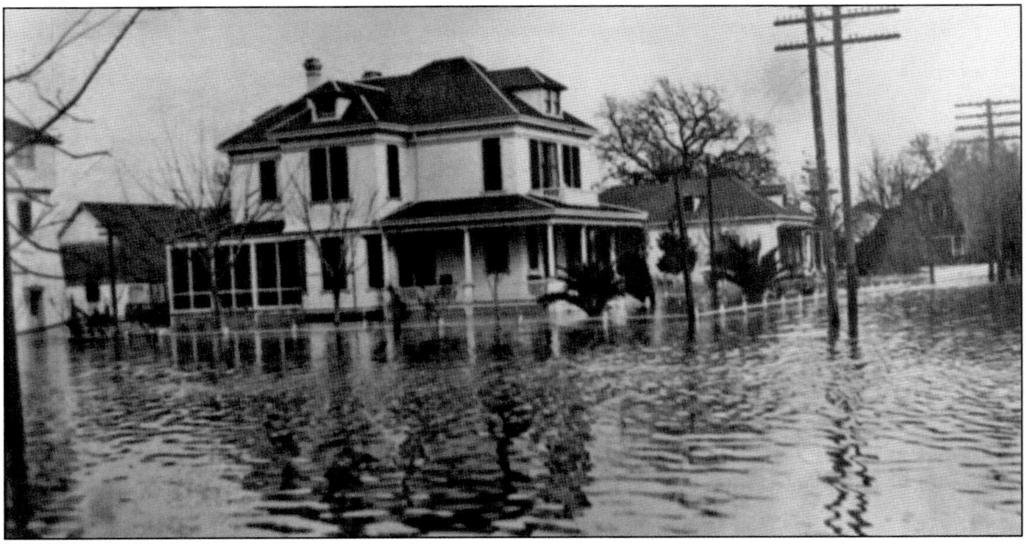

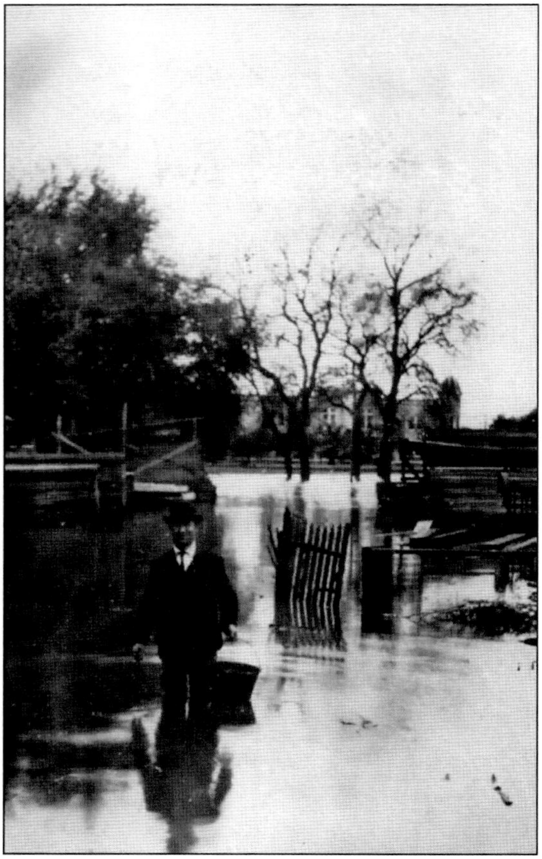

The following excerpt is from the *Gridley Herald* of Friday, March 22, 1907: "The rain which began last Friday night continued through Saturday, Sunday and Monday inducing flood conditions in the rivers of the northern part of the State. The Feather River rose very rapidly and by Monday morning the danger line had been reached." Gridley citizens gave their attention to repairing the old levee that was supposed to never be needed. Soon the east side of town was three feet under water. The west part of town south of Hazel Street was high and dry. (Both, courtesy of the Gridley Museum.)

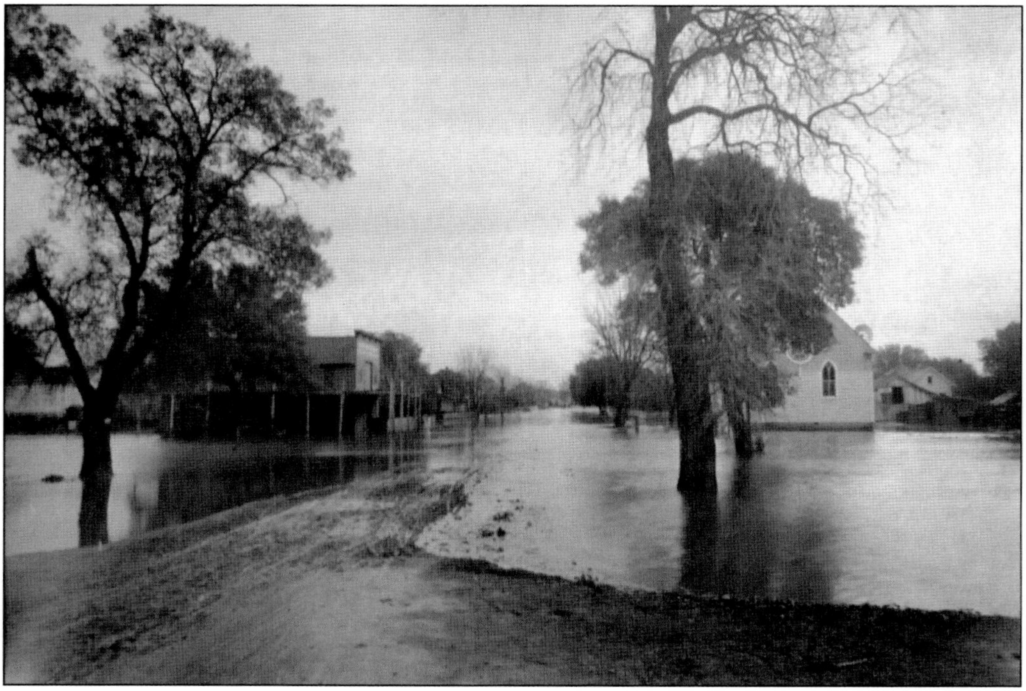

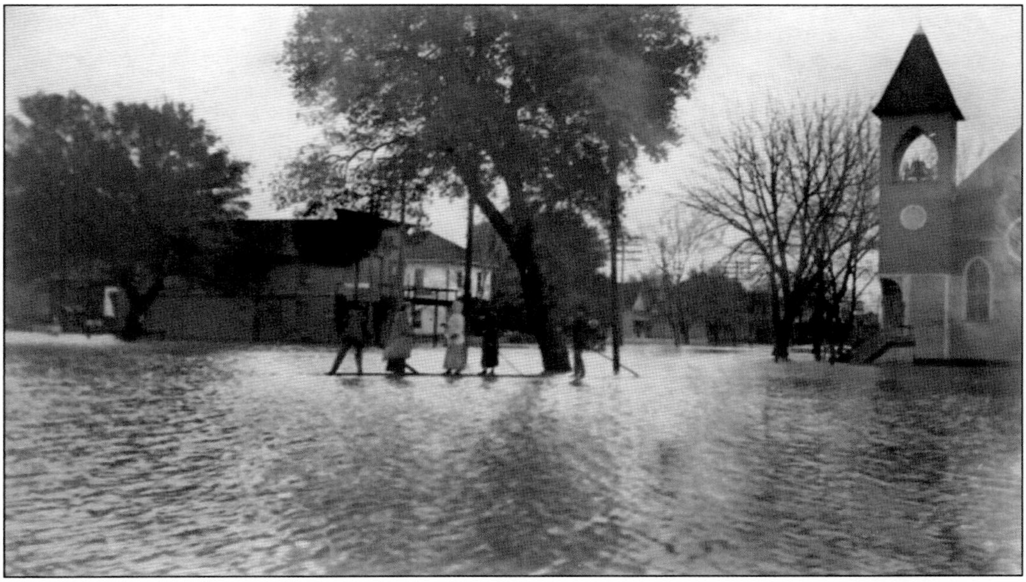

The most devastating flood in Gridley resulted when voluminous rains from tropical air masses melted a deep snow pack, causing tremendous run-off. Reportedly, the highest level attained since recording began was reached on March 18, 1907. Citizens of Gridley navigated the streets in rowboats. This image shows the corner of Hazel and Washington Streets. The Christian Church is at right. (Courtesy of the Gridley Museum.)

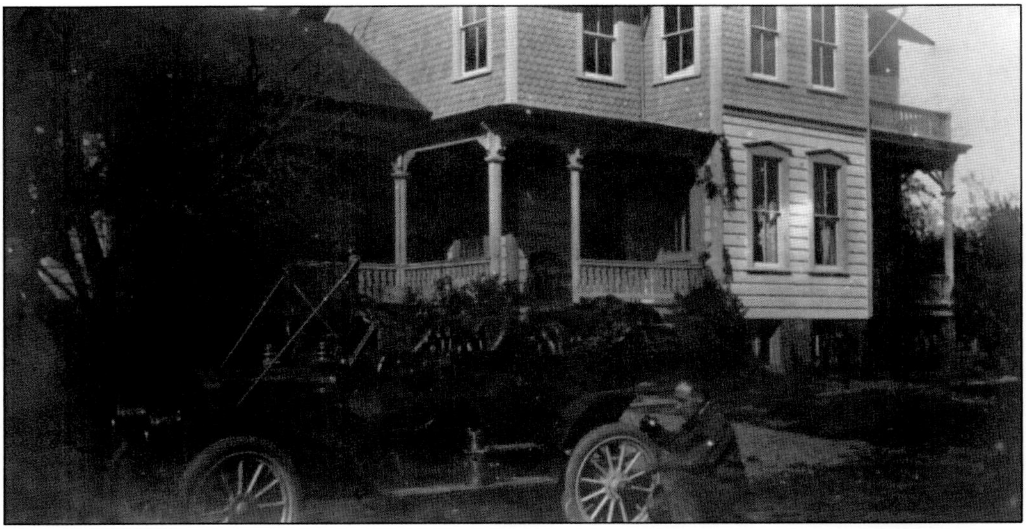

When the state constitution was changed in 1879, it paved the way for several additions to the duties of the county superintendent of schools' office. To assist the superintendent, Virgil Paris Richards was appointed to the first board of education for Butte County schools in May 1880. Richards's home stood on the corner of East Gridley Road and Highway 99E. Besides being a teacher, he was a farmer. (Courtesy of the Gridley Museum.)

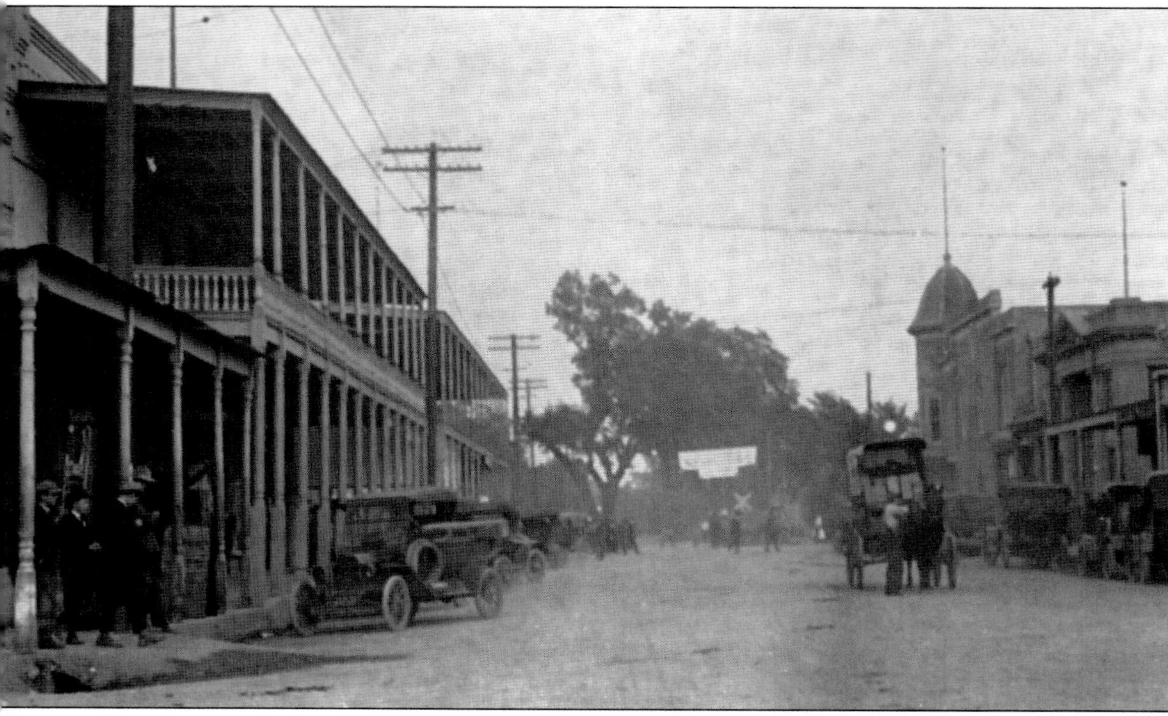

This photograph, dated November 3, 1915, shows Hazel Street looking east from Kentucky Street in Gridley's downtown business district. The old Leland Hotel building, erected in 1888, is at left. The rebuilt Stone Block can be seen up the street on the right. The porches that covered the sidewalk were removed in 1924 and 1925. (Courtesy of the Gridley Museum.)

Two

Early Businesses

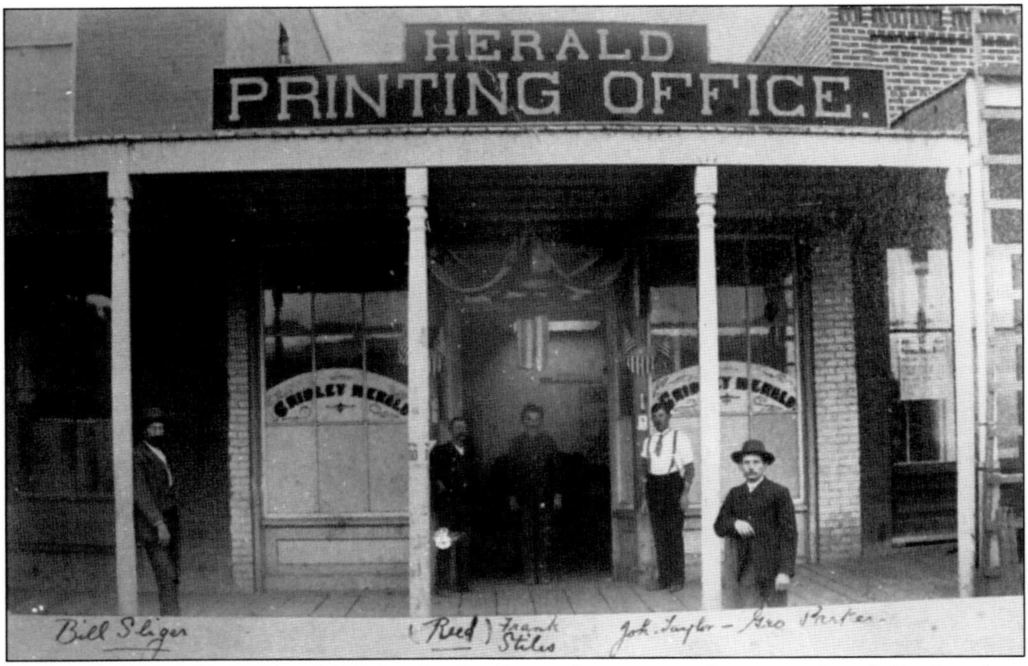

Charles Neff Reed saw a bright future for Gridley and its surrounding agricultural district when he published the first issue of the *Gridley Herald* on October 20, 1880, using a small lever-operated hand press. He vowed he would conduct the *Herald* as a "fearless" politically independent journal owning no allegiance to any "clique or faction." Reed is pictured here second from left. (Courtesy of the Gridley Museum.)

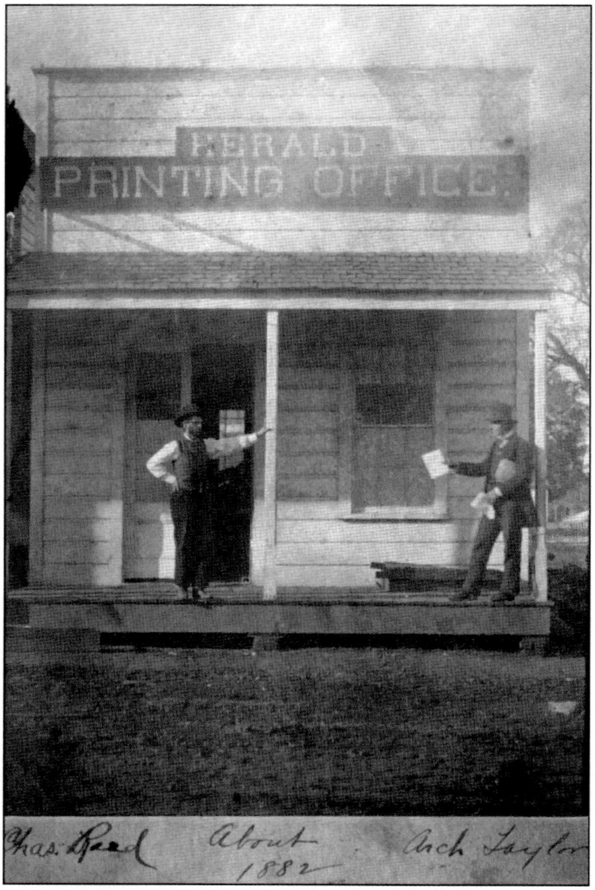

The *Gridley Herald*, a weekly, was founded in 1880 by Charles Neff Reed, who died in 1891. After trying for several months to run the paper herself, Mary Catherine Reed, Charles's widow, sold the paper to a group of farmers interested in bringing in irrigation. One of these was Columbus Washington Thresher and his brother George. The farmer ownership was shuffled a bit, but they still needed an editor. Charles Deuel, a young Oroville man, was hired as editor in 1895. Although he worked only two years in Gridley, he found a bride and moved to Chico, which created a need for another editor. (Both, courtesy of the Gridley Museum.)

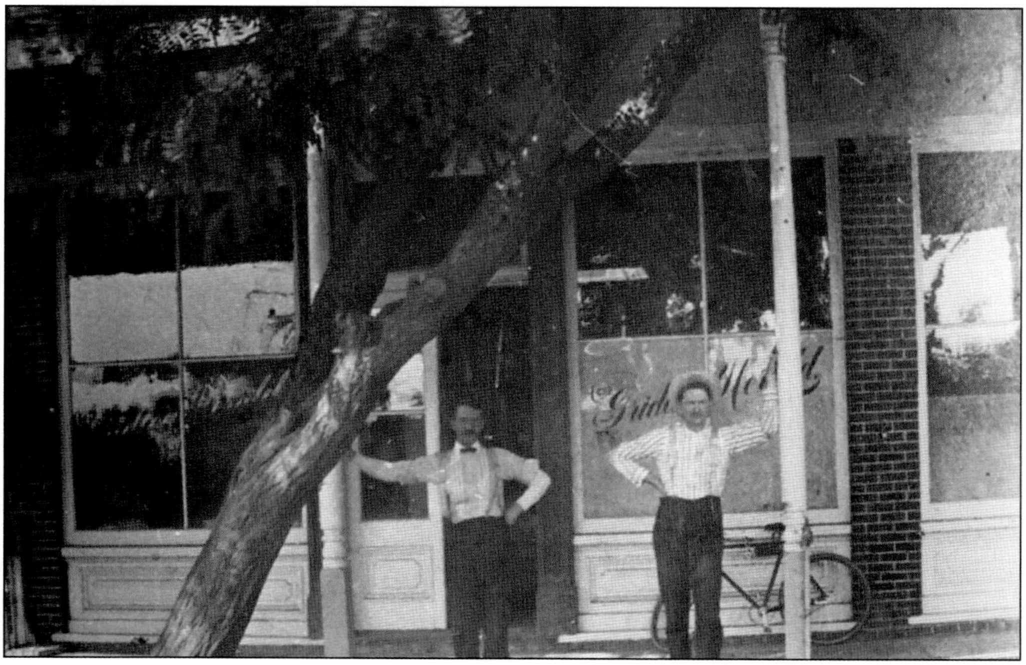

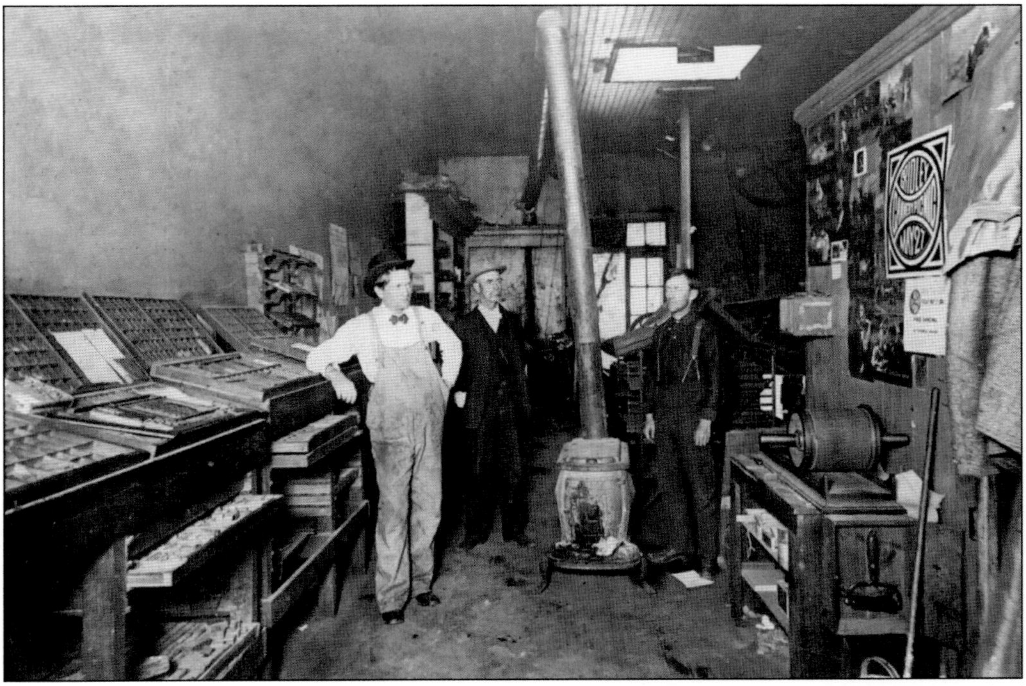

This scene inside the *Gridley Herald's* newspaper plant on Virginia Street in 1908 was typical of small-town print shops at that time. William David Burleson is standing at left in front of the cases that held the hand-set type that was still in use. (Courtesy of the Gridley Museum.)

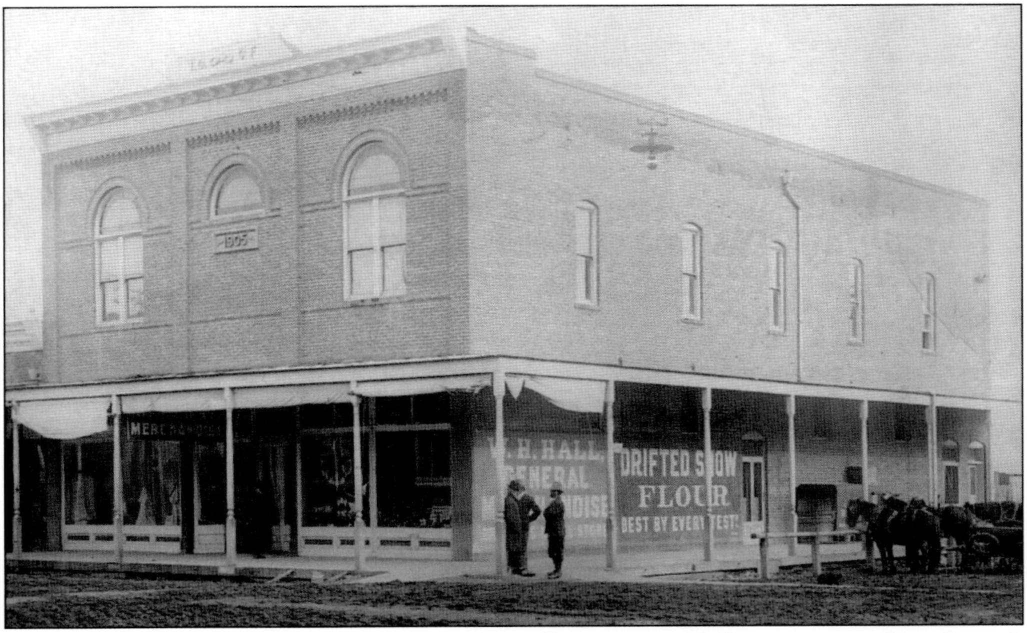

An advertisement in the city directory read, "William Henry Hall, proprietor, of gentlemen's clothing, furnishings, goods, boots and shoes." This two-story brick building, located at the southeast corner of Hazel and Kentucky Streets, is believed to have been built around 1885. It was used for stores on the ground floor and had a lodge room for the International Order of Odd Fellows upstairs. (Courtesy of Dan Boeger.)

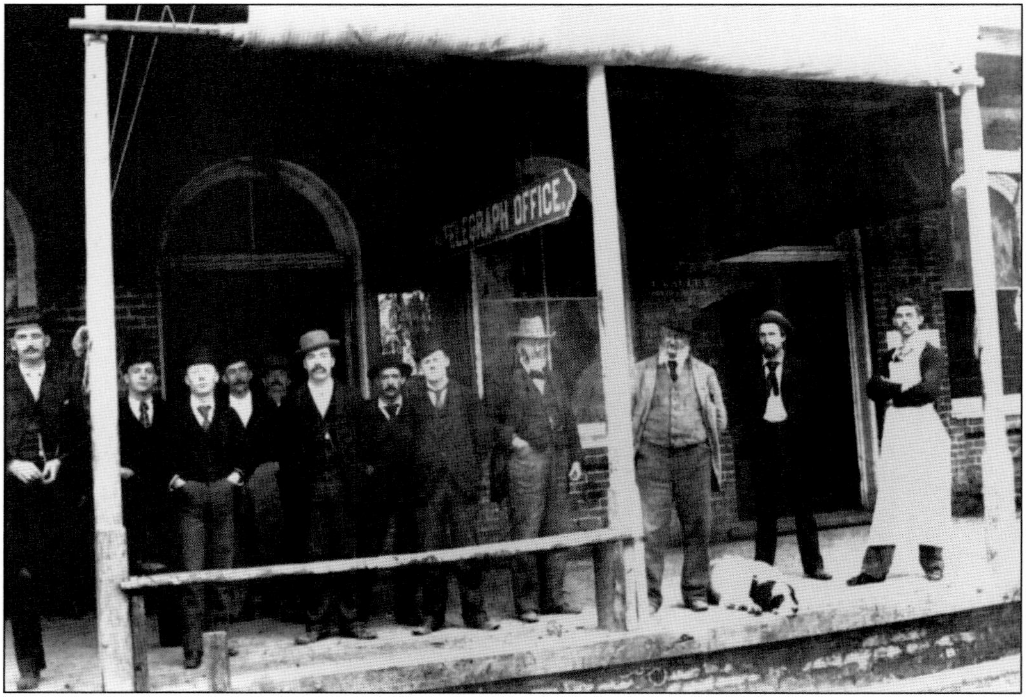

Pictured here are some local "good ol' boys" posing in front of Hackett and Jeffrey's Cigar Store. The sign on the building lists L. Tallen, justice of the peace, and William Brown's meat market. William Brown is at far right. This row of businesses was on Hazel Street between Virginia and Kentucky Streets in 1884. (Courtesy of Butte County Historical Society.)

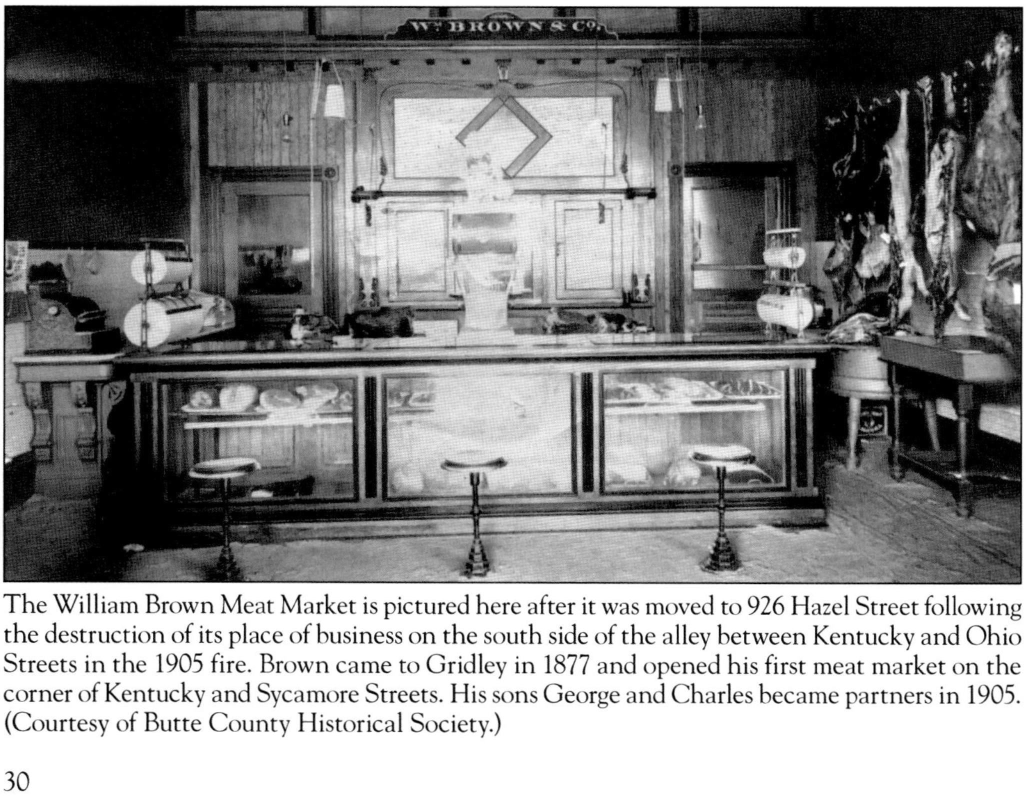

The William Brown Meat Market is pictured here after it was moved to 926 Hazel Street following the destruction of its place of business on the south side of the alley between Kentucky and Ohio Streets in the 1905 fire. Brown came to Gridley in 1877 and opened his first meat market on the corner of Kentucky and Sycamore Streets. His sons George and Charles became partners in 1905. (Courtesy of Butte County Historical Society.)

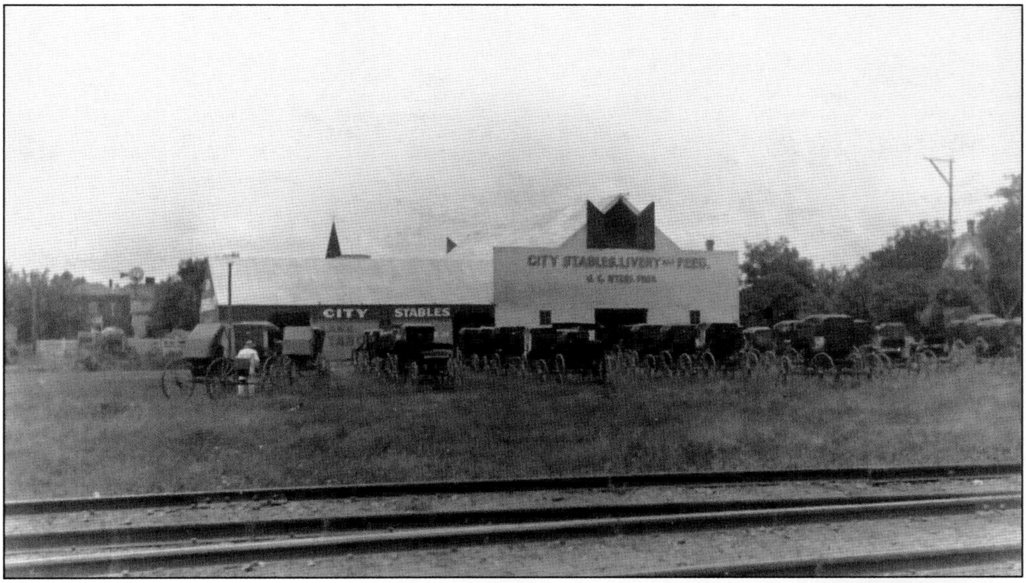

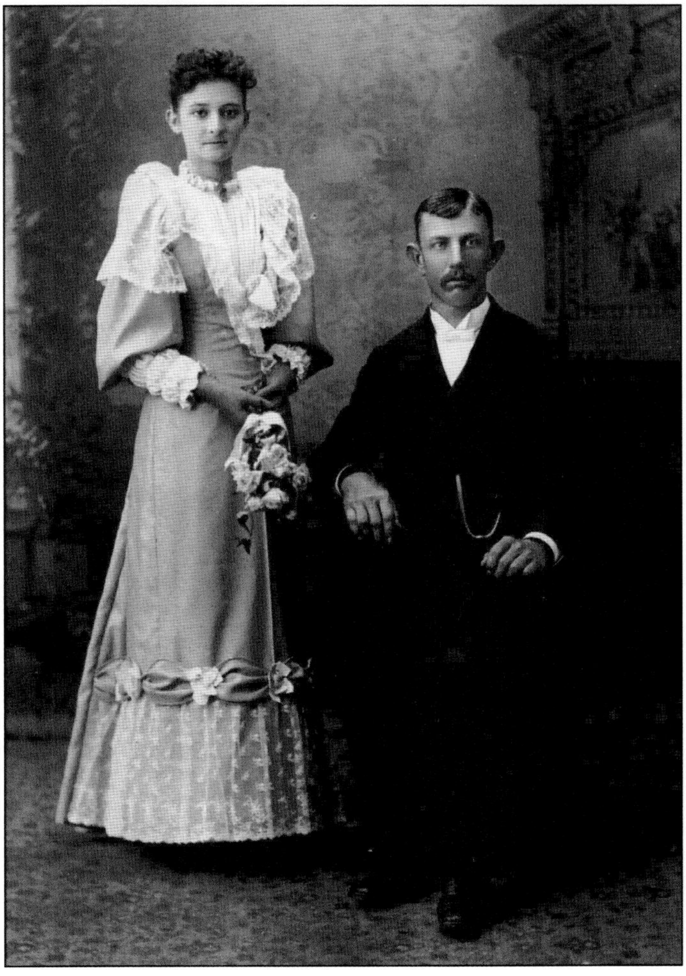

John Calvin Myers was born in 1867 on Myers' Ranch at Pennington and attended North Butte School. He followed his father in farming grain and stock raising. In August 1891, John married Anna Bertha Marr and established their home in the Sutter Buttes. In 1903, they moved to Gridley and built Myers Livery Stables at the corner of Virginia and Sycamore Streets. The barn had hardwood floors upstairs, making it easy to move hay, and was also used for community dances. After the automobile made the stable obsolete, Myers sold wood and coal with partner Ora Driskell. The coal they sold was Aberdeen coal, used by blacksmiths. They expanded the business to sell feed for livestock and chickens. Deliveries were made in a red wagon. John and Anna were active in many organizations and helped plan the yearly cannery picnic. (Both, courtesy of Tyrone Shaeffer.)

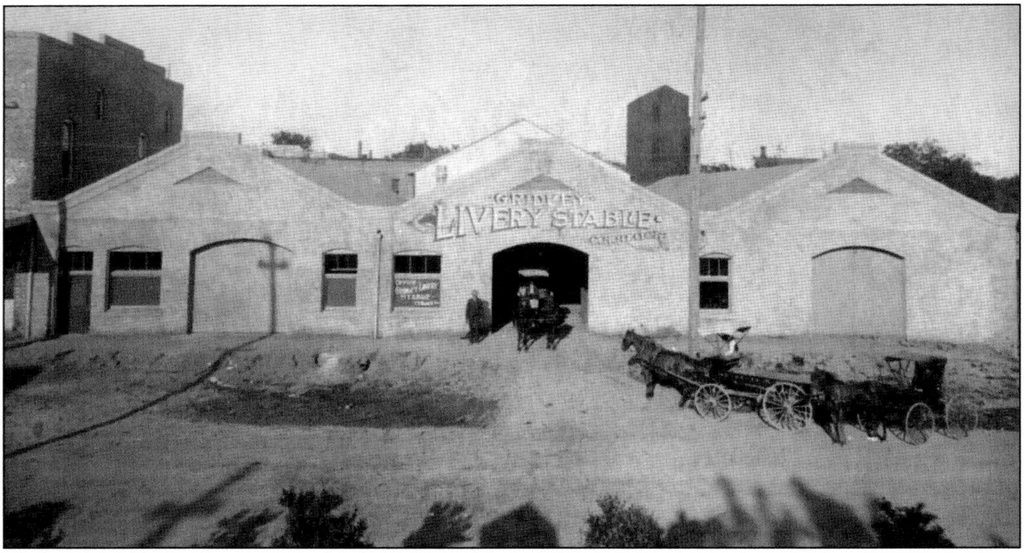

The Gridley Livery Stable, one of the most prominent and reliable establishments, was owned and operated by Charles Henry Block. Block had the best stock of buggies and carriages with reliable drivers, who could be hired any time of day or night for parties, weddings, or funerals. Block also operated the town mortuary in the same building. This arrangement provided horses for the trips to and from the cemetery. (Courtesy of the Gridley Museum.)

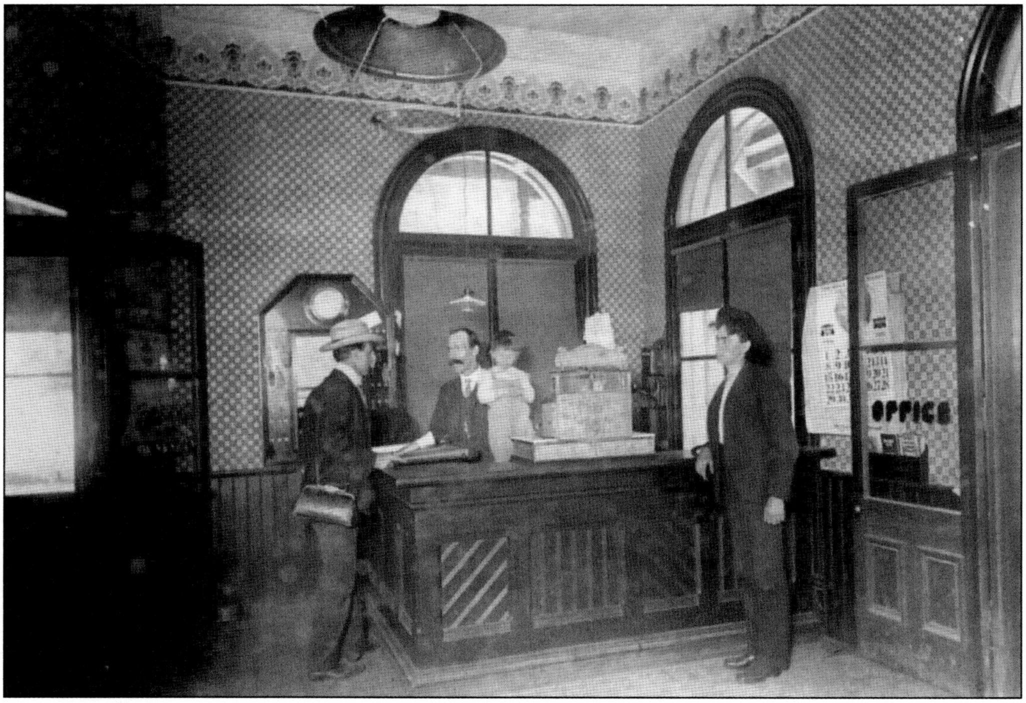

When Fred Fink Sr. was following his trade as a blacksmith in Colorado, he spoke to a man who had formerly lived in Gridley and learned about the attractive features of this section and decided to locate here. After he arrived, he became the proprietor of the Pacific Hotel, which was reported to have tables supplied with all delicacies. The rooms were said to be clean and airy. (Courtesy of the Gridley Museum.)

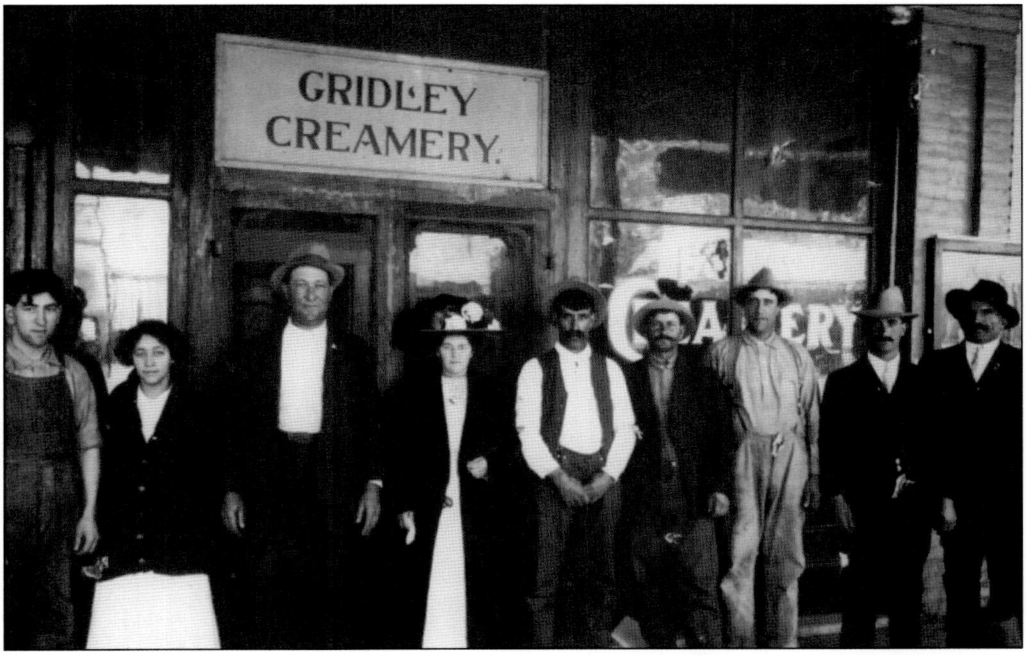

The Gridley Creamery and Ice Company, organized in the late 1800s, was a prosperous business and placed around $25,000 worth of treasury stock among the farmers. The sale of stock put the creamery in a position not only to vastly increase its output to make money for its stockholders but also to stimulate and encourage the dairy business of the vicinity. This ensured that the industry would increase in volume and importance in the future. In 1914, local dairymen working with a San Francisco creamery concern took over the plant. The concern was a cooperative affair, and local men took shares of stock liberally. Some of those who invested were Frederick Arbow Onstott, Edward Fay Biggs, and Manual Machado. (Both, courtesy of the *Gridley Herald*.)

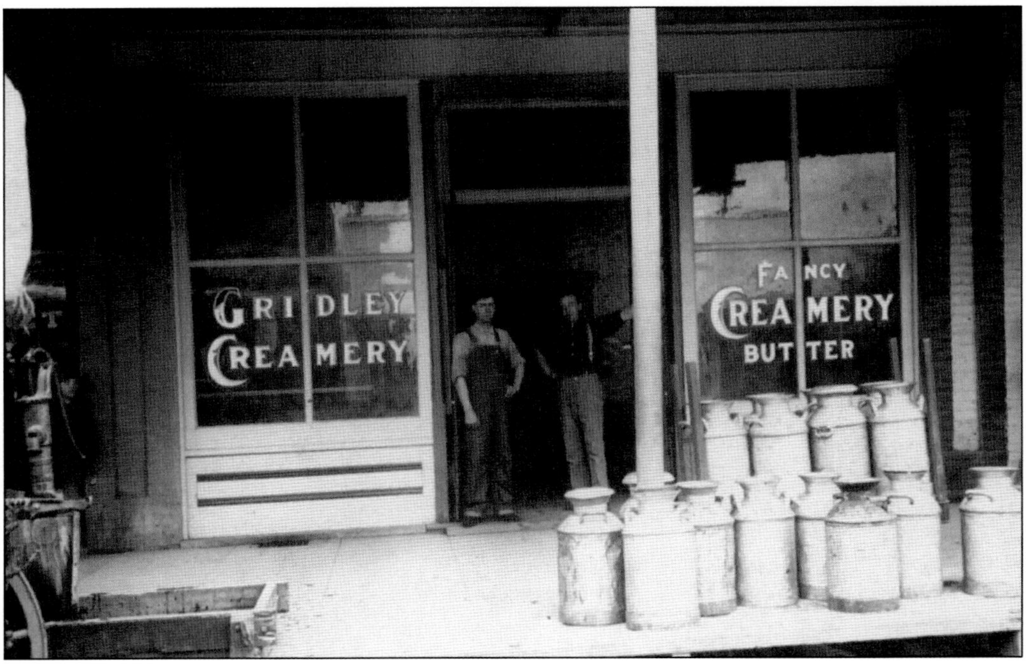

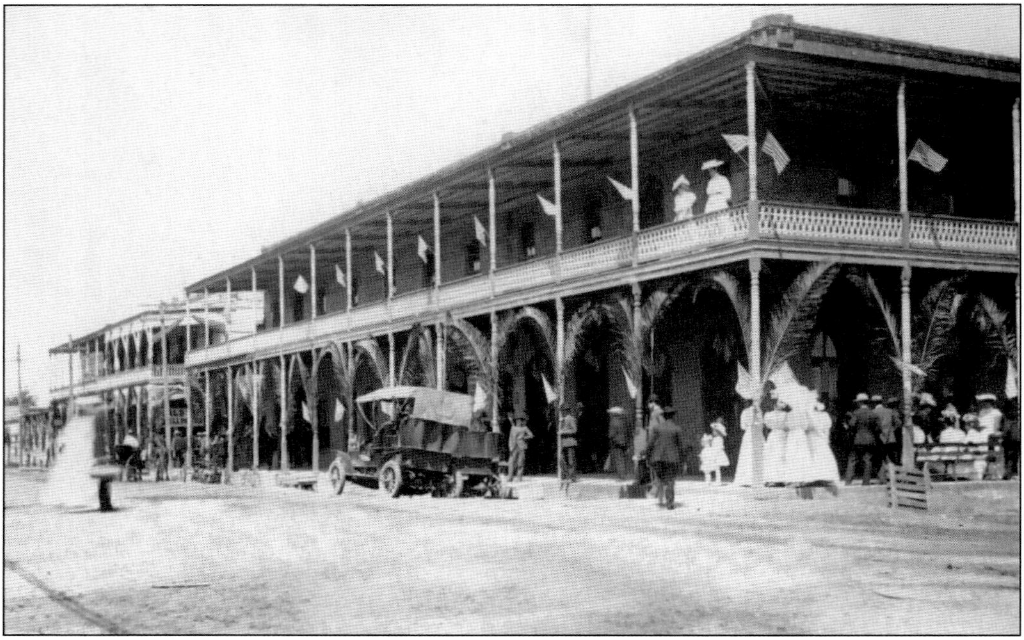

Edward Taylor maintained the Gridley Hotel at the corner of Hazel and Virginia Streets. Advertisements in the *Gridley Herald* boasted, "First-Class House; Table Supplied with the Best in Market; Rooms Comfortable and Airy; Gridley, California; near Railroad Depot." The *Herald* also announced that "Phillip Maul has opened his Shoe Shop in the building formerly occupied as a barber shop in the rear of the Gridley Hotel." (Courtesy of the Gridley Museum.)

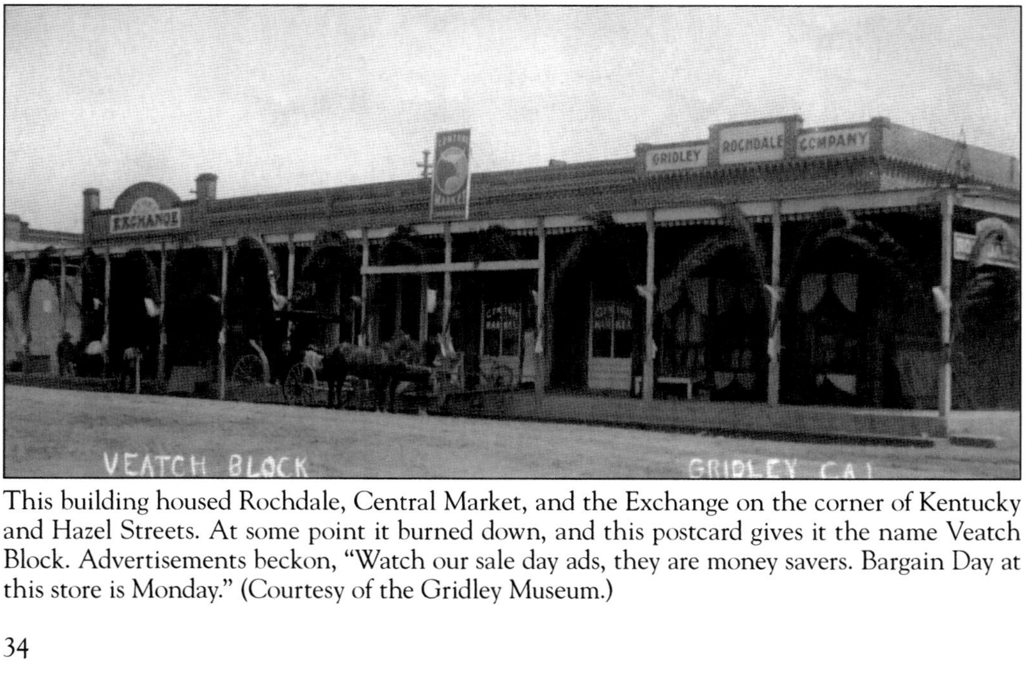

This building housed Rochdale, Central Market, and the Exchange on the corner of Kentucky and Hazel Streets. At some point it burned down, and this postcard gives it the name Veatch Block. Advertisements beckon, "Watch our sale day ads, they are money savers. Bargain Day at this store is Monday." (Courtesy of the Gridley Museum.)

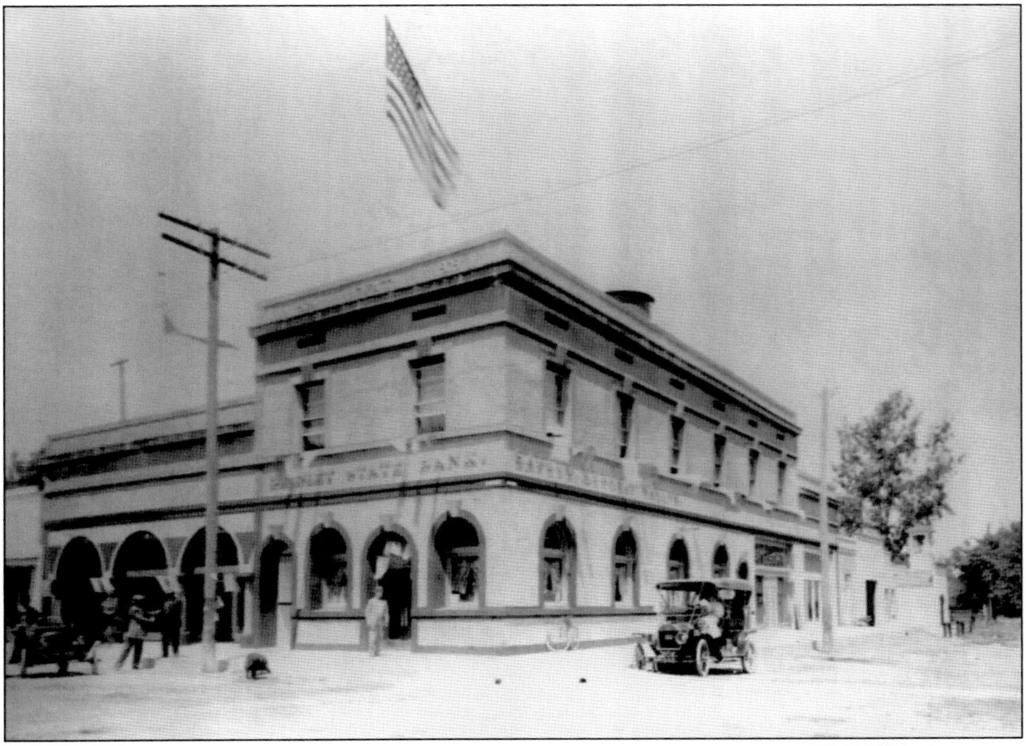

An excerpt from the minutes of a City of Gridley meeting reads: "The City Clerk read a letter from Henry Clay Veatch dated August 2, 1909, asking permission to build a reinforced concrete and brick building on Hazel and Kentucky Streets, with fire-proof roofing as approved by the Board of Underwriters. Permission was granted." The Gridley State Bank was designed and erected by Thomas Boulware, a contractor and builder. This building is known as the Veatch Building. Veatch was in real estate also. He owned the Gridley Investment Company, was instrumental in the Gridley State Bank, and developed the Veatch & McCallum and Parkside editions in Gridley. (Both, courtesy of RuthAnn Cassady King.)

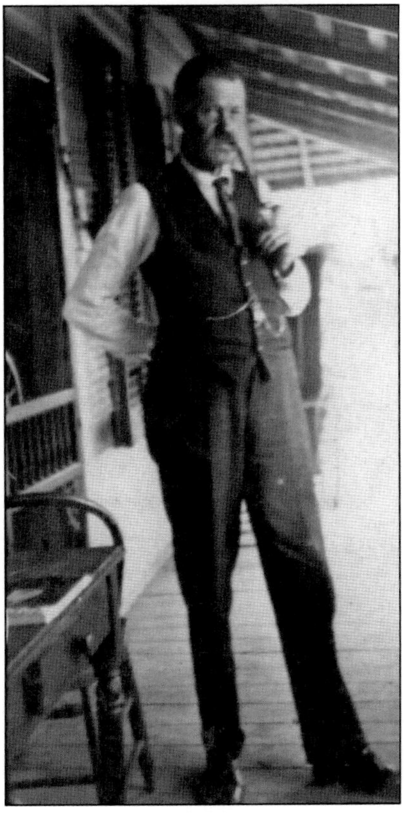

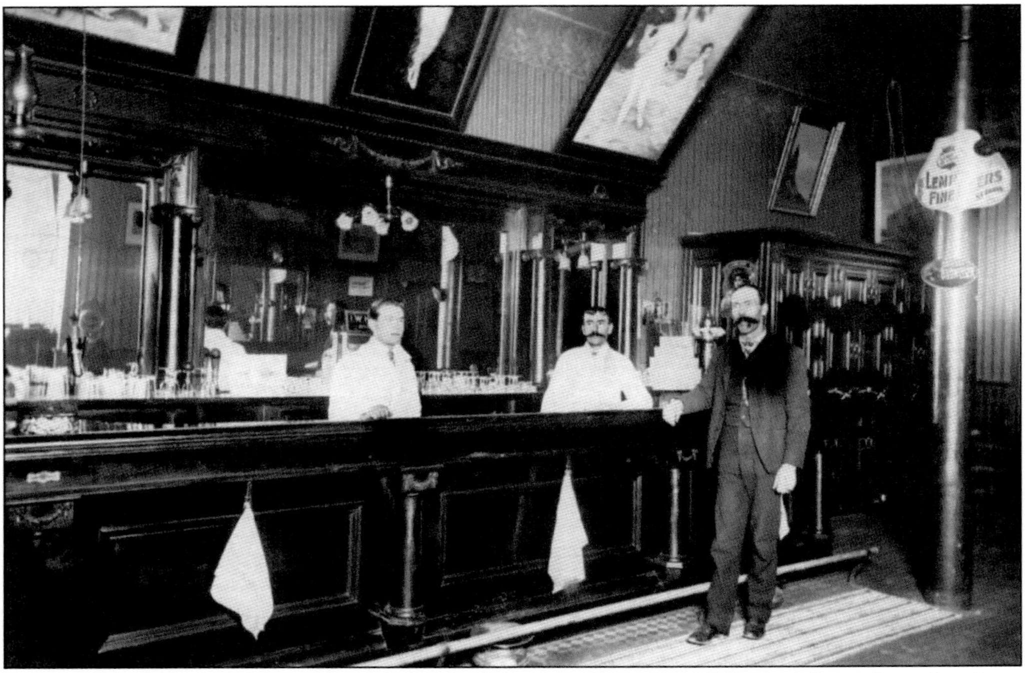

Frederick Fink leased the Pacific Hotel, which he named the Hotel Fink and conducted in first-class style for 10 years. During that time, he leased the Fink annex, a rooming house next to the hotel. For several years he was disconnected with the hotel management but still managed the rooming house on Hazel Street. Fink opened a restaurant on Hazel Street and later added a bakery. (Courtesy of the Gridley Museum.)

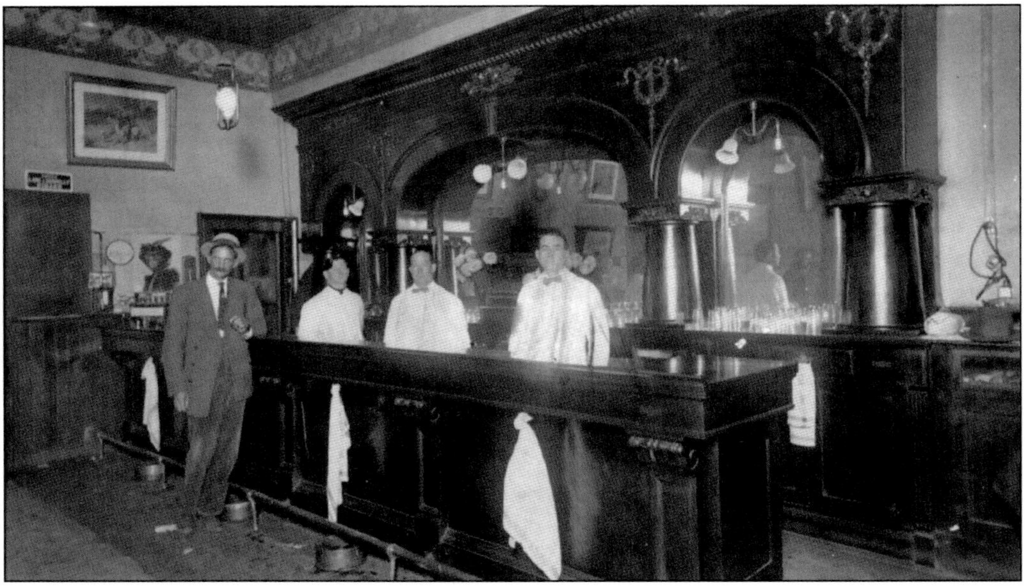

Although this saloon is unidentified, the *Chico Weekly Record* reported, "Let Gridley go ahead with its woolen mill. Gridley will have to pay for all the wool it gets, while Chico will be the daisy town of Northern California while commanding the trade in 'sheepherders delight.' " In the opinion of that paper, Gridley, with only nine saloons, had no hope of becoming a "daisy town." (Courtesy of the Gridley Museum.)

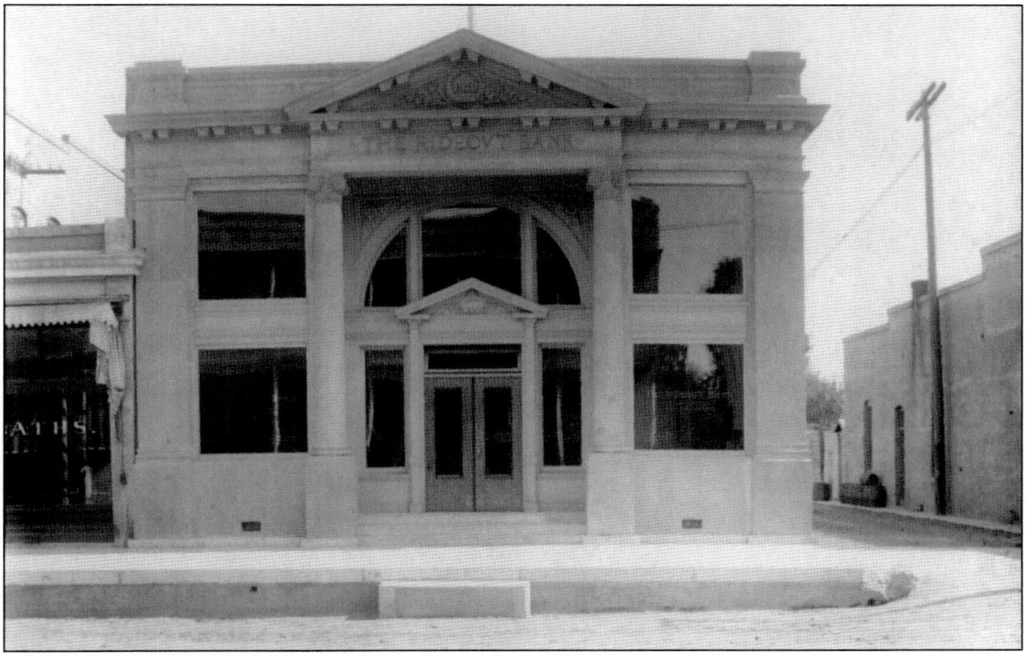

When Henry Veatch constructed a new two-story building for the Gridley State Bank in 1909, the Rideout Bank of Marysville, which had a branch in Gridley since 1884, was not to be outdone. The result was an elegant structure complete with sandstone facade located on the south side of Hazel Street on the east side of the alley between Kentucky and Virginia Streets. On August 1, 1910, manager Edward Biggs was granted permission by the Gridley City board of trustees to remove the old building on the site and erect a new structure. The contract for constructing the building was signed to James Newman of Napa, who sublet the carpenter work to John Palmer and Richard Jenkins of Gridley. The floor and ceiling of the bank's vault were interlaced with thick steel bars. (Both, courtesy of the Gridley Museum.)

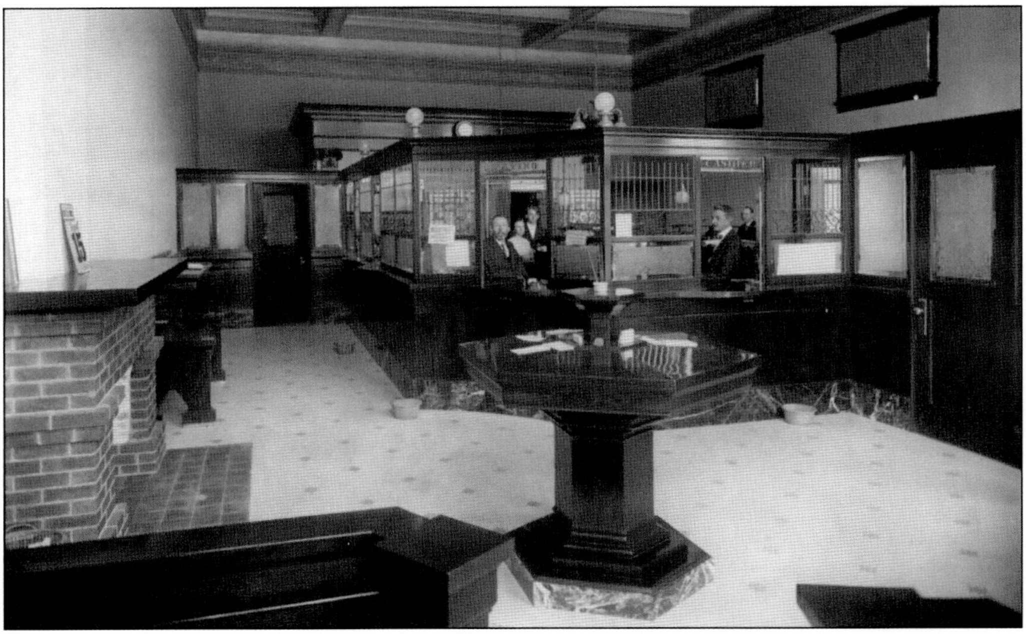

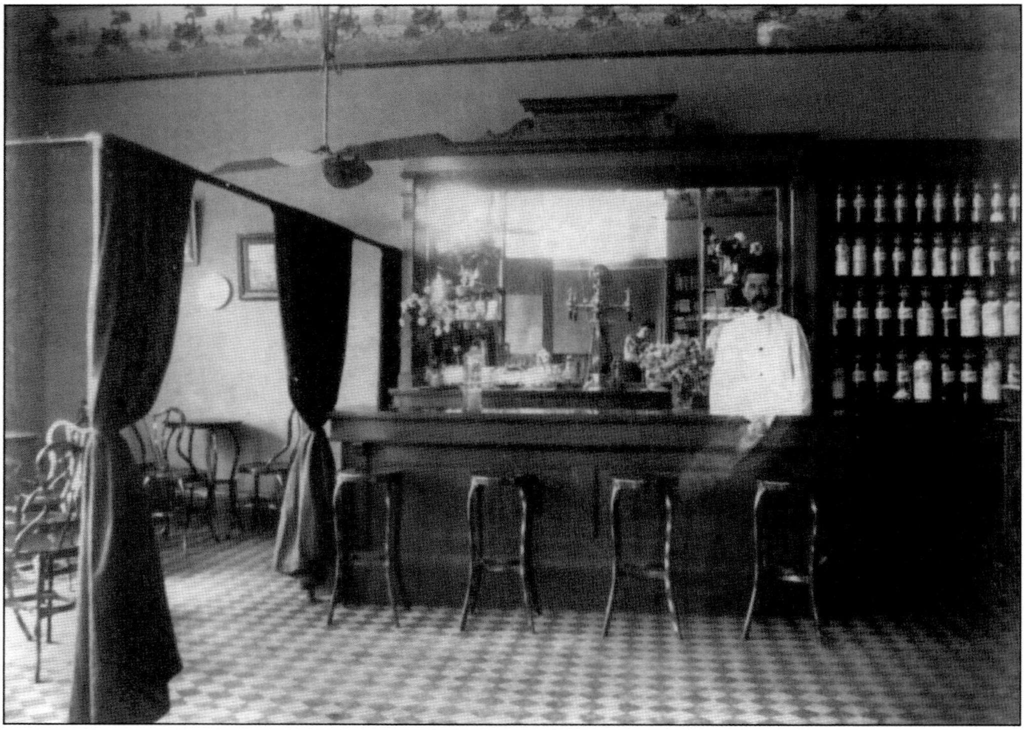

Drugstores usually came to an area along with population growth. When people arrived, along came the first druggist. About 1880, the first drugstore in Gridley was established. It was called the Pioneer, or Norman Drug Store, and was located at the southwest corner of Hazel and Virginia Streets. Pictured here is Norman's Drug Store. (Courtesy of the Gridley Museum.)

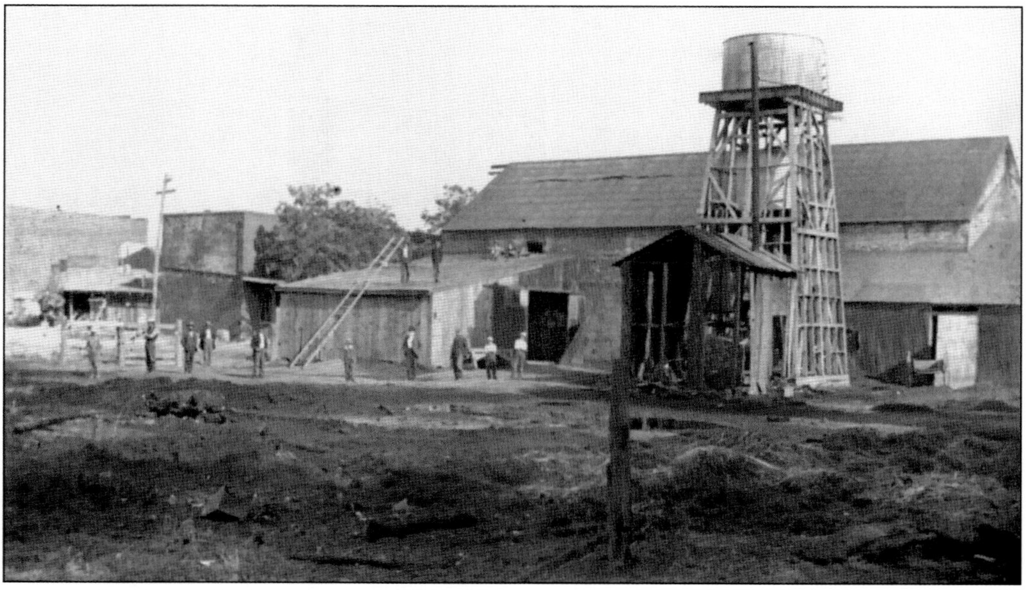

The Gridley Steam Flouring Mills were erected by the joint-stock company of Stone & Gridley in 1875. These mills were among the finest in the valley, costing over $40,000. They had a grinding capacity of 250 barrels of flour per day. In 1881, the machinery was kept running night and day to fill large orders of flour to be shipped to San Francisco. (Courtesy of the Gridley Museum.)

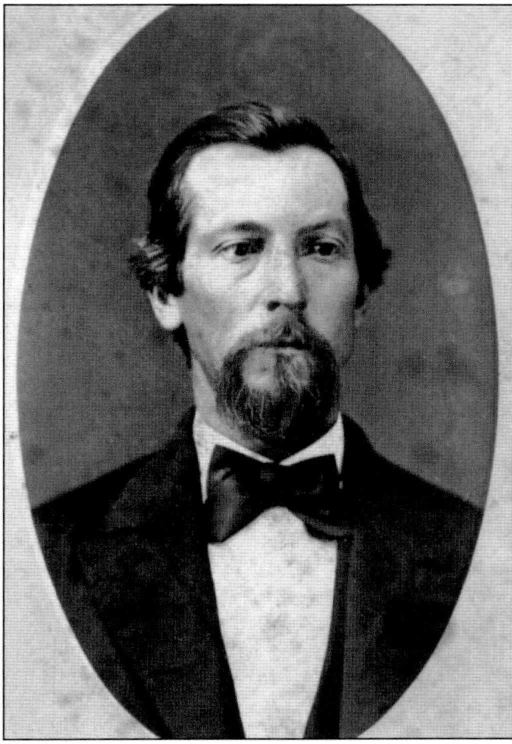
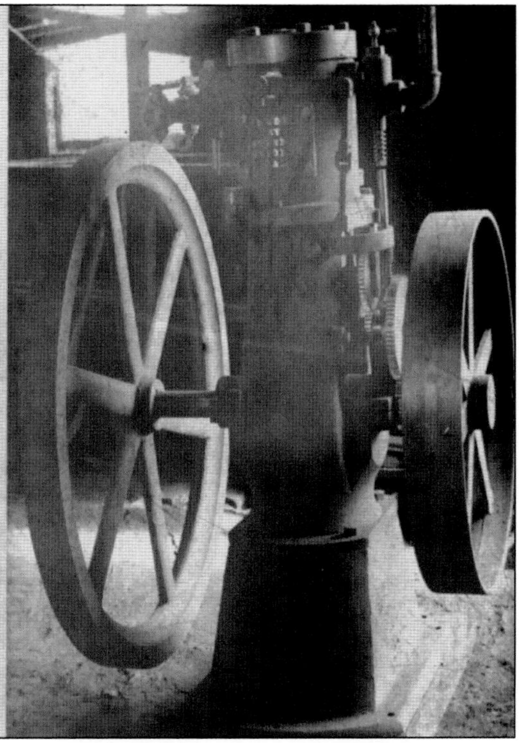

In the mid-1880s, Soranus Standish, a descendant of Miles Standish of Pilgrim fame, maintained a busy foundry and workshop in Gridley. The shop was located at the south end of Kentucky Street. Standish built what he described to his grandson as "the first gas engine built in the United States." (Courtesy of Lorry Dunning.)

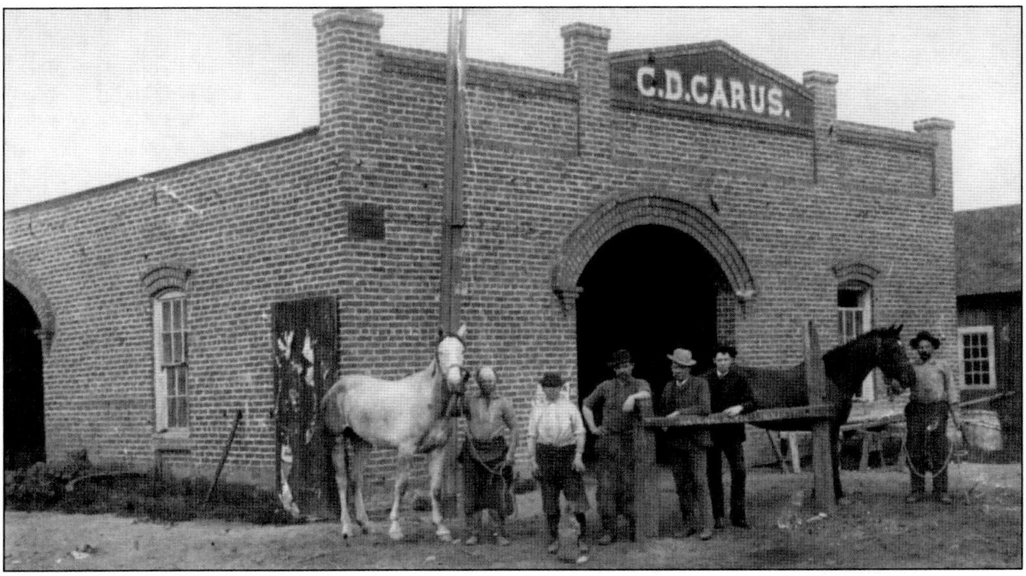

As quoted in the *Gridley Herald* on August 14, 1884, "Carus' new shop is the tastiest one story brick building in the county." Chester Delos Carus, a blacksmith by trade, came from Michigan and settled in Gridley. He also was a volunteer fireman and was elected Gridley's first fire chief. The fire equipment was stored at his place of business. (Courtesy of the Gridley Museum.)

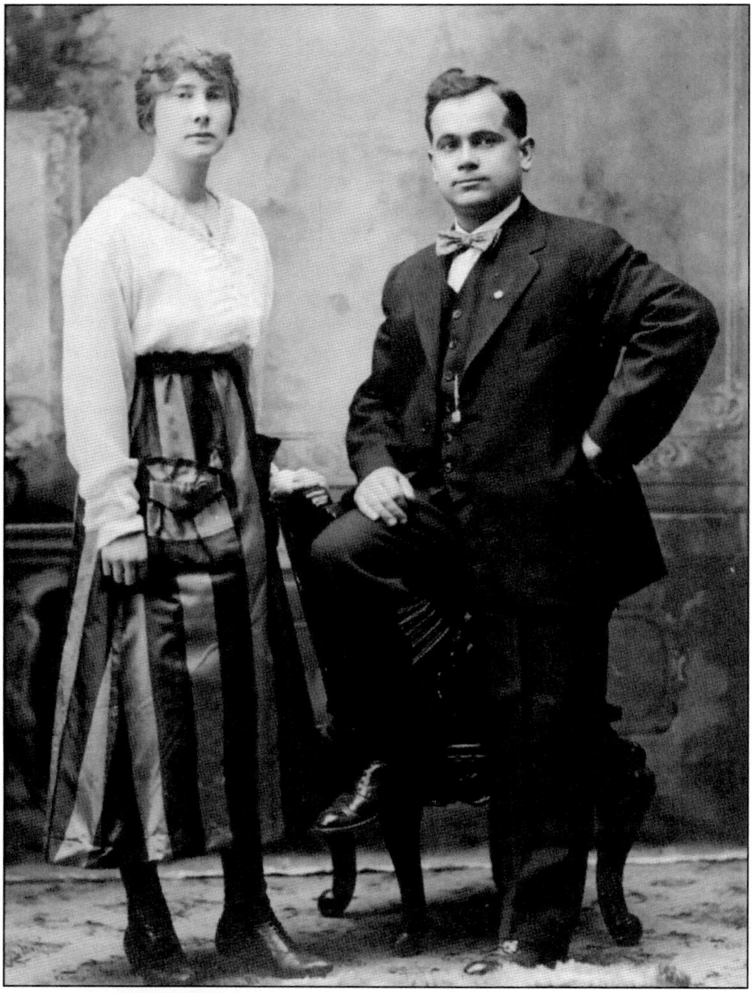

Nellie and Loreto Antonio Panecaldo were married in 1913 in Shasta County, and he proudly became an American citizen. He was among the merchants who sustained the enviable reputation of Gridley as a business center and a desirable place of residence. Before he came to the United States, Tony learned the baker's trade while in the Italian army, which equipped him to start his own bakery. Pictured below is the bakery wagon used to deliver loaves of bread to Durham, Richvale, Biggs, and other parts of southern Butte County. (Both, courtesy of the Gridley Museum.)

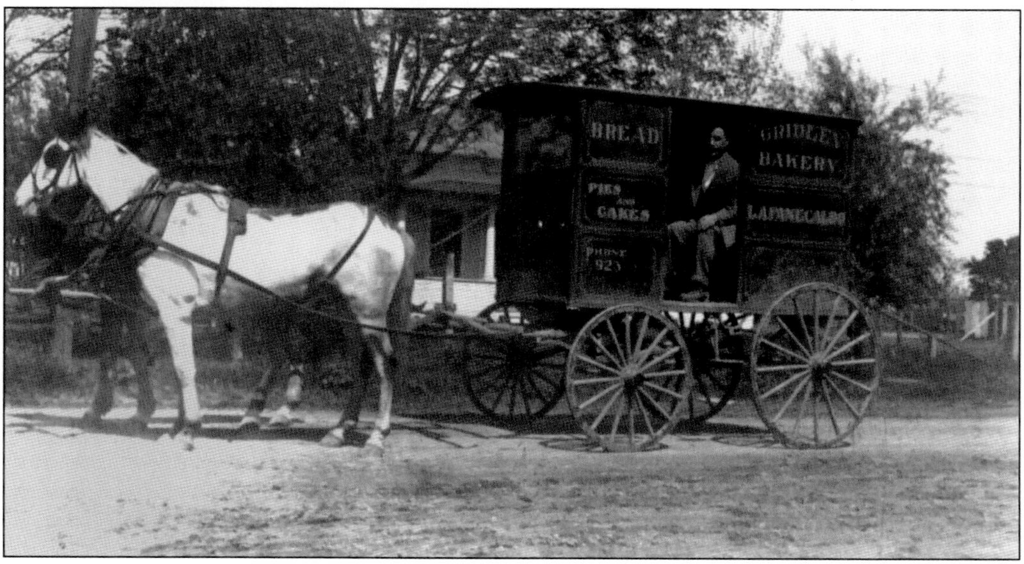

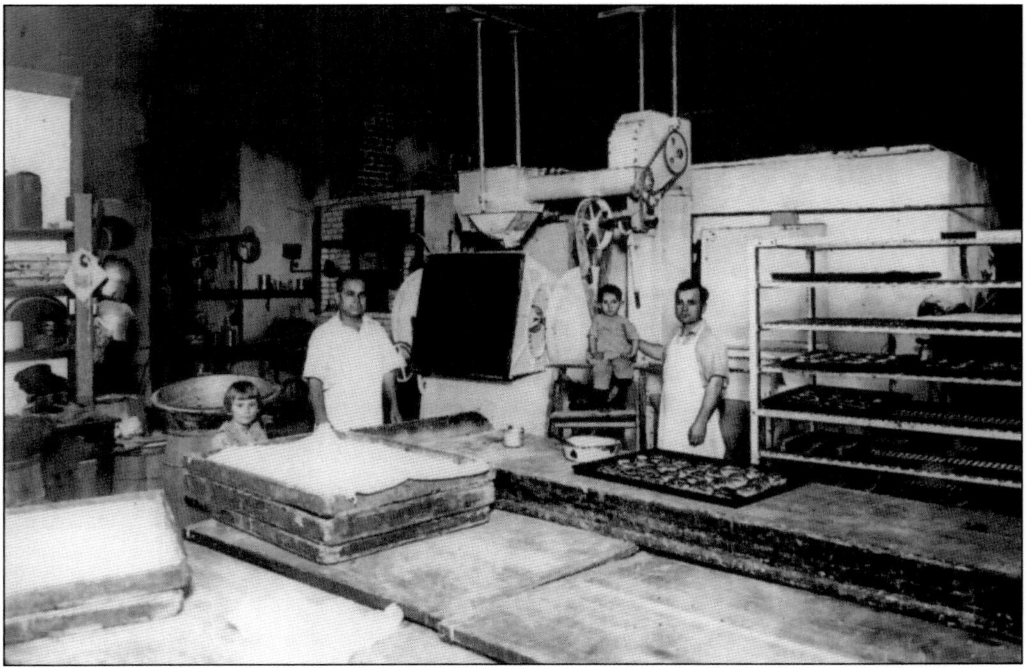

Loreto Antonio Panecaldo, one of Gridley's most enterprising businessmen, bought out a small bakery and made many needed improvements, including a new oven and the most modern machinery, making his business the best well-equipped bakery in all of Butte County. Now that he had the most modern equipment available, Panecaldo was able to bake 1,000 loaves of bread and more daily. He wisely invested his profits and expanded and opened a liquor store named Old Roma. Panecaldo is pictured below in Old Roma. (Both, courtesy of the Gridley Museum.)

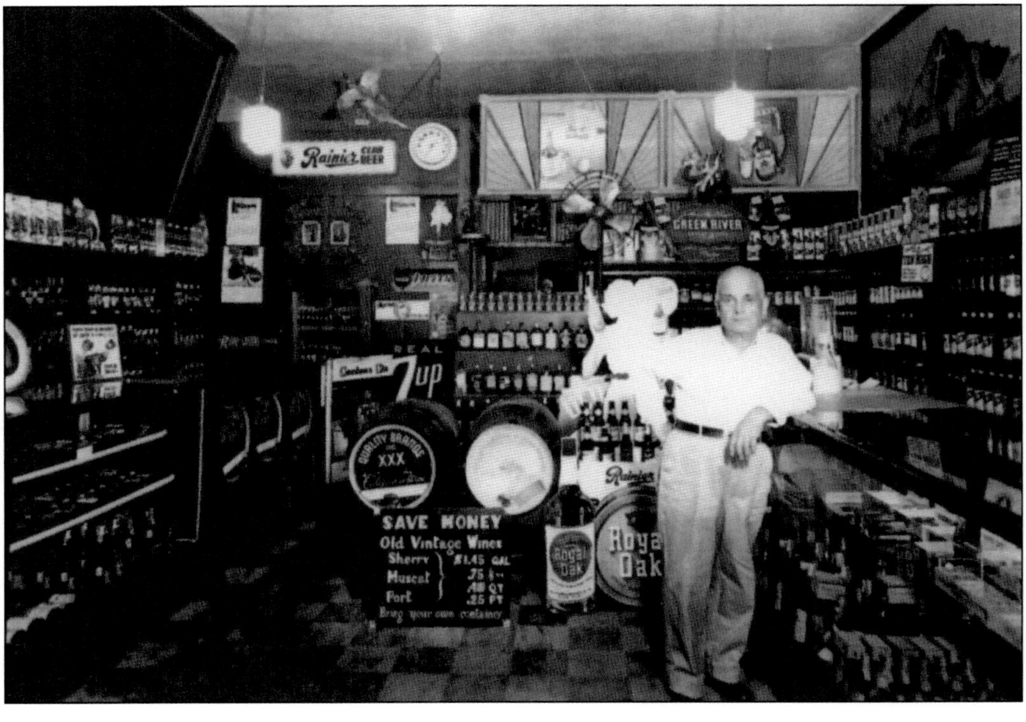

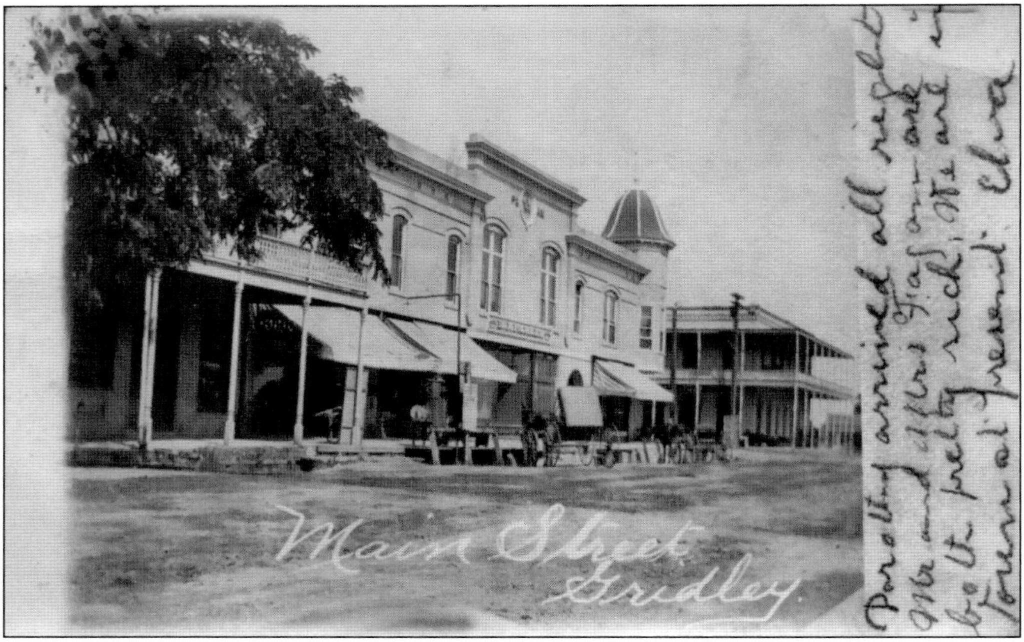

After the town of Gridley was platted in 1870, the arrival of merchants and agents rendering essential services was immediate. A poor money lender had been farming south of town and became the town's first merchant. Lewis Charles Stone opened a store in a cabin on Virginia Street. Two years later, a two-story building was needed to accommodate the growing demand. Stone became an express agent and the postmaster as well as a general merchant. In 1877, a two-story brick building was erected by Stone on the southwest corner of Hazel and Virginia Streets. A saloon and druggist moved there as well as the first physician, Dr. France. The first school was held in a storefront, where Miss Calhoun was the teacher. These two views show the Stone Building looking from south to north and north to the south. (Both, courtesy of the Gridley Museum.)

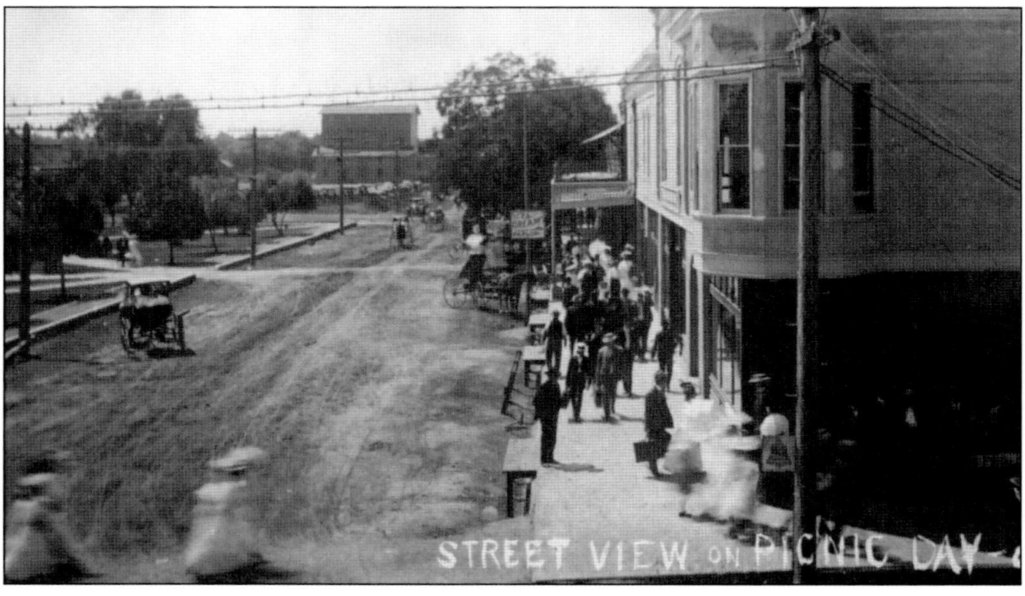

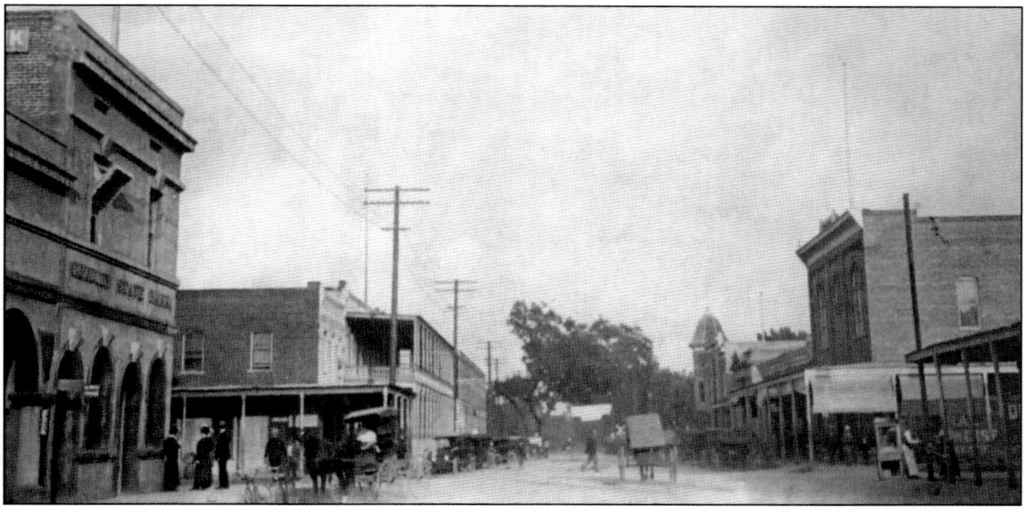

Pictured here in 1915 is the downtown business district on Hazel Street, looking east. The 1888 Leland Hotel is at left. The rebuilt Stone Block building is up the street on the right. The city council adopted an ordinance in 1924 that required the removal of porches that had shaded a number of businesses. The porches were taken down later that year and during the early part of 1925. (Courtesy of the Gridley Museum.)

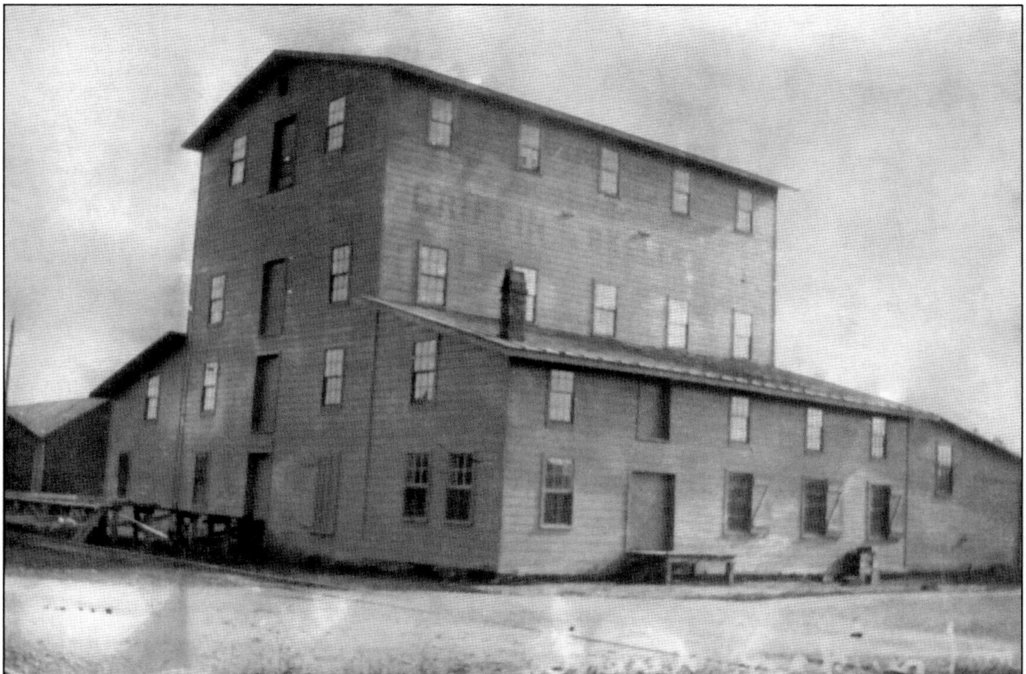

The Gridley Flour Mill, located at the southeast corner of Virginia and Magnolia Streets, was erected in 1875. In 1903, the Griffin-Skelly Company leased the building for packing dried fruit. The Gridley Rice Milling Company took over the building and held a celebration the evening of January 1, 1915. Malinda Schaeffer pulled the whistle and started the engine. John Schaeffer, representing the Gridley Businessmen's Association, gave the opening address. (Courtesy of the Gridley Museum.)

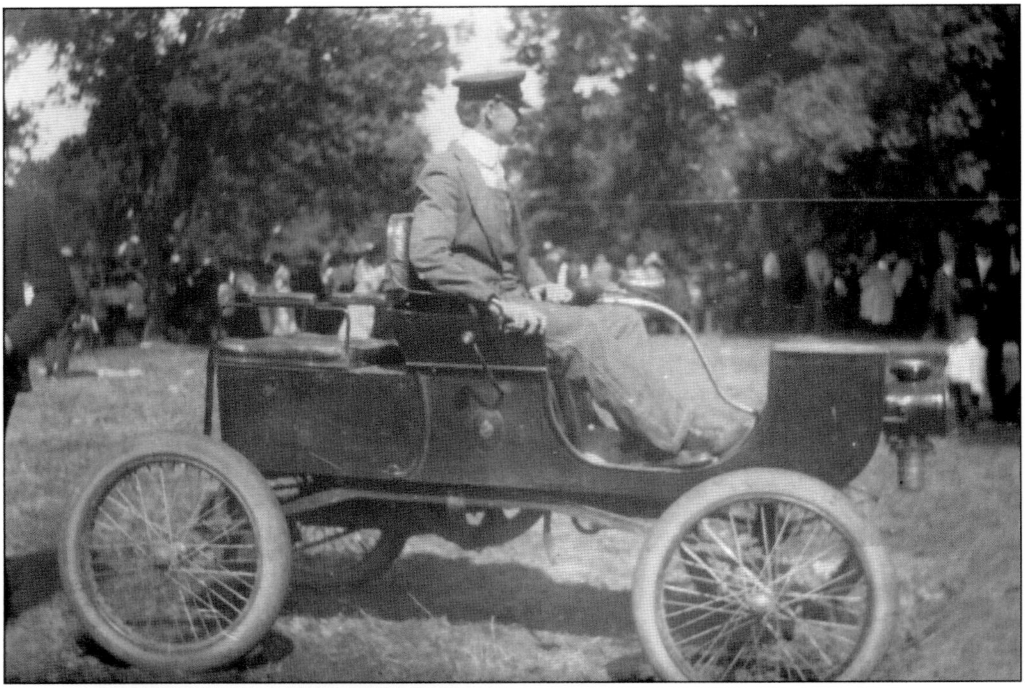

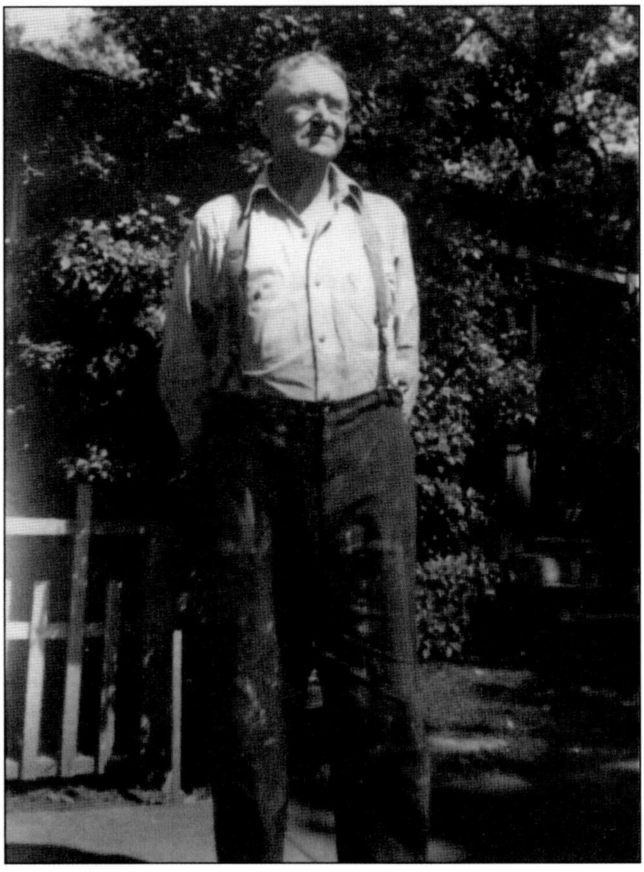

William Southard Simpson, born August 24, 1879, in Minden, Michigan, came to Gridley at the age of five. He opened Gridley's first garage, named the Pioneer Garage, in 1910 and was one of the first owners of an automobile in Northern California. Southard also owned and operated a variety store for a number of years. Prior to his retirement, he managed Simpson's Court, a group of rental cottages on Jackson Street. His wife was named Rhoda, and they had two children, Noeme and George. (Both, courtesy of the Gridley Museum.)

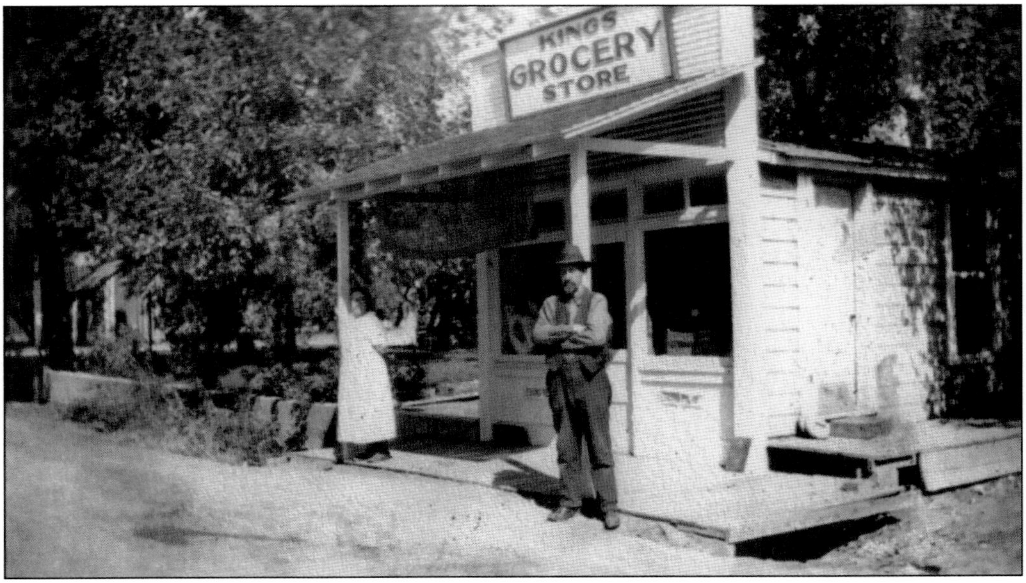

Above, Catherine and John King are standing in front of their grocery store on the West Biggs-Gridley Road between Hazel and Sycamore Streets. John, a farmer, used some of his profits to start a small grocery store in town. His son Leo Emmett followed in the business, managing a Kilpatrick's (a small Northern California grocery chain), later owning his own store. Sometime later, the Quist family ran the business. The image below shows how they added on to the building. (Both, courtesy of the Gridley Museum.)

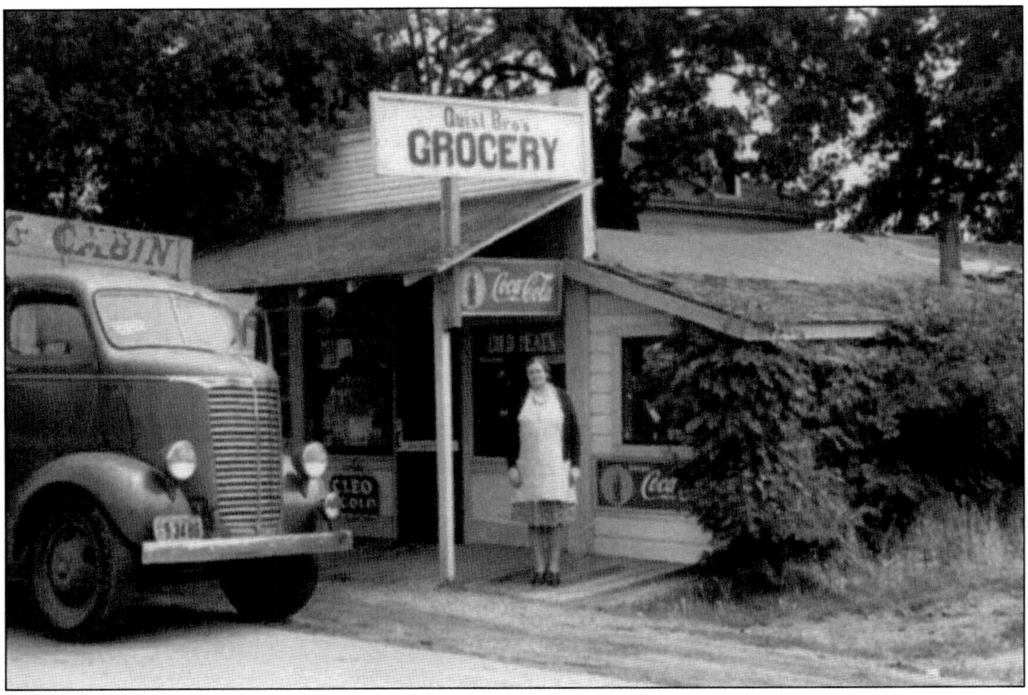

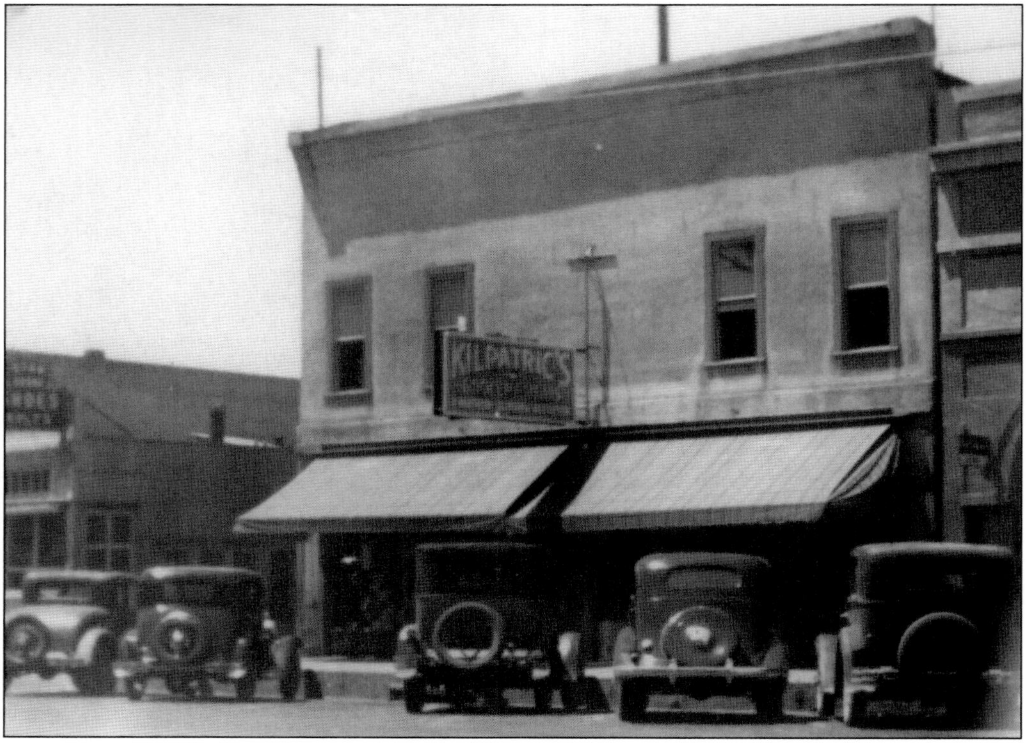

The interior of this Kilpatrick's store is narrow and deep, with only one aisle. Notice the stool for the customers to sit on while the clerk gathered their groceries. This location is on the north side of Hazel Street, between Kentucky and Ohio Streets, next to the Gridley Pharmacy. It burned in 1942 and was relocated on Kentucky Street next to the library. Leo King was a manager at this store from the age of 21 until it was sold to Wentz Markets in 1957. (Both, courtesy of the Gridley Museum.)

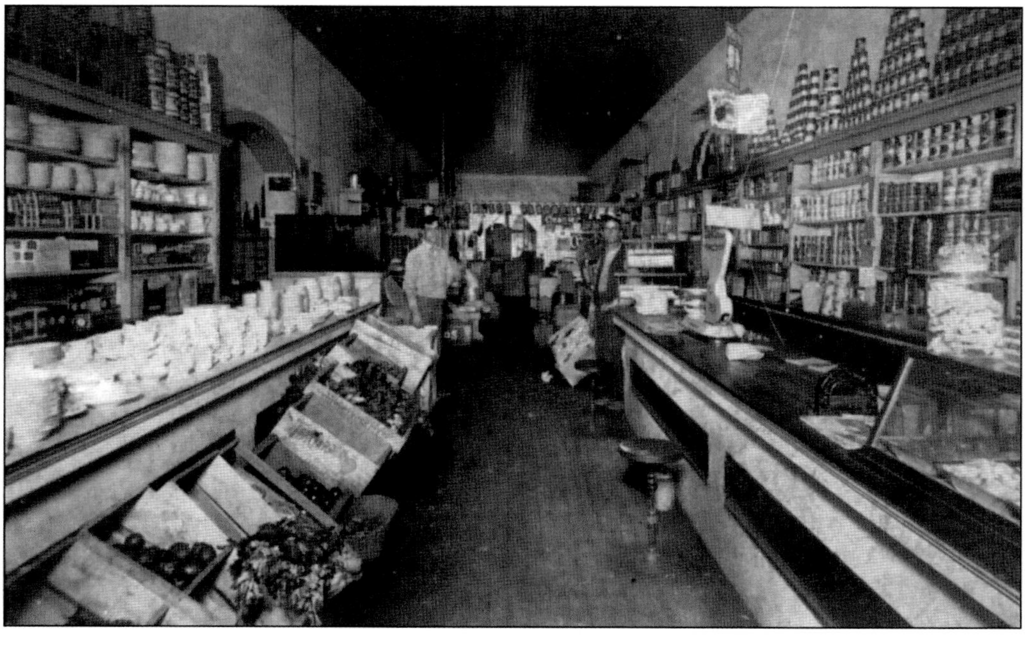

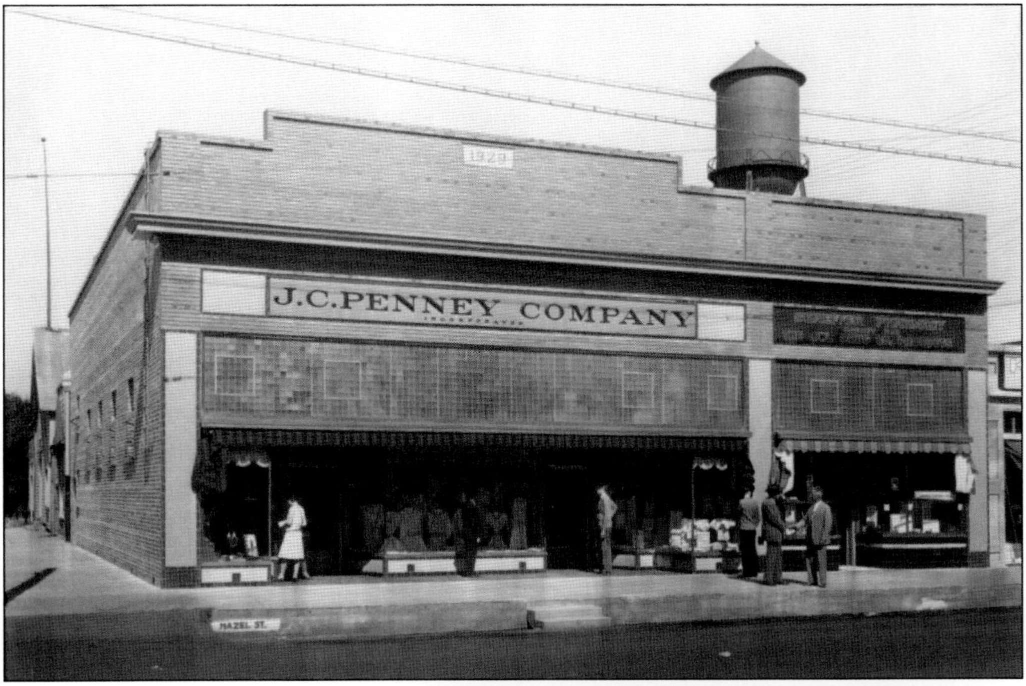

J.C. Penney came to Gridley in 1929, and the building was specifically built and owned by Henry Veatch. The tile entrances spell out J. C. Penney. This store had all the newest innovations, with two balconies at the front and back and pneumatic tubes at the checkout stations that sent payments upstairs to a central location and back down with the change. (Courtesy of the Gridley Museum.)

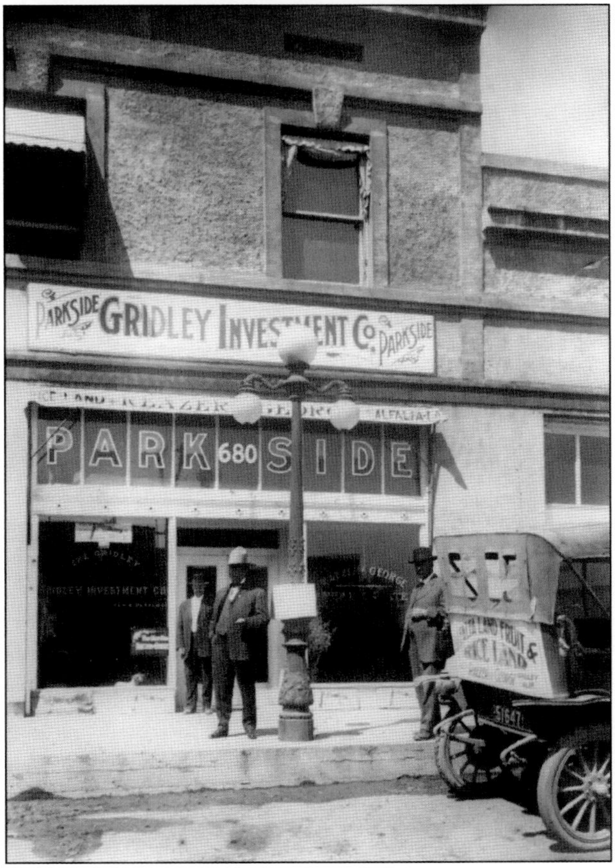

The agricultural future of Gridley took off at a high gallop with the establishment of the Gridley Investment Company. Pictured here are Henry Clay Veatch (standing by 1914 Overland automobile) and Duncan McCallum (center). These men were among those who brought the first irrigation district into being. This photograph, taken on the east side of the Veatch building, shows the upstairs office of Dr. Ida Beck. (Courtesy of the Gridley Museum.)

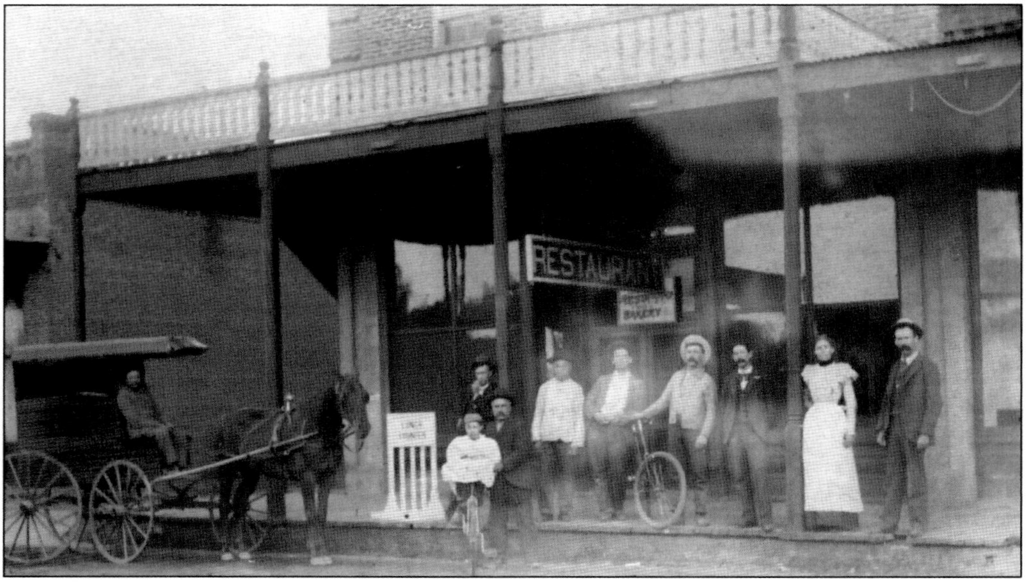

This is possibly the restaurant and delivery wagon owned by Fred Fink. It has been reported that the gentleman in the wagon is Fink himself. Standing on the porch-covered boardwalk are patrons and waitstaff of the eatery. (Courtesy of Butte County Historical Society.)

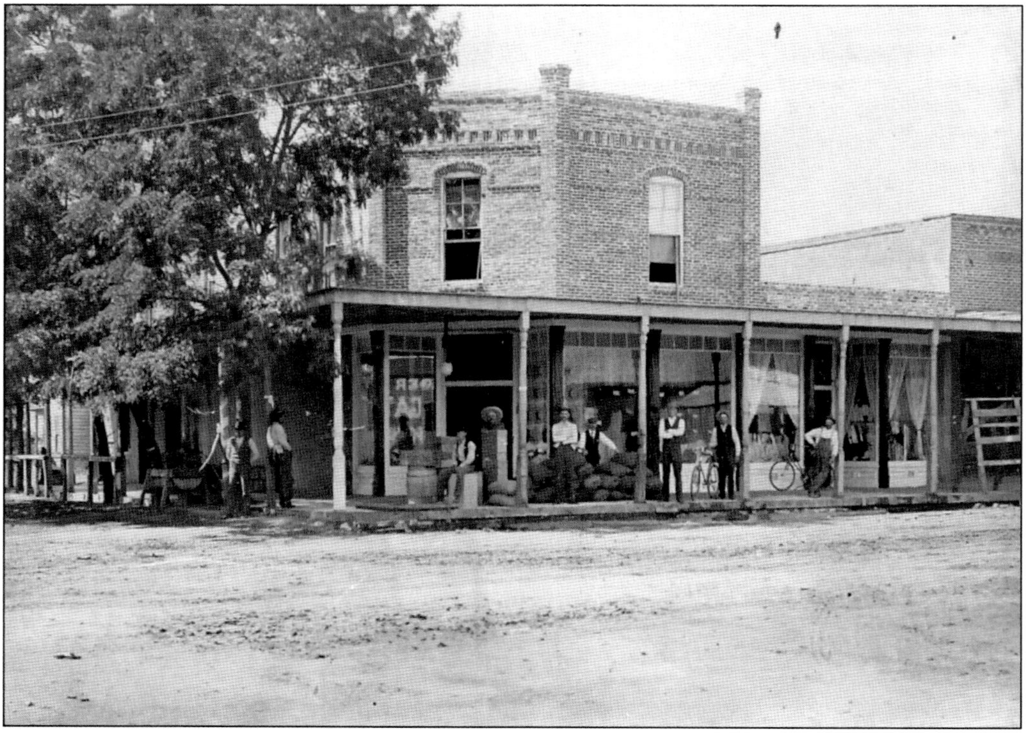

Farmers' Mechanics' Merchandise Store sat on the southwest corner of Hazel and Kentucky Streets in 1884. According to a Gridley city directory, a Mr. Schwarz was the manager at one time. (Courtesy of Butte County Historical Society.)

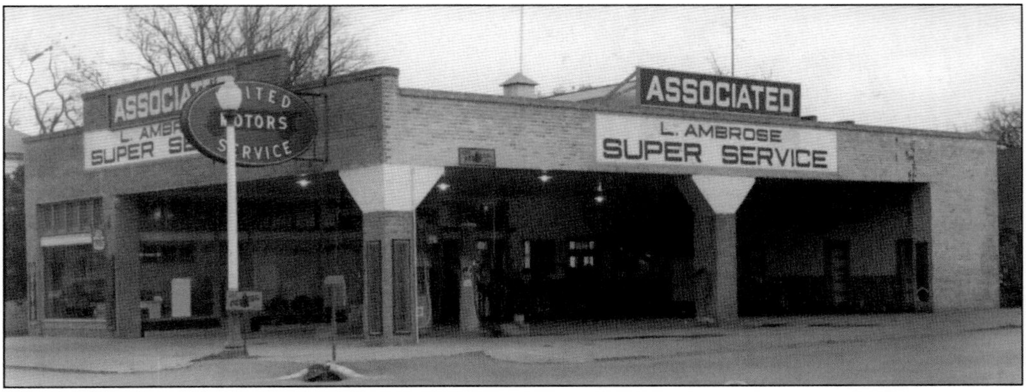

Associated Oil, owned by Louis Ambrose, was a full-service gas station. It was located on the corner of Hazel and Vermont Streets. Not only could one fill up on gas, it was a place that did repairs on carburetors. Associated Oil was the precursor to Chevron and Flying A. (Courtesy of Gridley Museum.)

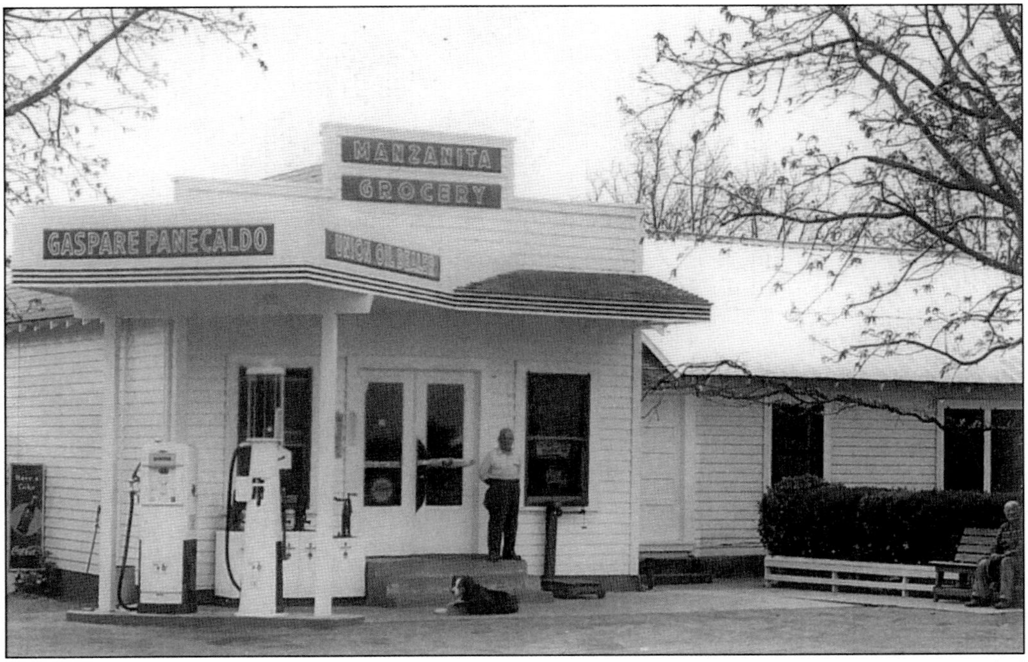

When he was 16 or 17, Gaspar Panecaldo came to the United States from Italy alone and traveled from New York to California on the train. He went to work with his brother in the bakery, but because of allergies to the flour, had to find other work. On 10 acres in the Manzanita area he built a small grocery store. The family lived behind the store. (Courtesy of the Gridley Museum.)

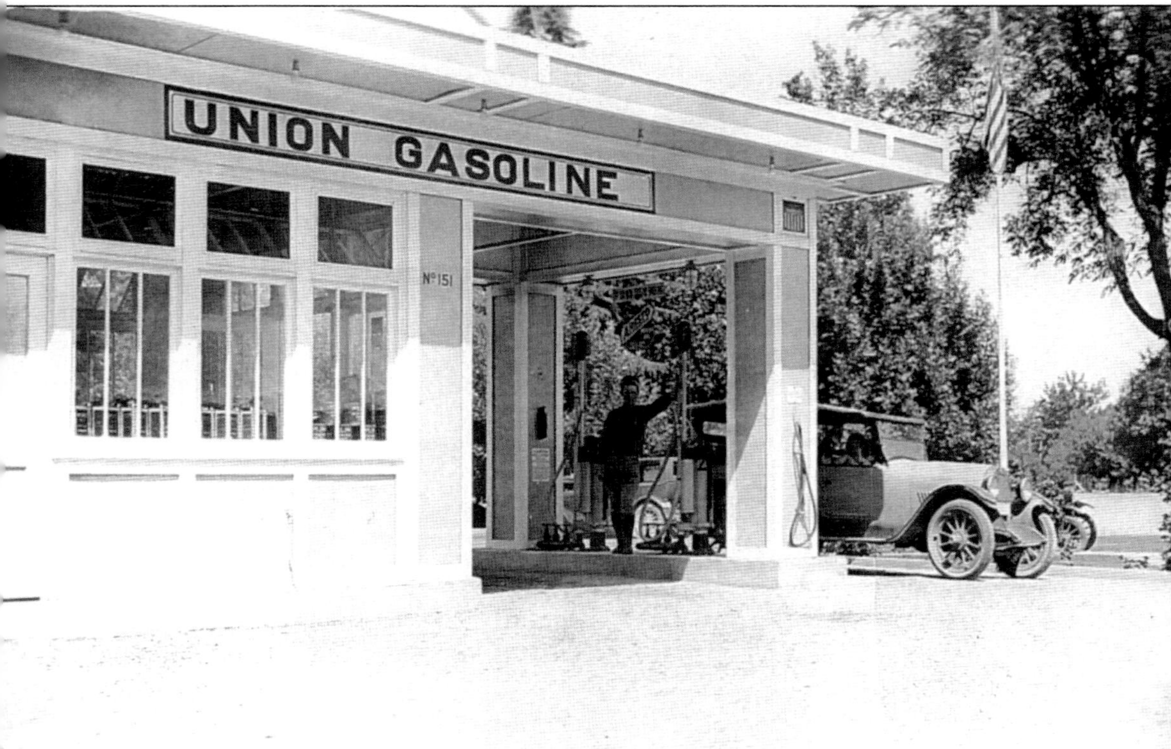

Charles Stohlman, son of Allen Stohlman, a Shell Oil distributor in East Gridley, bought his own Union Oil station in 1948. It is interesting he would continue in the petroleum business, following in his father's footsteps. The business is located on the northwest corner of Sycamore and Virginia Streets, still run by his family. (Courtesy of the Gridley Museum.)

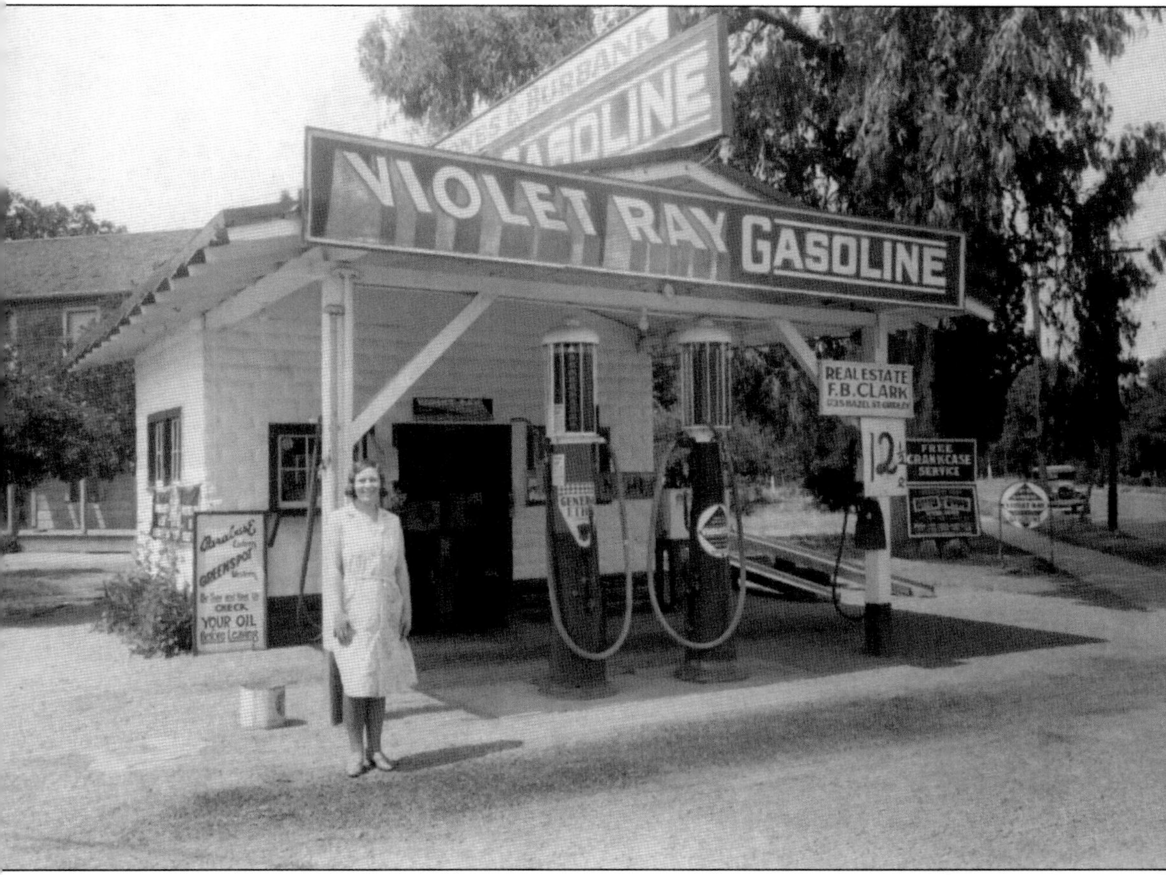

Violet Ray was General Petroleum's new anti-knock gasoline in 1928, with a major advertising campaign involving 3,500 West Coast dealers "from Canada on down." Shown here is Charlotte Burbank, whose father was the owner of this local gas station. Charlotte married Ned Davis of Gridley. This station sat on the corner of Wilson Street and Highway 99E and later became the Mobil station. (Courtesy of the Ned Davis family.)

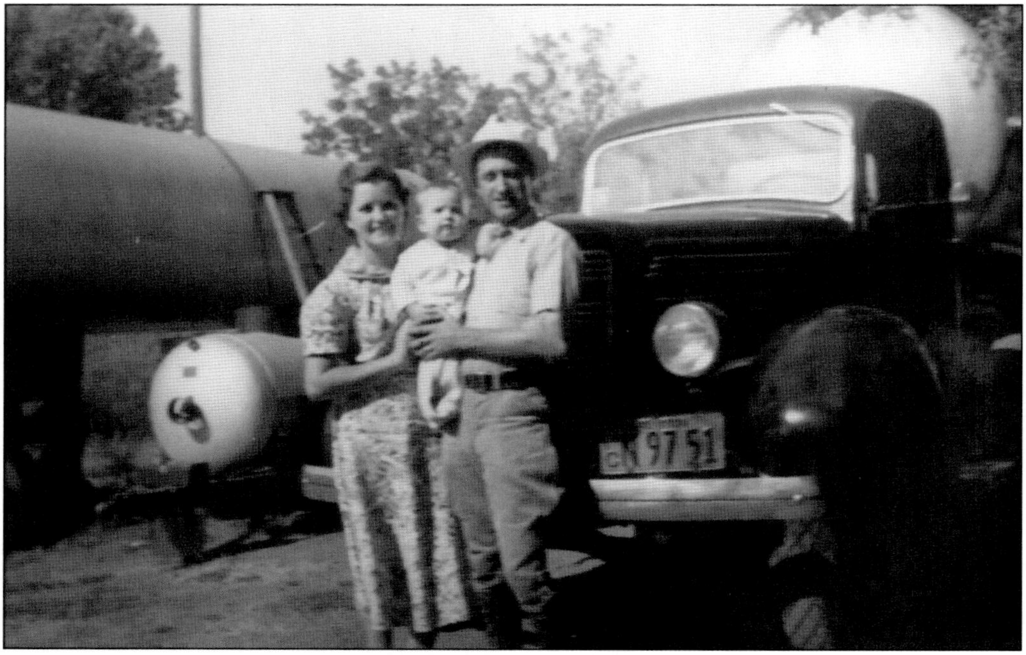

Albert Dunning, born in 1906 to Lewis and Antoinette Dunning, after determining the need for cheaper fuel, partnered with his father in Dunning and Dunning Butane Supply in 1933. Specializing in converting Caterpillar tractors from gasoline to butane during World War II, he became the sole owner under the name Albert Dunning Butane. His son Lorry filled fuel tanks and repaired carburetors, with Albert working in the field. In 1945, he expanded his business to include Albert Dunning's Appliance, featuring Tappan and Westinghouse brands. (Both, courtesy of Lorry Dunning.)

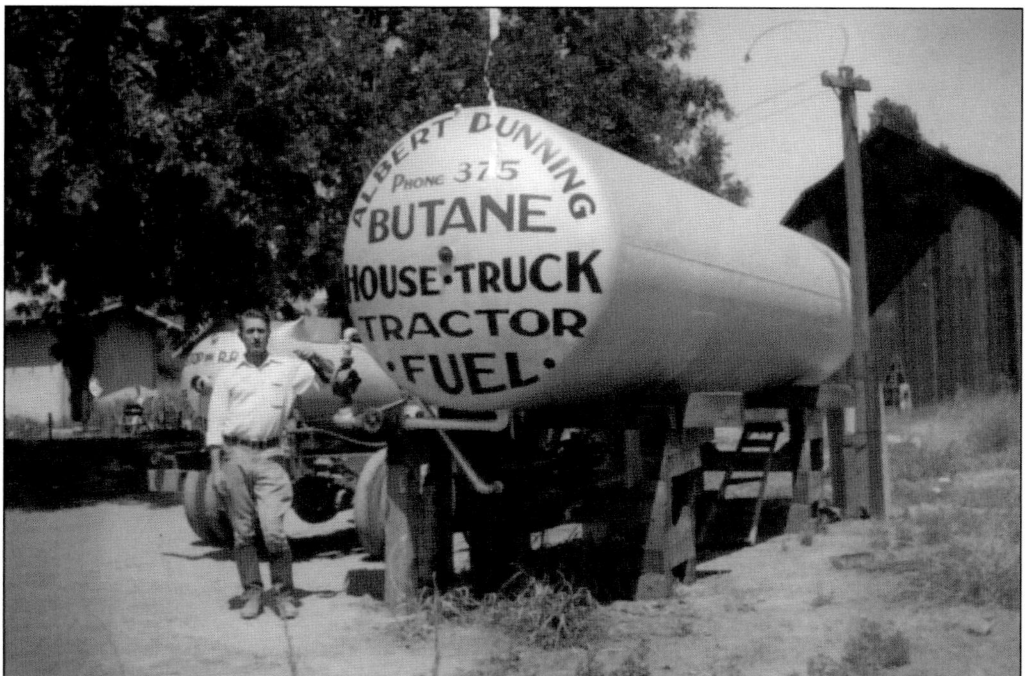

Three

SCHOOLS

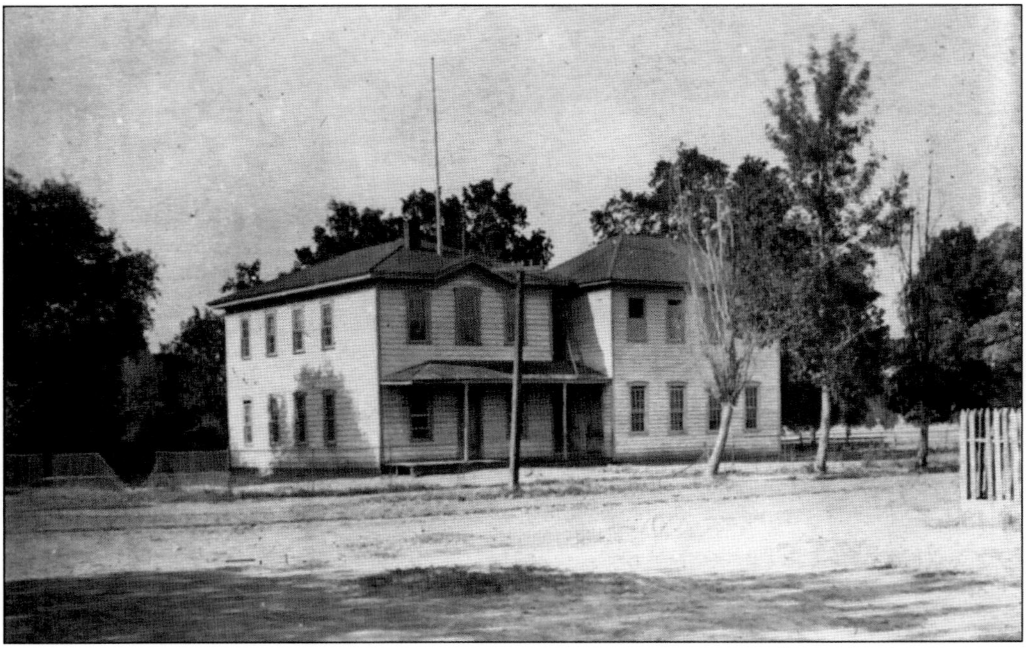

The Wells and Chambers *History of Butte County* of 1882 states, "The Gridley School District was formed on February 6, 1873. It comprised the territory of a mile and a half square from the railroad station as a center. In 1874, a two-story schoolhouse was very well equipped, for the time. This building later became known as the old 'Orange Hotel,' 'Vi's Rooms,' and the 'Gridley House.' " (Courtesy of the Gridley Museum.)

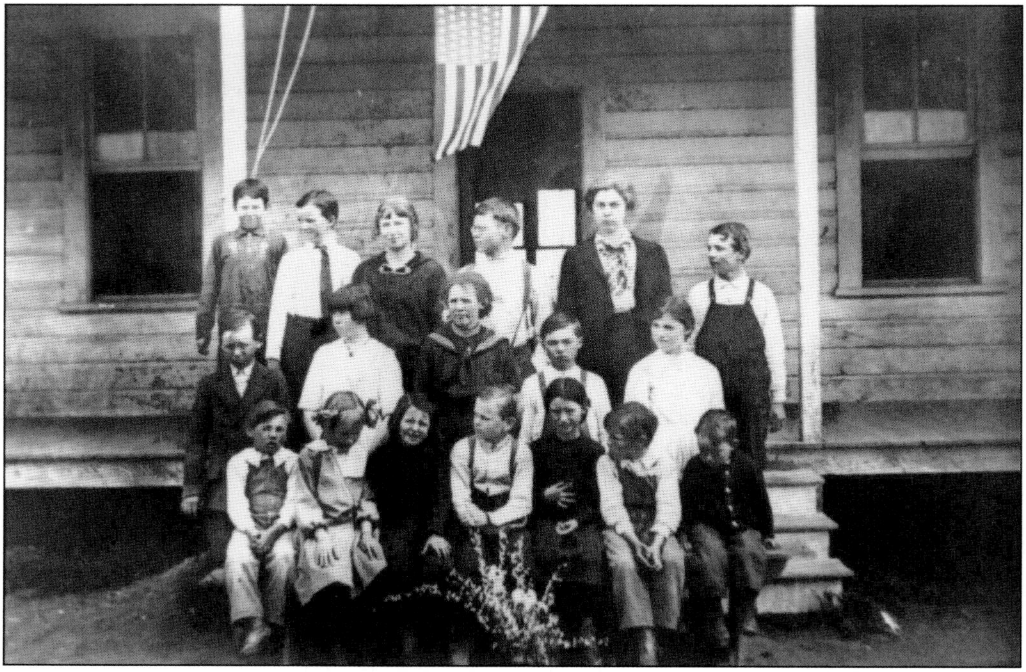

Butte District School formed in 1873 west of the town of Gridley at a distance five or six miles on Pennington Road. Students pictured here are (first row) Leta Fairlee, Adelaline Watson, Angeline ?, Willie Ashbury, and Lyle Fairlee; (second row) Joseph Nugent, Ester Nugent, Violet ?, Joe Ashbury, and Stella Ashbury; (third row) Frank Watson, Marvin Cassady, Gertrude Watson, Norman Nugent, and Lester Dow (teacher). (Courtesy of Richard Watson.)

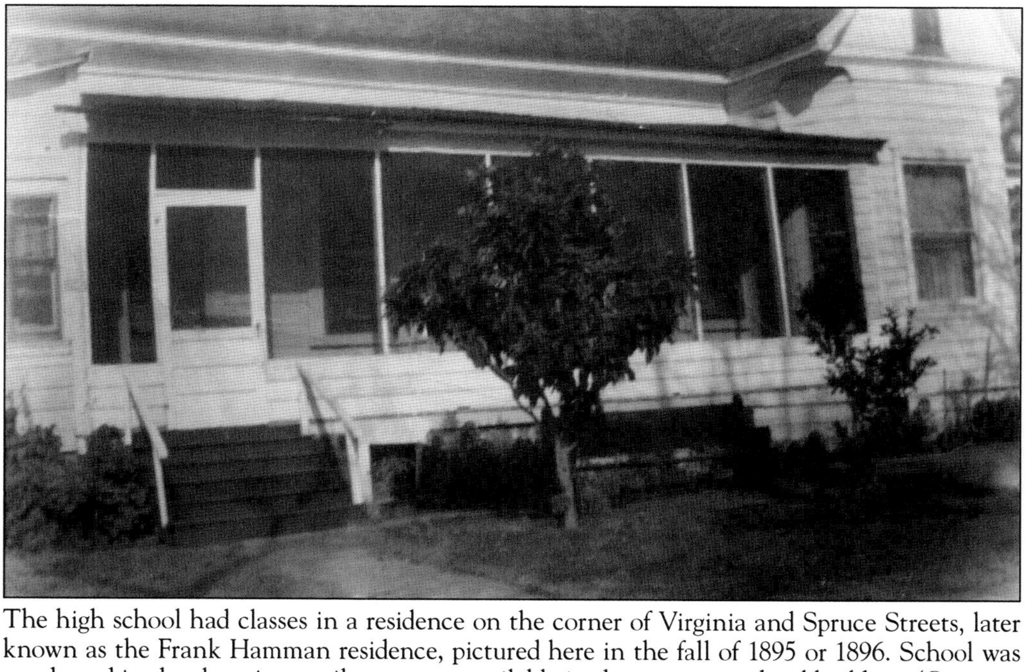

The high school had classes in a residence on the corner of Virginia and Spruce Streets, later known as the Frank Hamman residence, pictured here in the fall of 1895 or 1896. School was conducted in that location until space was available in the grammar school building. (Courtesy of the Gridley Museum.)

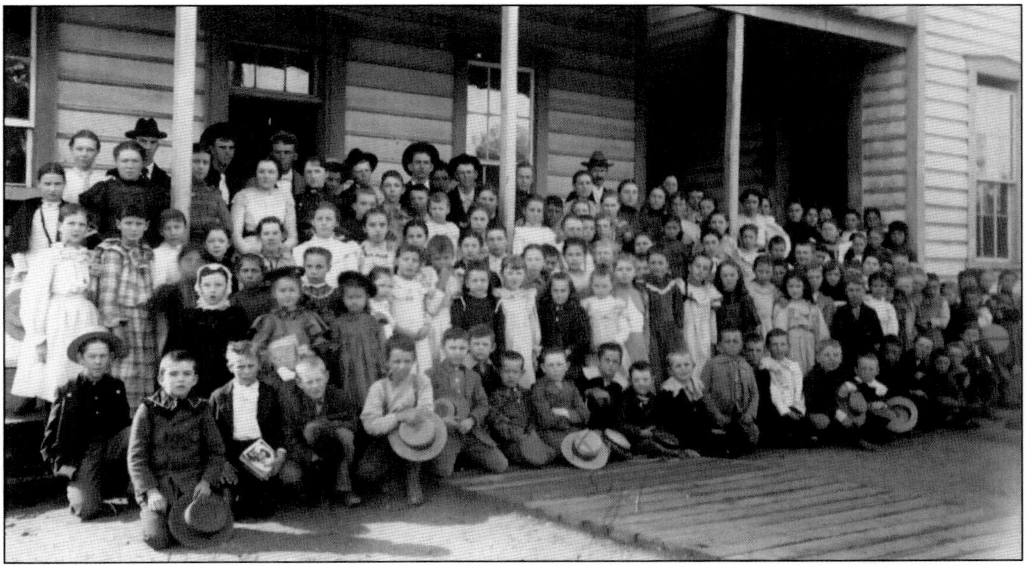

The date of this photograph is unknown, but school was held in this big grammar school building that later became known as the Orange Hotel and Vi's Rooming House on Ohio Street. It is likely the entire school posing for this photograph. (Courtesy of the Gridley Museum.)

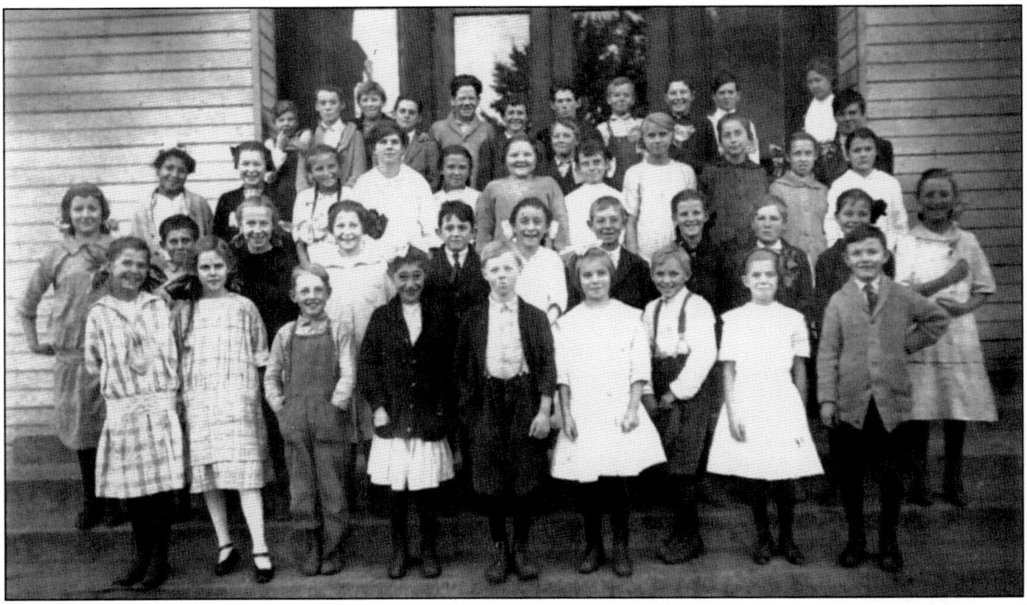

The new grammar school was built in 1907 on the Sycamore Street property between Ohio and Vermont Streets. Although there is no clear evidence, the previous building may have been moved from this location to Ohio Street, providing space for the new building. Dorothy May Crum is standing at far left in the first row of this photograph of the school taken around 1911–1915. (Courtesy of the Gridley Museum.)

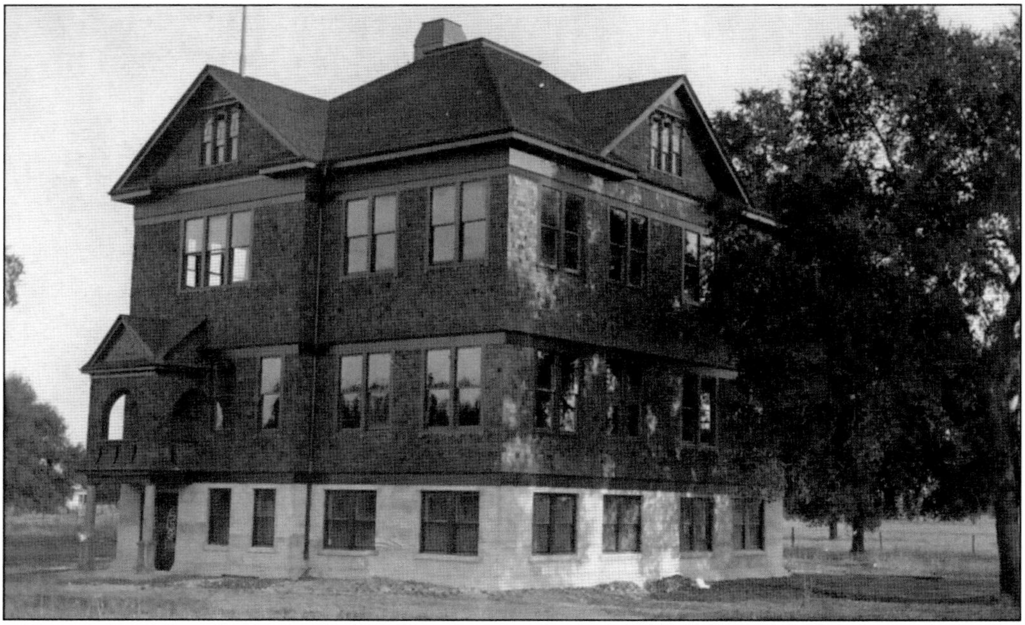

The Gridley Union High School was formed in 1892, one of the first in the county. The first records for Gridley showed a monthly expense of $150 for a teacher. When attendance was low, some of the businessmen's wives attended part time to keep up the averages. The first commencement exercises were held in June 1897 with graduates Nellie Long, Charlotte Channon, and Charles English. (Courtesy of the Gridley Museum.)

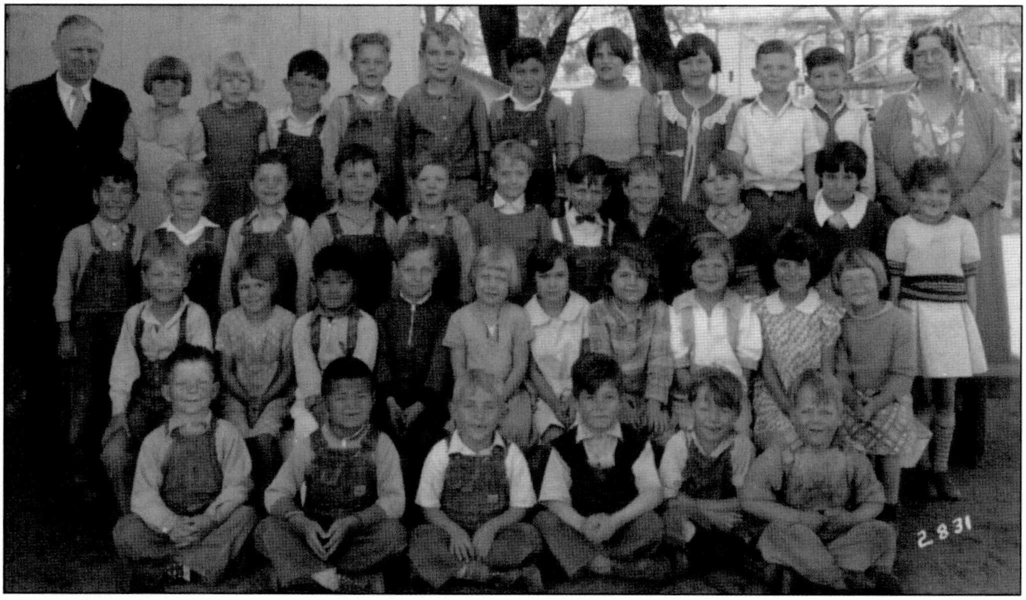

This McKinley School photograph was taken around 1935, with Principal Nugent on the left and teacher Jessie Burleson on the right. The first grade class that year included Dick Cassady, Beatrice Brady, Betty Justeson, Frances McKinney, Gerald Thompson, Philip Huston, Lou (Gus) Martine, Marie Vines, Nettie Wheeler, Betty Boyett, Jackie Clements, Flora Kelly, Bill Dukes, June Longacre, Leland Dewsnup, Fred Little, Tommy Miho, Les Ozawa, and Bob Francis. (Courtesy of the Gridley Museum.)

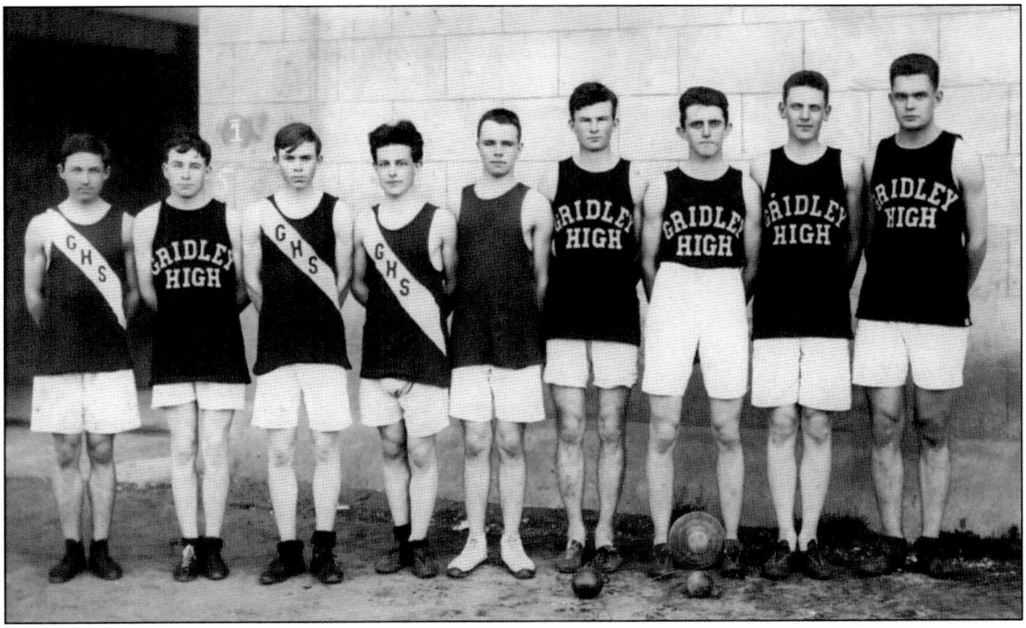

The 1913 Gridley High men's track team members pictured here are, from left to right, Alvin Harry, Lloyd Craig, Clyde Hamer, Bert Garner, Leo Post, Jim Clark, Morris Wood (captain), Willard Gerry, and Elwood DeRuchie. A few of the team were underclassmen, and they had hopes of developing into a first-rate track team. Wood and DeRuchie were the team's two track stars. (Courtesy of the Gridley Museum.)

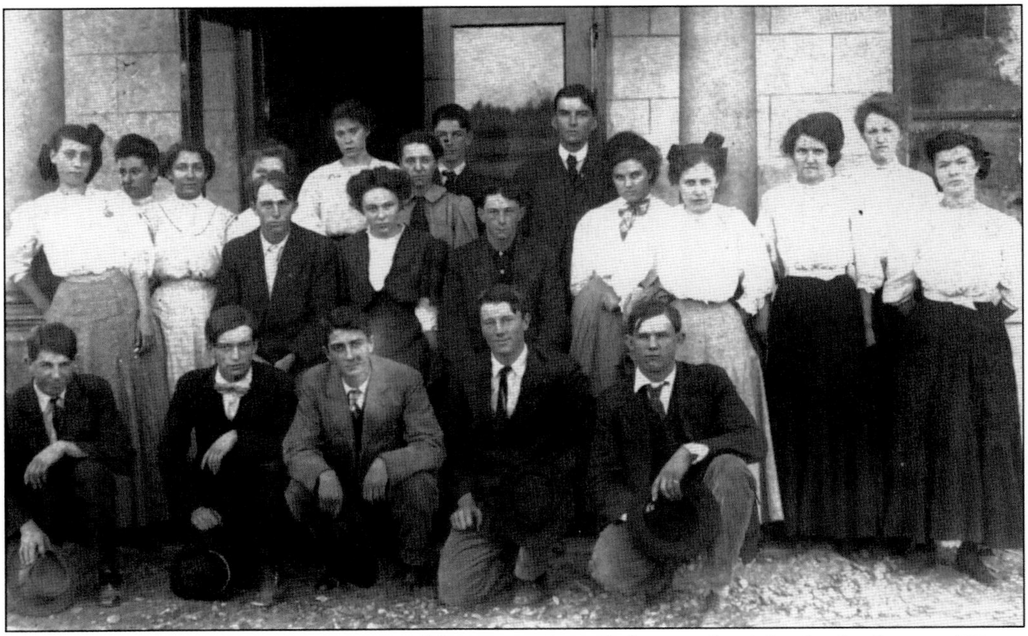

Members of the class of 1909 pictured here are, from left to right, Myrtle Anderson, Diana Simpson, Ethel Nichols, Una Boulware, Eda Bishop, Robert Golway, Sidney Smith, Jimmie Allen, Vada Wells, Velma Lewis, Hattie Cape, Ross Lewis, Eva Moody, Lizzie Osborn, Amy Culver, Ada Ambrose, George Knoop, Lyman Doty, Jake Allen, Leon Hampton, and Roy Barker. (Courtesy of the Gridley Museum.)

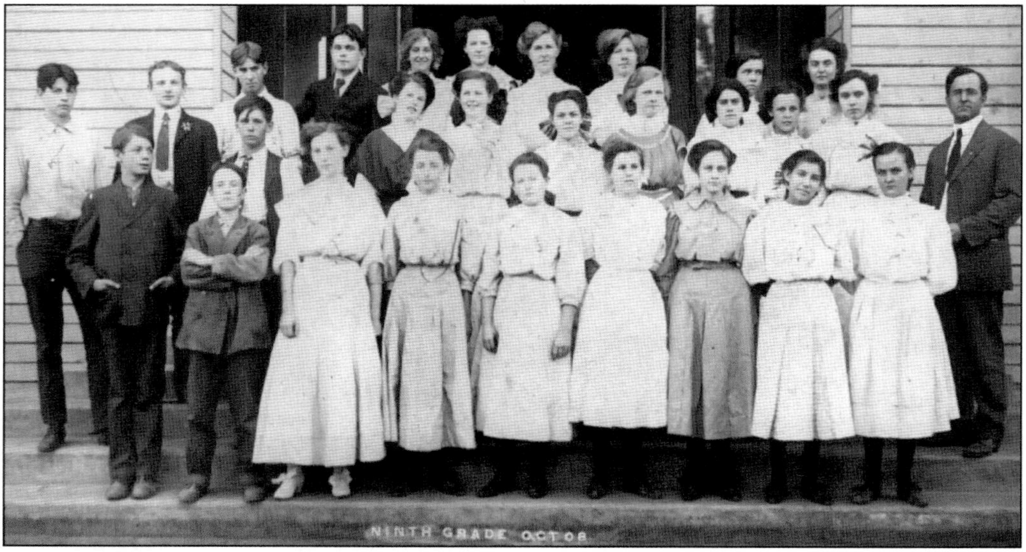

Ninth graders pictured here in 1909 are, from left to right, (first row) Harold Simpson, Joe Sheridan, Myrtle Clarenback, Helen Bonslett, Mamie Condon, Elma Nichols, Florence Robinson, Katie Osborn, and Dorothy Moody; (second row) Ambrose Burleson, Harold Evans, Ernie Williams, Ramona Quimby, Florence Moore, Edith McDaniel, Elwood DeRuchie, Alma Gerst, Ola Porter, Sadie Duus, Carrie Duus, and Louise Treadgold. Principal Howard Short is standing on the right. (Courtesy of the Gridley Museum.)

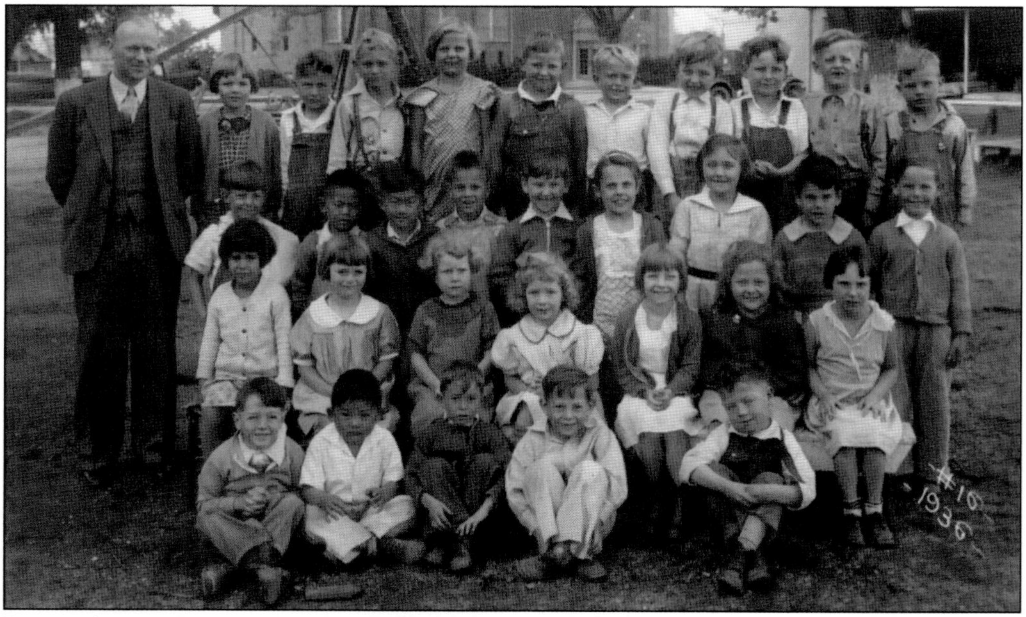

First graders pictured here in 1937 are, from left to right, (first row) Hyrum Horn, Kay Fukushima, Joe Taylor, Donald Payne, and Jimmy LeValley; (second row) Mary Loy Lopez, Barbara Wheeler, Bertie Lou Stenzel, Lucille Mitchell, Evelyn Robinson, Genevieve Stohlman, and Victoria Olschowska; (third row) Howard Mulkins, Dick Ozawa, Jimmy Miho, John Hunter, Dickie Perrine, Hazel Lively, Annabelle James, Jimmy Vines, and Max Woodward; (fourth row) Charley Thompson, Byron Campbell, Wallace Womack, Mavis Benish, George Harrington, Jimmy Randolph, David Porter, Charles Clark, ? Swallow, and Billie Hampton. (Courtesy of the Gridley Museum.)

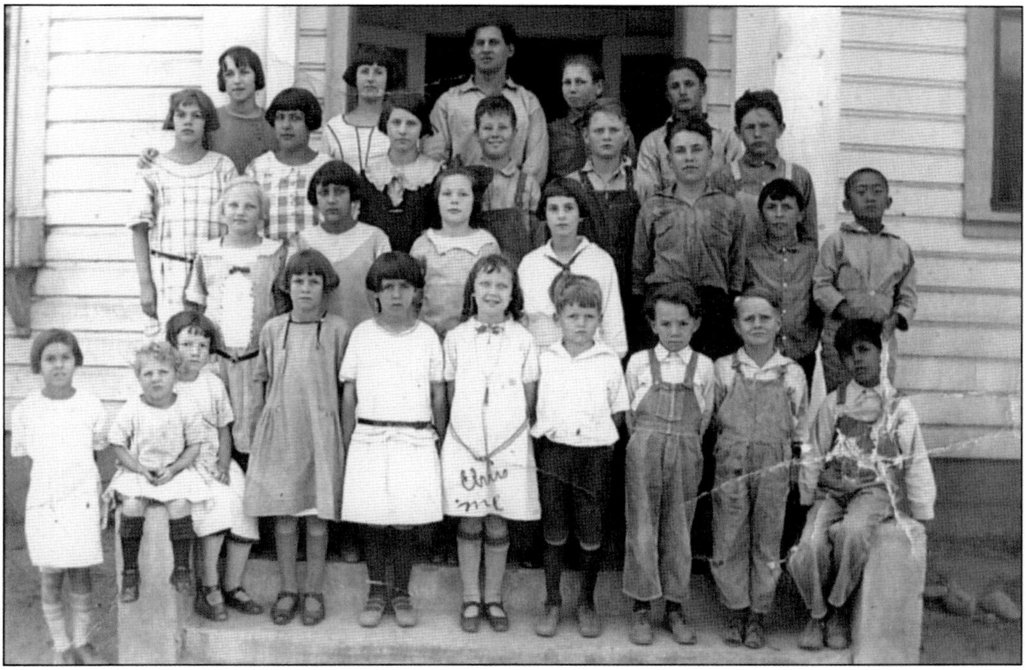

In the early days of the East Gridley School District, the students spent a portion of their school days in a tent under the shade of a valley oak. Instead of deer and wildcats, they saw electric cars going past at a great speed and overhead, a 66,000-volt electric power line. Mrs. Hillhouse, the teacher, opened the school with about a dozen children. Christina Cassady is sixth from the left. (Courtesy of the Gridley Museum.)

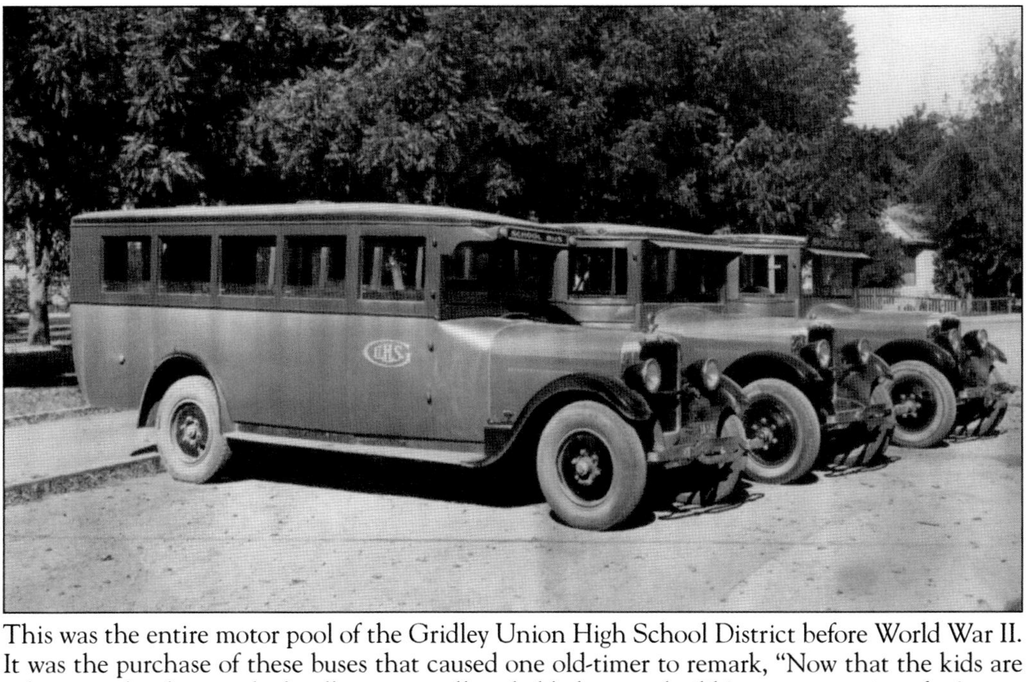

This was the entire motor pool of the Gridley Union High School District before World War II. It was the purchase of these buses that caused one old-timer to remark, "Now that the kids are riding to school instead of walking, we will probably have to build 'em a gymnasium for 'em to get their exercise in." (Courtesy of the Gridley Museum.)

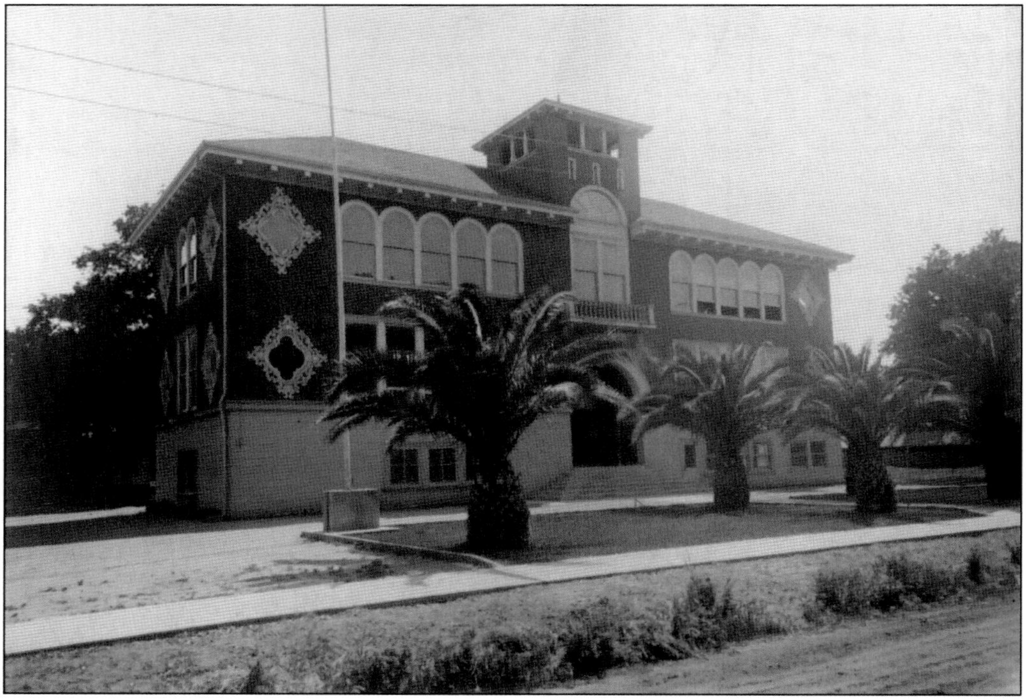

McKinley School stood on Sycamore Street between Ohio and Vermont Streets. Gridleyans are pictured below surveying the damage to the first McKinley School, which burned on January 7, 1915. The *Gridley Herald* reported in its February 3, 1915, edition that the original plans, which were drawn by a San Francisco architect in 1902, had been lost in the fire that followed the 1906 earthquake there. Therefore, Chester Cole, the architect retained for rebuilding the school, had secured photographs of the old building for use in drawing plans to reproduce it. (Both, courtesy of the Gridley Museum.)

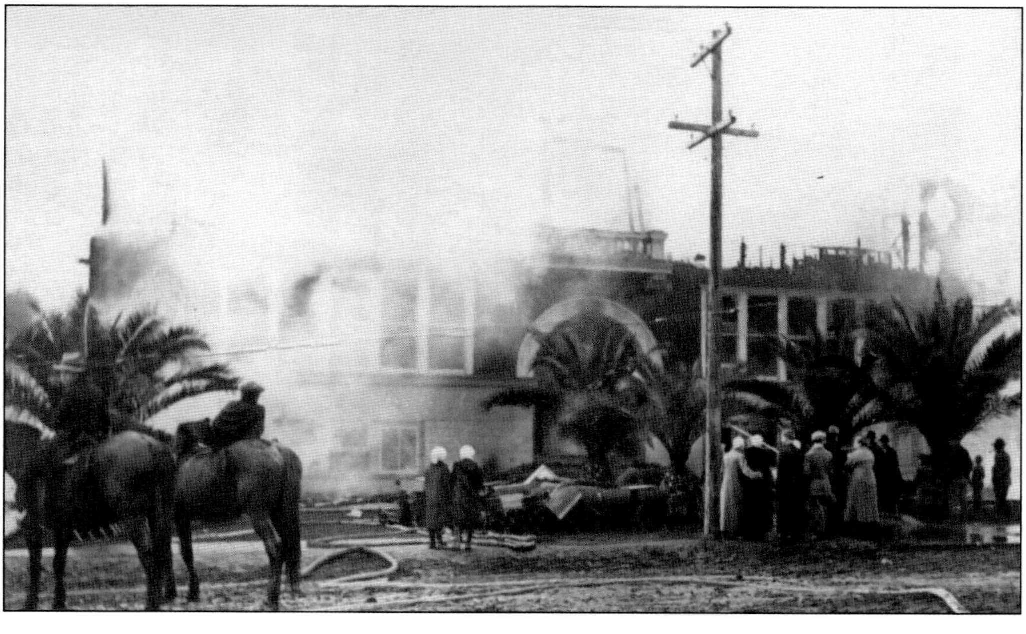

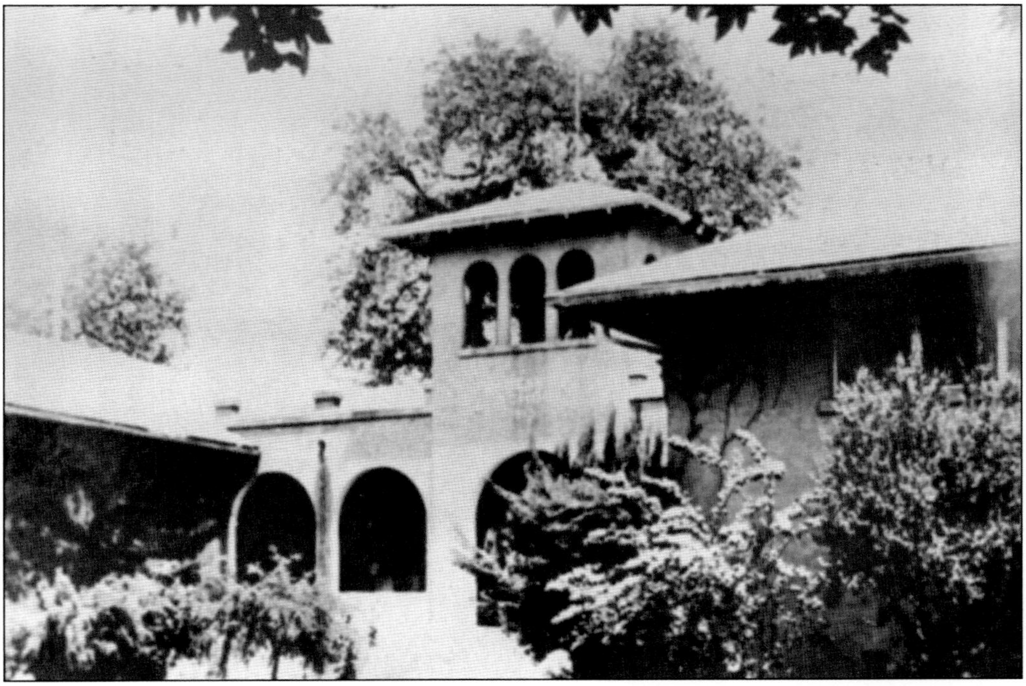

The one-room Early Manzanita Schoolhouse was built in 1873. In 1908, another room was added with windows on each side. The middle of the room had a large cast-iron stove on which the children often sat to keep warm or get dry. Games played were ante-over, shinny (with homemade sticks and tin cans), tag, dare-base, and some baseball. Shown here is the second school building for Manzanita. (Courtesy of the Gridley Museum.)

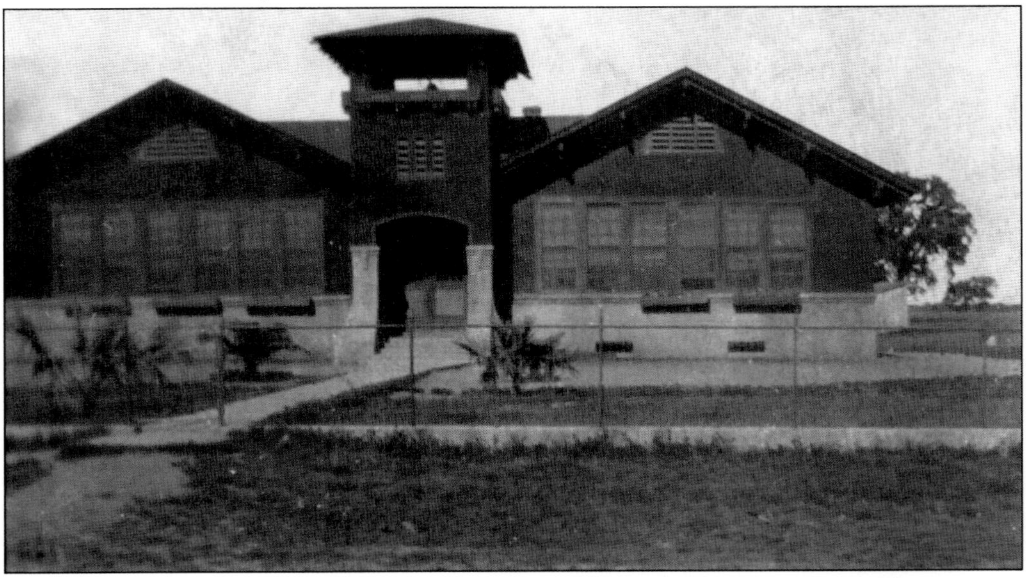

West Liberty School District formed in 1863, serving southwest Butte County. There was an altercation with Gridley residents in 1876, and a petition to abolish the district in favor of the Gridley district was signed by Gridley town residents and the West Liberty Board. George Gridley and ranchers in the area rose up in wrath, hired an attorney, appeared before the board of supervisors, and won. The school was saved. (Courtesy of the Gridley Museum.)

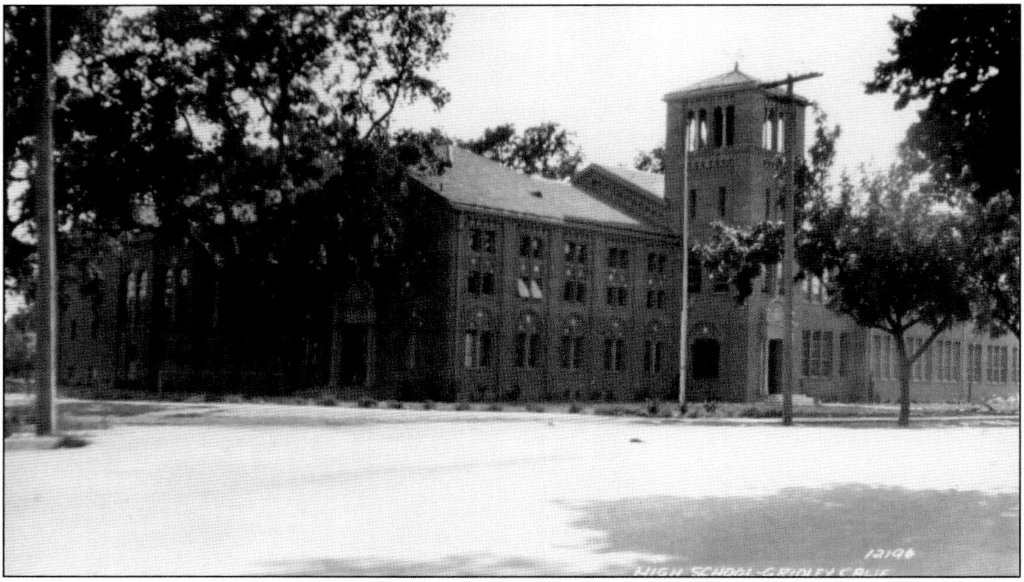

This is the second high school that replaced the building of 1907. The winning bid of $121,441 set off the construction of an architecturally beautiful redbrick building two stories high, with adequate classrooms and a large auditorium with an excellent stage. When completed, it was one of the most attractive buildings in Gridley. This school was later destroyed by fire on July 4, 1942. (Courtesy of the Gridley Museum.)

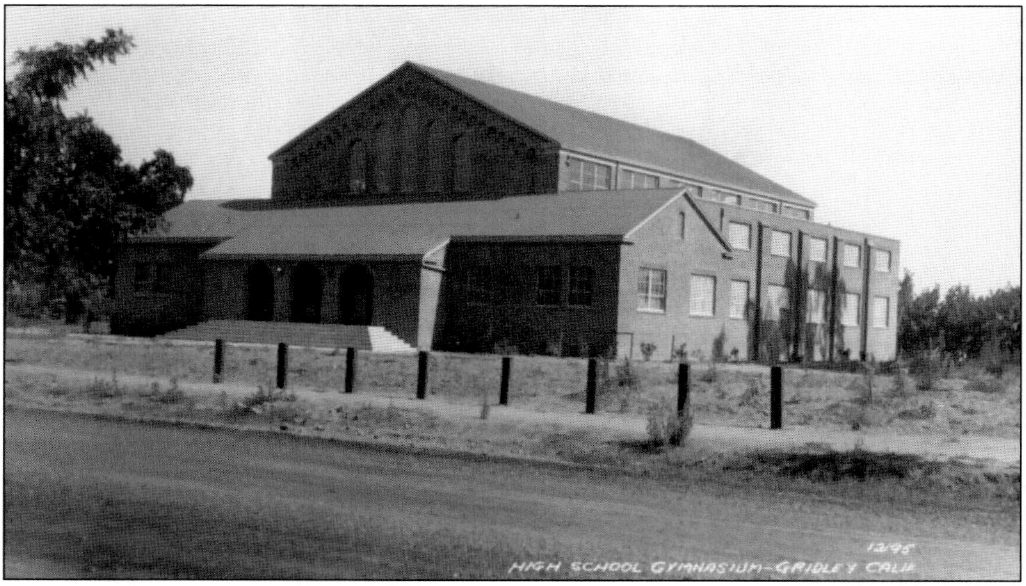

The gymnasium was next to the new high school. The basketball court had hardwood floors with raised seating along both sides. Ample space provided dressing and shower rooms below. This magnificent gym was available every weeknight for scheduled use by the high school basketball teams, as well as men and women of different athletic teams of the community. (Courtesy of the Gridley Museum.)

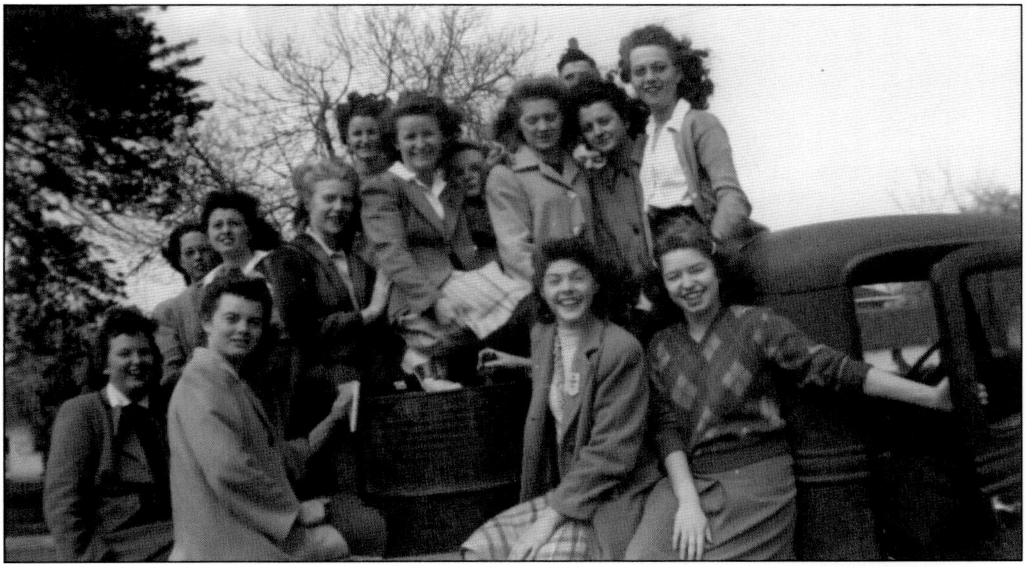

This photograph was taken around 1944. These high school beauties are having a good time posing. Not in any particular order, some of them are identified as Mabel Fife, Barbara Bond, Pat Hubbell, Dora Farr, Mildred Robinson, Helen Robinson, Barbara Olsen, Mary Kossow, Dorothy Nelson, and Barbara Johnson. (Courtesy of the Gridley Museum.)

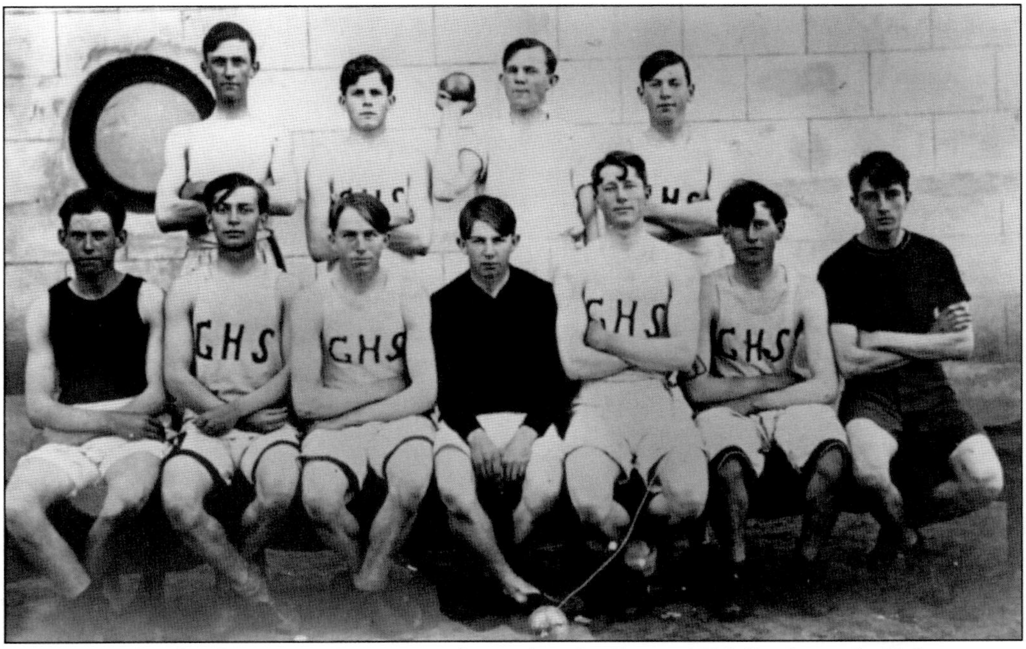

The first high school in Butte County was located in Gridley in 1892. By the early 20th century, other high schools had been established, and athletic teams were meeting in competition. This Gridley track team more than held its own until rival schools grew larger, with bigger student bodies to draw from. (Courtesy of the Gridley Museum.)

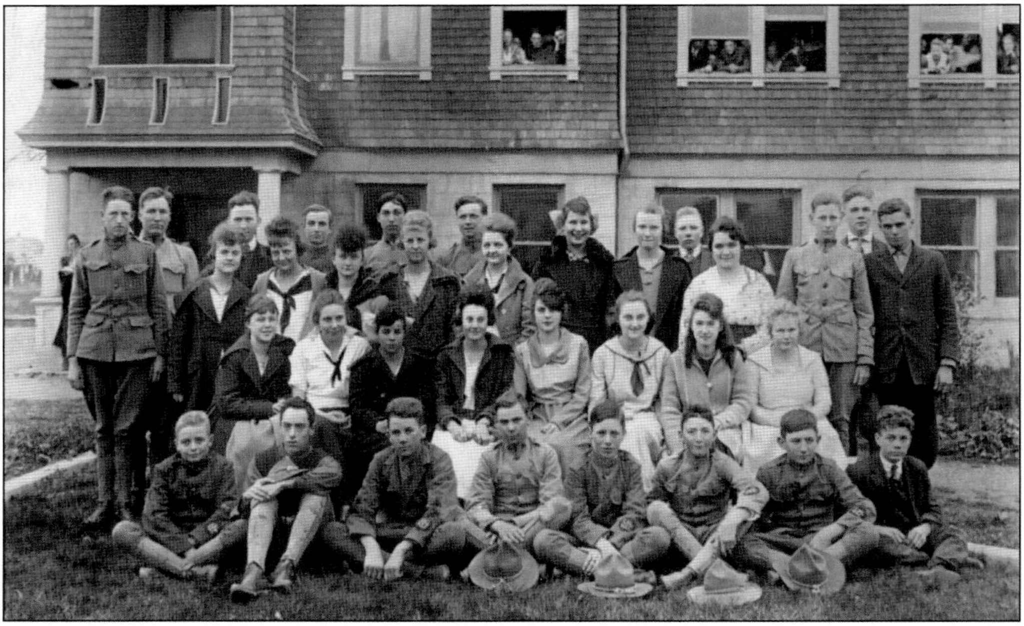

The Gridley High yearbook, *The Spider*, wrote, "We, the Class of 1921, knowing that our untimely end is near, due to long assignments and complications thereof, while here together in these dying moments, do hereby bequeath the following: the juniors, we bequeath our sympathy, knowing well the trial and tribulations they will have to experience next year, sophomores, our brilliancy, self-conceit and our love of poetry, and freshmen, our brilliancy, self-conceit and our other characteristics." (Courtesy of the Gridley Museum.)

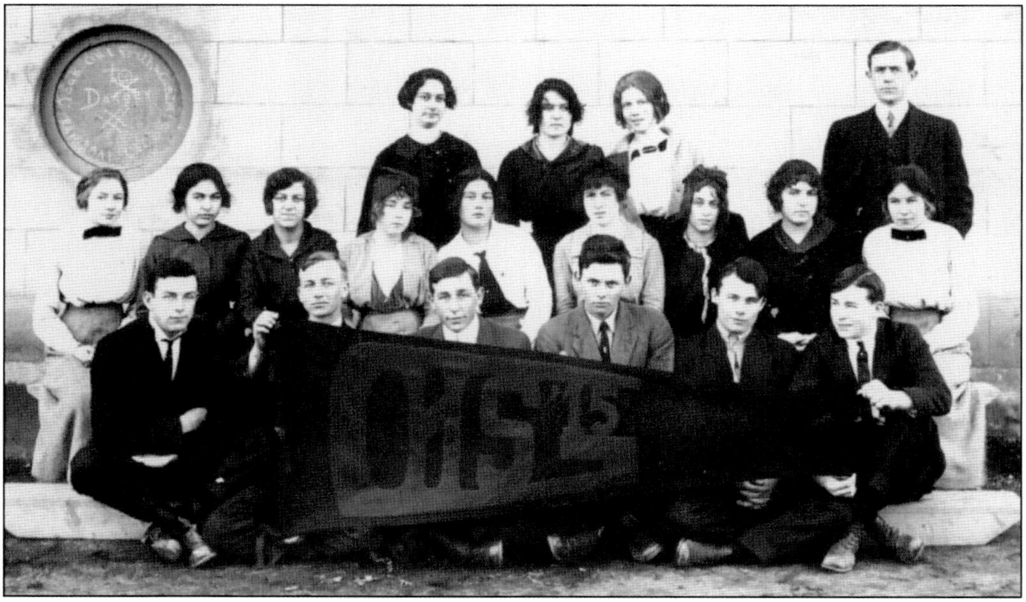

The Gridley High class of 1915 is pictured here. The students are, in no particular order, Ada Cowee, Gladys Myers, Anita Neilson, Bertha Neilson, Lloyd Craig, Leo Post, Willard Gerry, Iona Craig, Georgiana Johnson, Amelia Quados, James Fannin Presley, William Evans, Charles Porter, Marguerite Williams, Alyce Orr, Leigh Ahlstrom, Thomas Ryan Block, Walter Emery, and Annabelle Barker. (Courtesy of the Gridley Museum.)

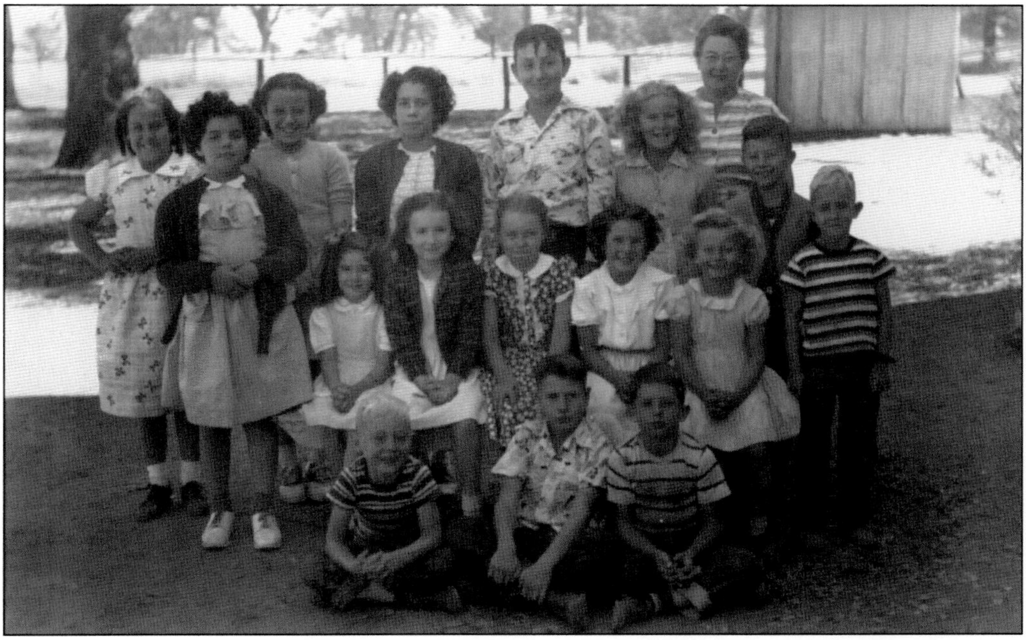

Central House School was located on Highway 40A just south of Robinson's Corner on the road toward Marysville. The school served the children of that area east of Gridley. The entire school is pictured here from left to right: (first row) Rodger Biggs, Allen Hill, and Gary Mills; (second row) Florinda Aquiar, Lavern Alves, Margo Robinson, Laura Lee Allen, Amy Hill, and Jerry Biggs; (third row) Margaret Bettencourt, Jean Bettencourt, Del Aguiar, Anthony Bettencourt, and Thelda Biggs (teacher). (Courtesy of Margaret Bettencourt Stanton.)

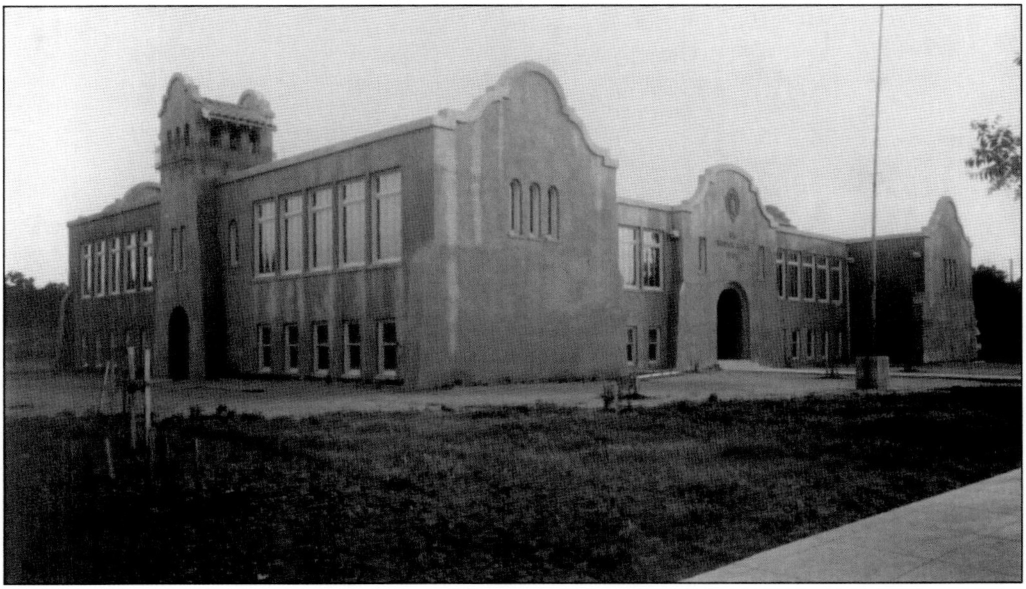

The original Woodrow Wilson School was constructed in 1914 and had a large unpaved basement and classrooms upstairs with oiled pine floors. Its first stage provided six classrooms upstairs. A few years later, a southeast wing was added, providing two more classrooms upstairs and additional basement space in the southeast wing. The school housed kindergarten through eighth grade into the 1950s. (Courtesy of the Gridley Museum.)

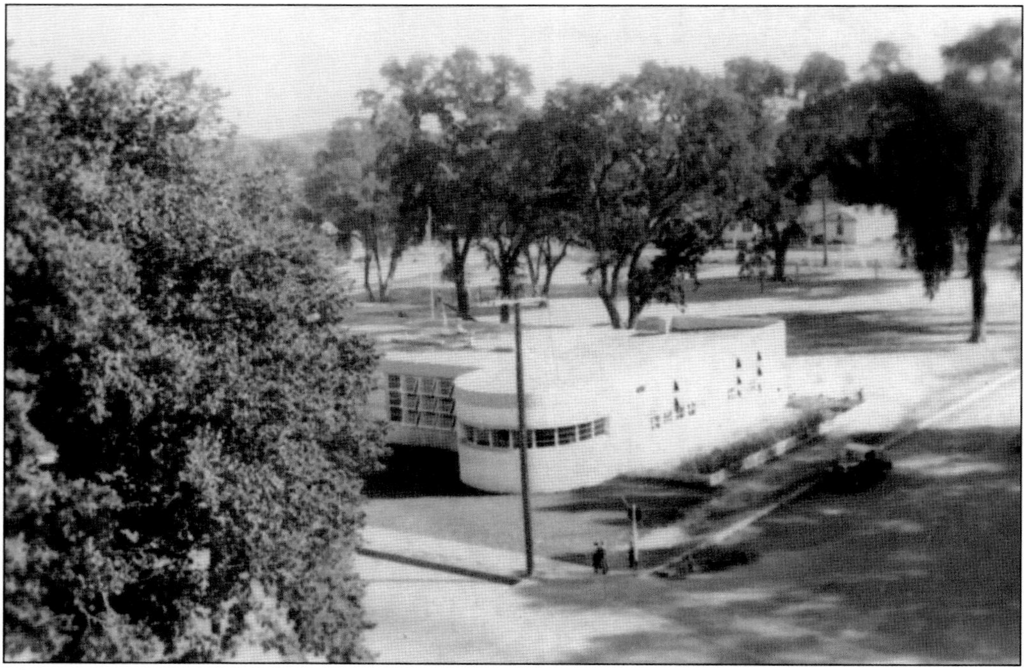

The Works Progress Administration, the largest and most ambitious New Deal agency, paid for the building of the new McKinley School in 1938. The previous school had been torn down to make room for the new one. (Courtesy of the Gridley Museum.)

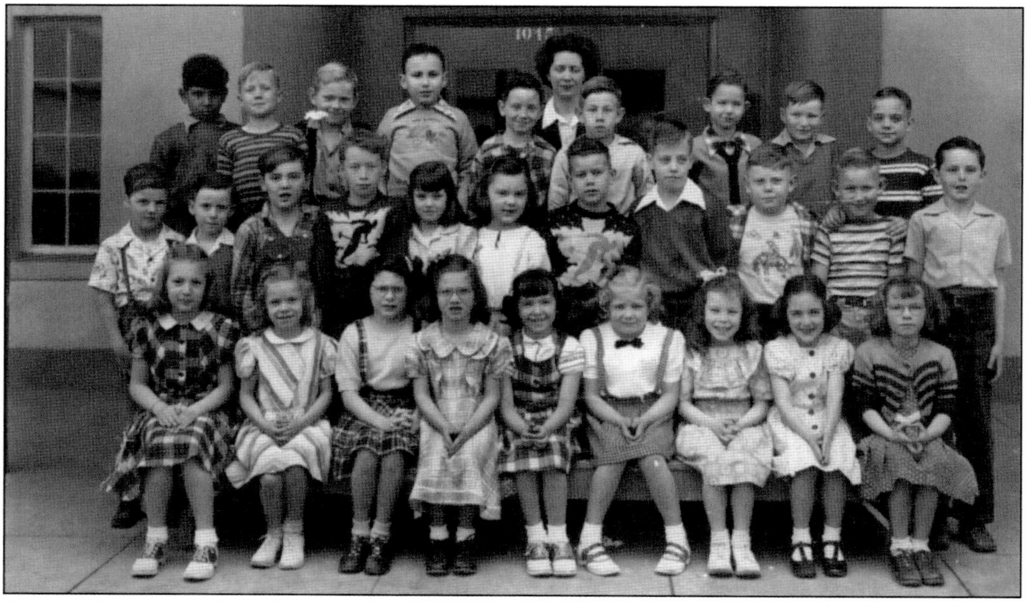

First graders from McKinley school in 1947 are, from left to right, (first row) Judy Gage, Loretta Burkes, unidentified, Davine Cushman, Athena Nicholau, Leanne Roberson, Joan Adams, and unidentified; (second row) Leon Longacre, unidentified, William Rose, Dennis Back, Thelma Tabor, Sharon Lawrence, Frank Stenzel, Gary Carlin, Howard Hamman, Robert Albert, and Jerry Sannar; (third row) Raymond Din, David Richins, Gene Almo, Michael Hanson, Steve Pantaleoni, Arnold Stewart, and Palmer Hatch. (Courtesy of the Gridley Museum.)

Four

Farming

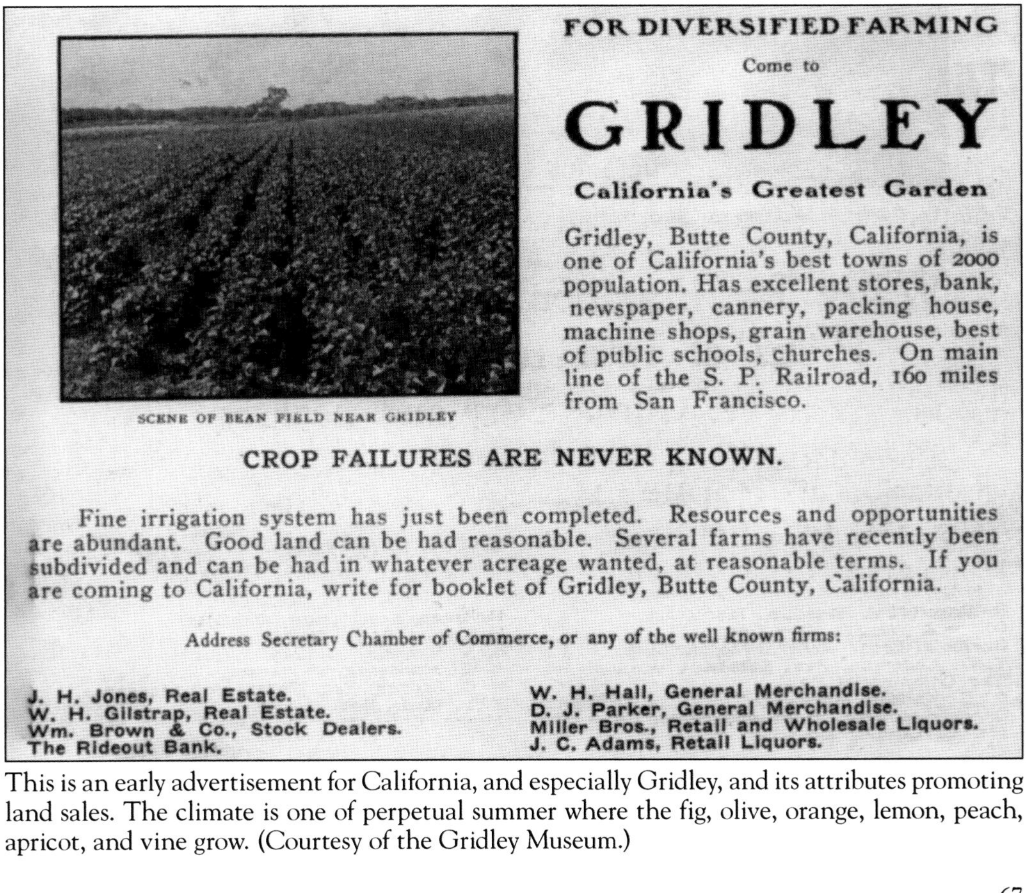

This is an early advertisement for California, and especially Gridley, and its attributes promoting land sales. The climate is one of perpetual summer where the fig, olive, orange, lemon, peach, apricot, and vine grow. (Courtesy of the Gridley Museum.)

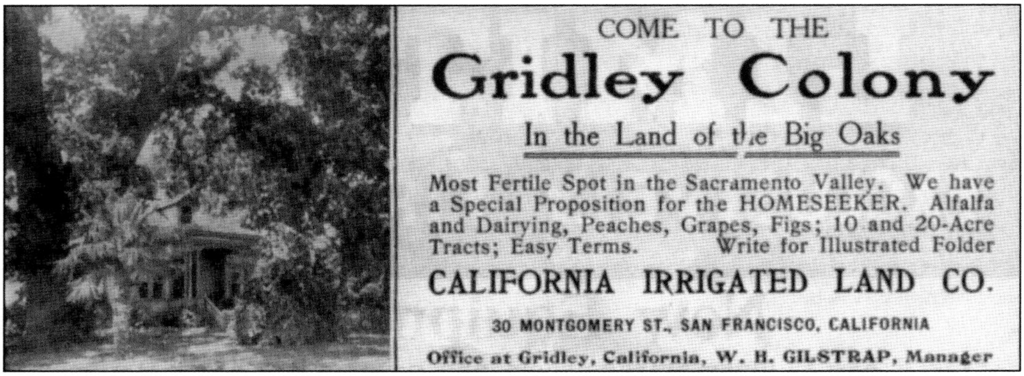

The price of land ranged from $15 or $20 per acre for the unimproved, up to as much as $175 for the more highly improved river bottom land. In 1937, Gridley had no ambitions to become an industrial city but prided itself on being a "farmers' town," according to a local merchant. In all directions there were farms producing rice, grain, orchards, poultry, dairy products, and spinach. (Both, courtesy of the Gridley Museum.)

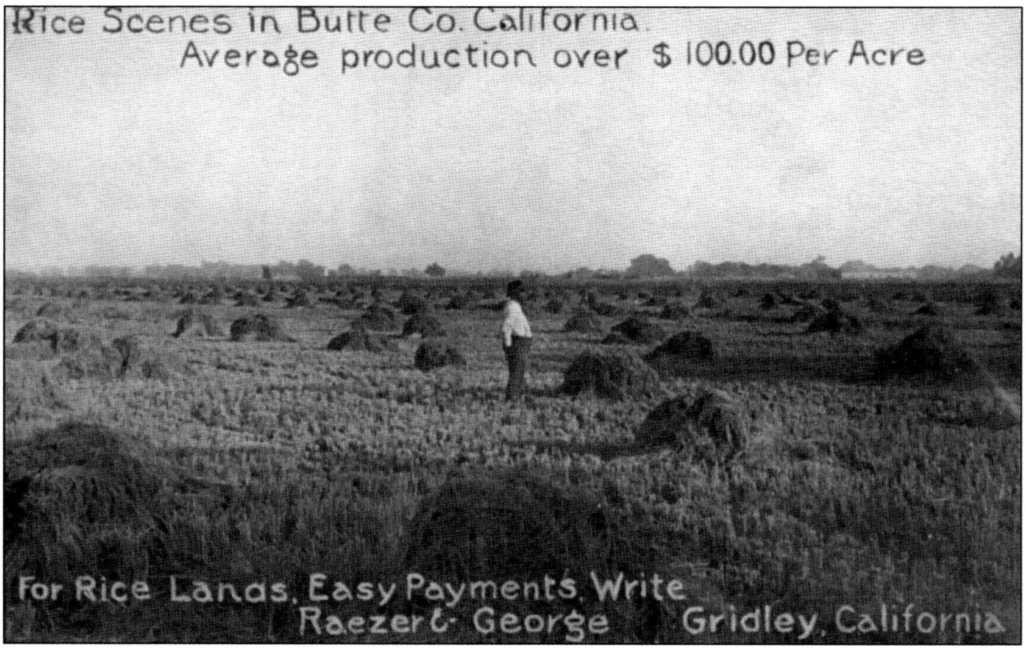

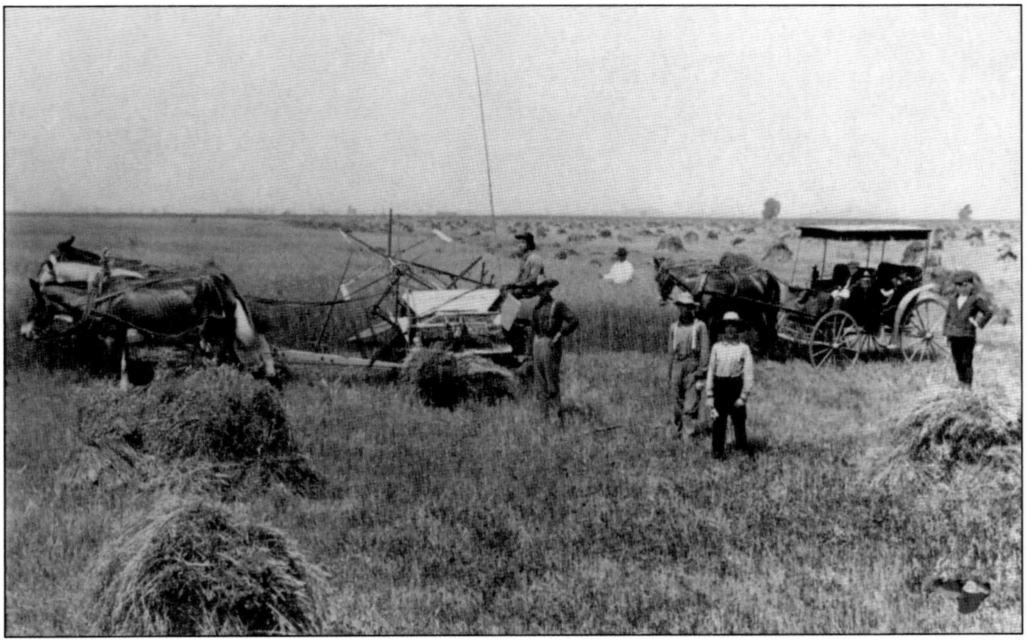

These photographs feature early harvest in the Gridley area around the late 1800s. Below is a 24-mule team pulling a harvester in wheat fields on the Harkey Ranch on Township Road, just south of Gridley. William Pinkney "Bill" Harkey is driving. This photograph is from around 1912, when Harkey was about 20 years old. (Both, courtesy of Edgar Stanton III.)

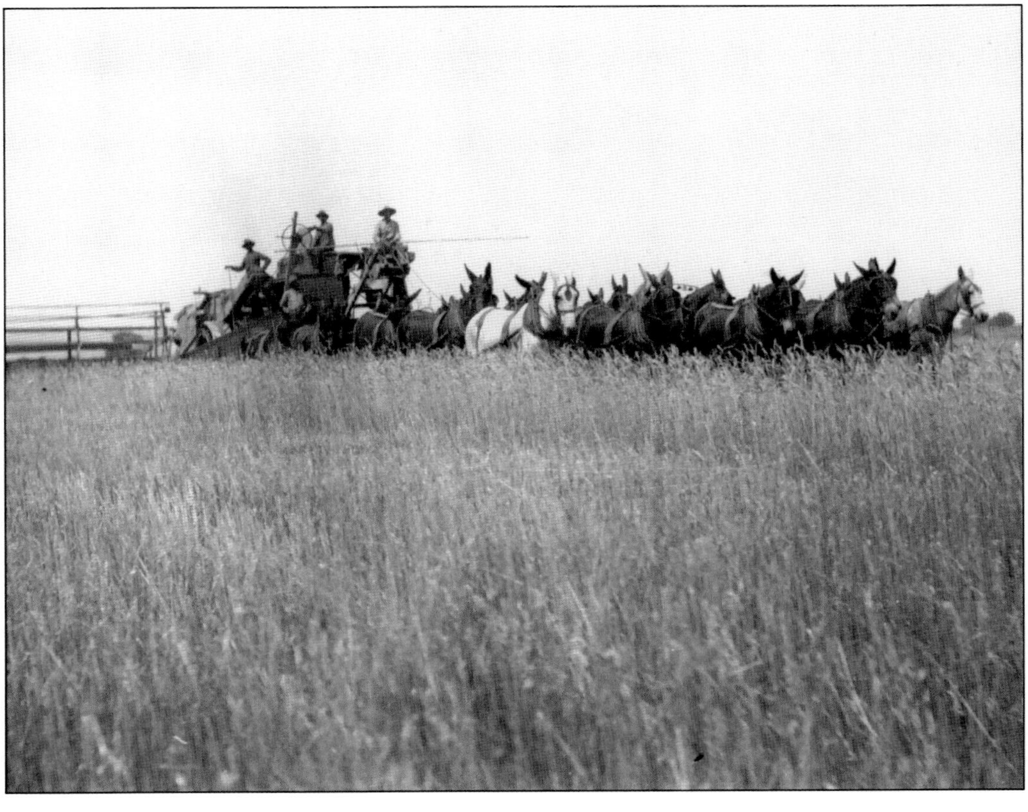

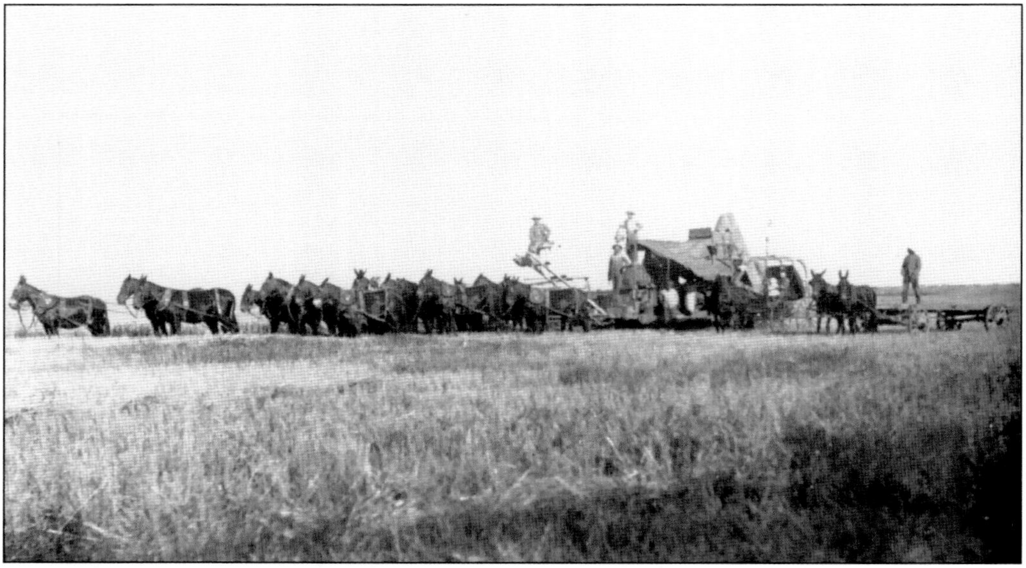

Pictured here is the Shaeffer Ranch crew hard at work at harvest time in the valley in the early 1900s, when wheat was big. Large acreages were farmed with horses or mules with ground combines. Later, engine-powered tractors and combines were used. (Courtesy of Tyrone Shaeffer.)

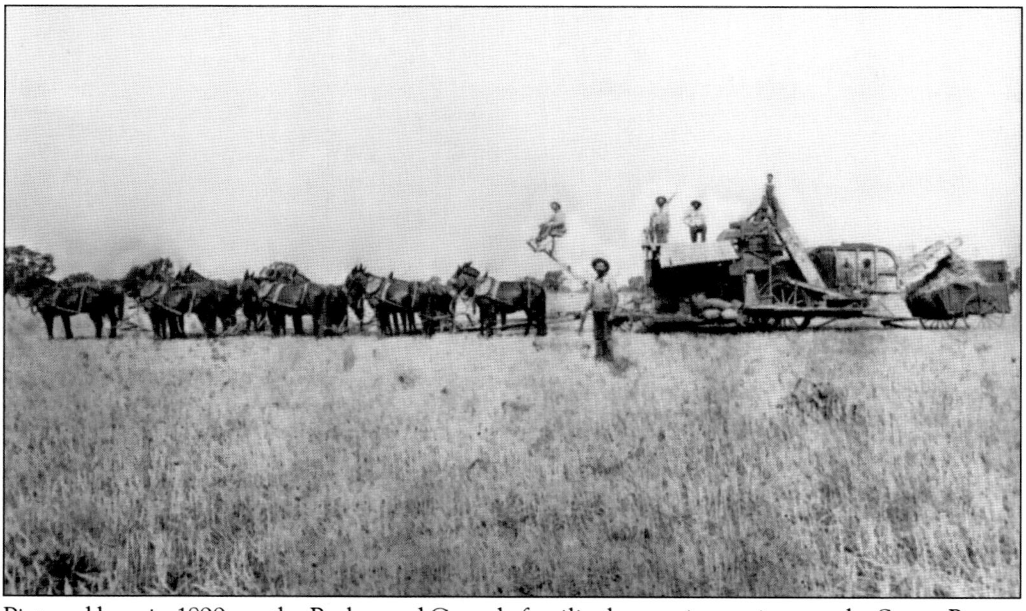

Pictured here in 1899 are the Barker and Cassady families harvesting grain near the Sutter-Buttes. This wooden ground-driven Holt harvester is driven by Alexander Cassady. The header runner is James Barker, with Washington Barker standing in the field. Melvin Bigelow is in the doghouse sewing sacks. Many times they would have a chuck wagon and cook to bring the noontime meal to the crew. (Courtesy of the Barker and Cassady families.)

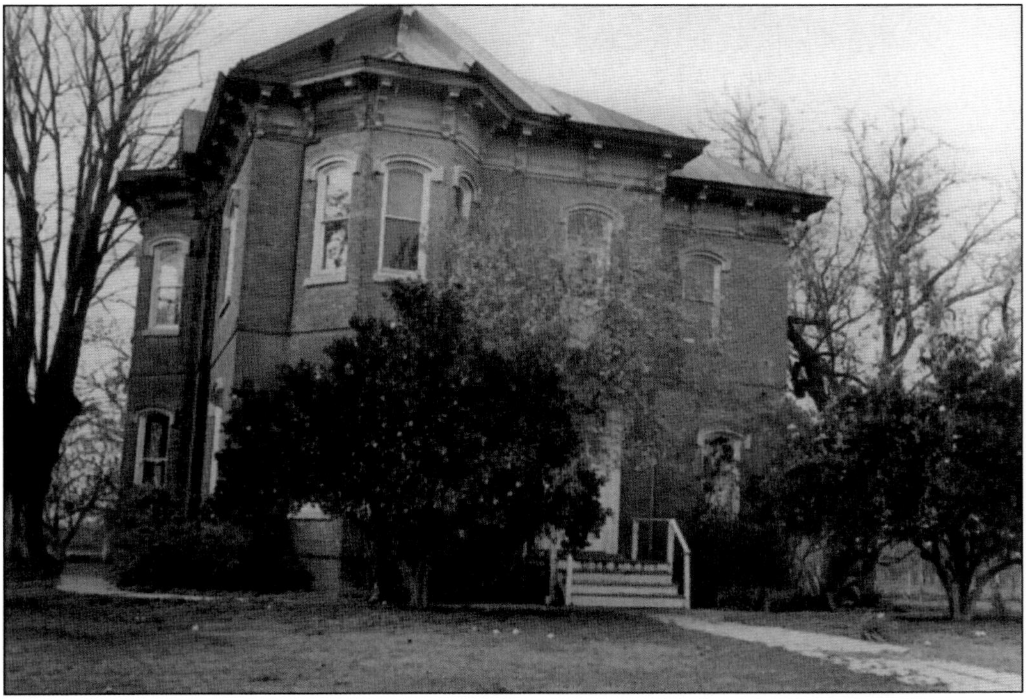

The Edward Fagan home, pictured above, was the headquarters of the Butte County Canal Company. Below, in 1904, George Thresher (left) is signing the first water contract with the Butte County Canal Company at the Thresher Ranch east of Gridley. Across an impromptu desk is Duncan McCallum, who helped pioneer the project. Looking on is Judge Eugene Allen Bridgeford, the first president of the canal company. (Both, courtesy of Butte Water District.)

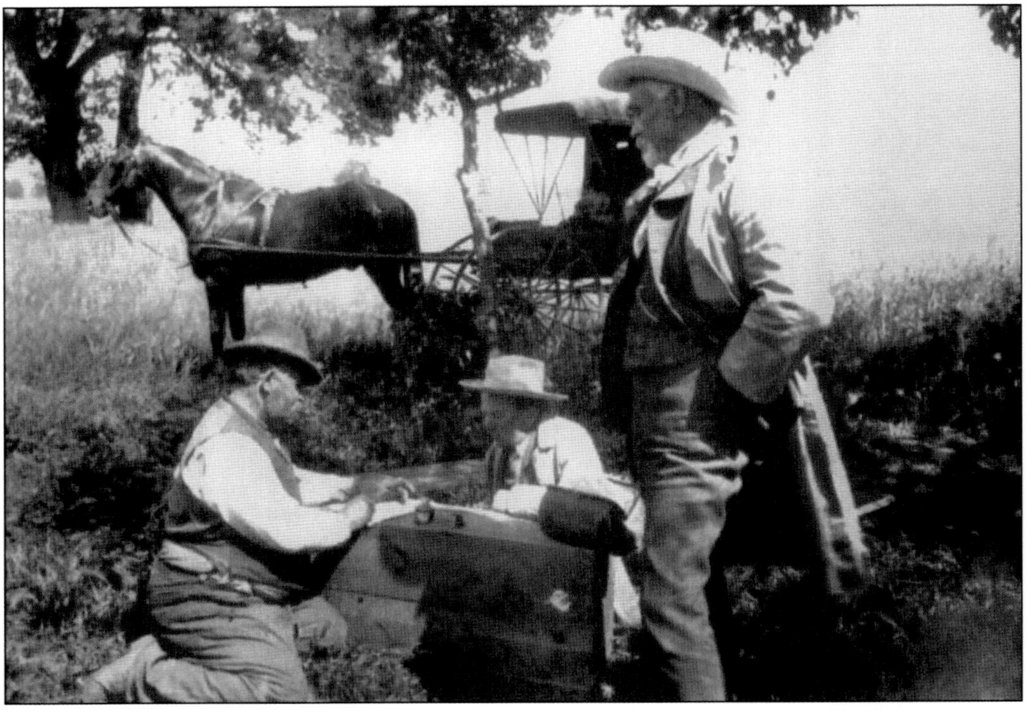

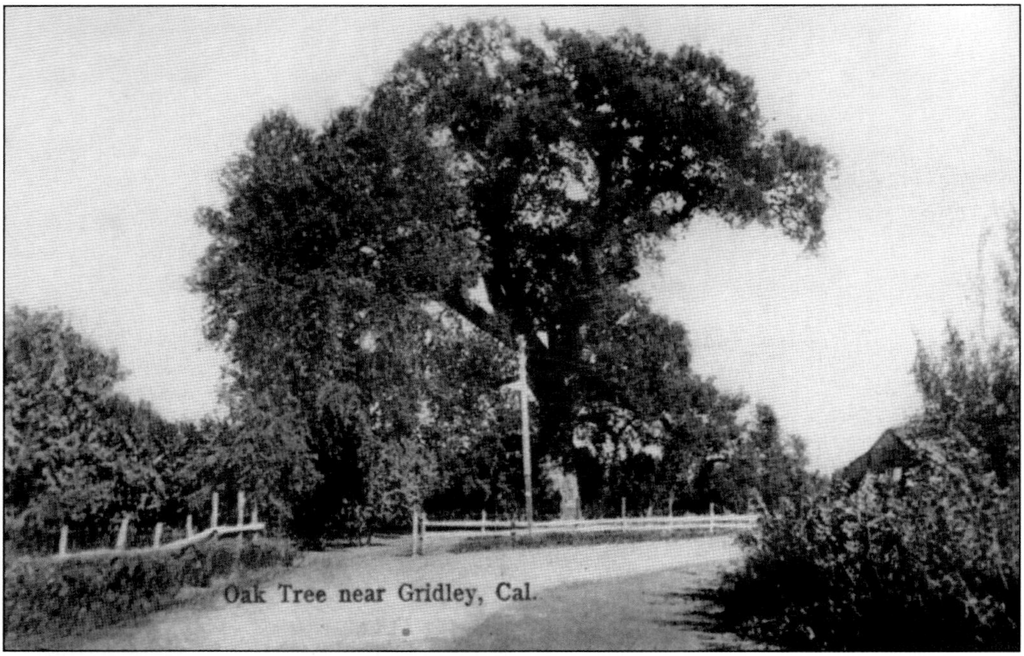

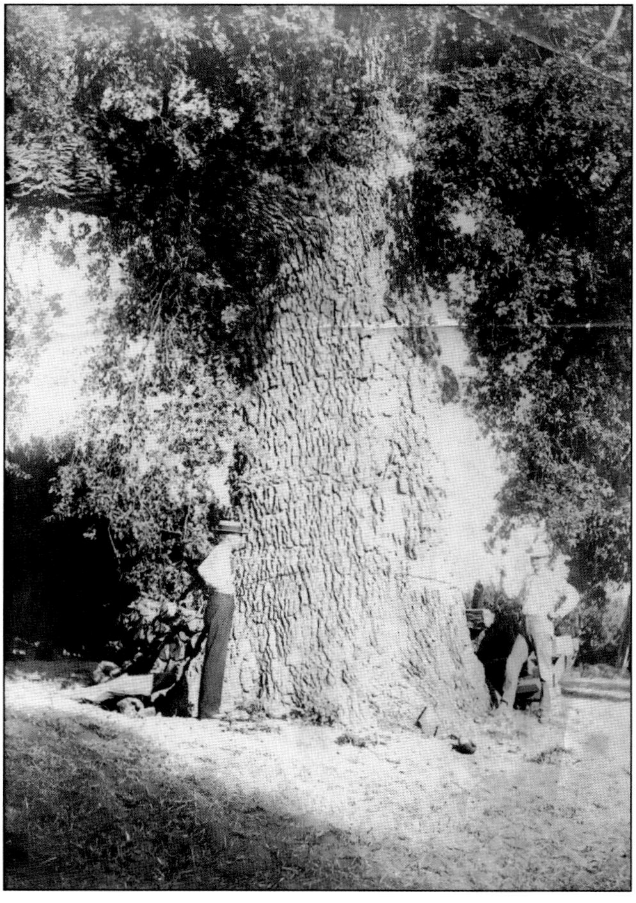

The Hutchins Oak, purported to be the largest oak tree in California, sat on the property of well-known farmer Thomas Boyd Hutchins adjacent the Feather River. It was eight feet in diameter, measured 93 feet high, and had an 84-foot spread of branches. (Both, courtesy of the Gridley Museum.)

This beautiful young lady in the white dress is Thomas Hutchins's daughter Bessie. She received her education at the University of California in Berkeley, as did Hutchins's son Thomas. (Courtesy of the Gridley Museum.)

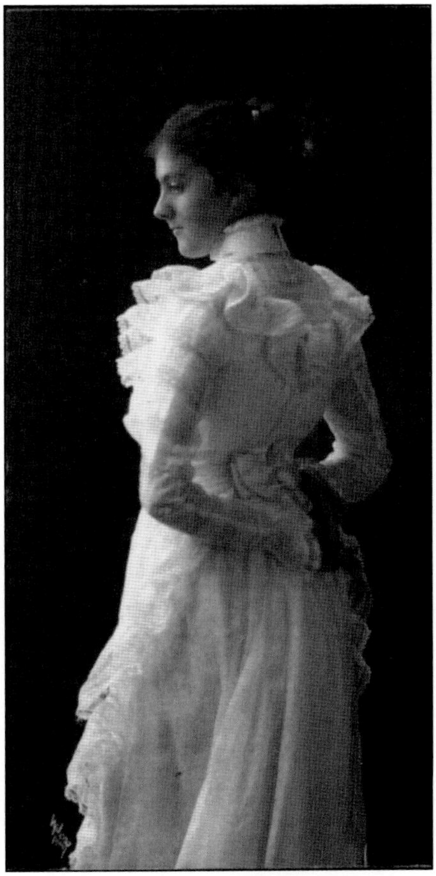

Thomas Hutchins's wife, Alice, christened the Gridley–Central House Bridge with a bottle of wine on December 6, 1884. Music was furnished by the Moore's Station Band. The 300-foot wooden bridge was built across the Feather River at a cost of $23,000, linking Gridley to Oroville and Marysville. Warnings included: no smoking on bridge, no crossing faster than a walk, no driving more than 25 head of cattle or horses at one time, and no driving more than one heavily loaded team and wagon at a time. Failure to comply resulted in a fine of $60. (Courtesy of the Gridley Museum.)

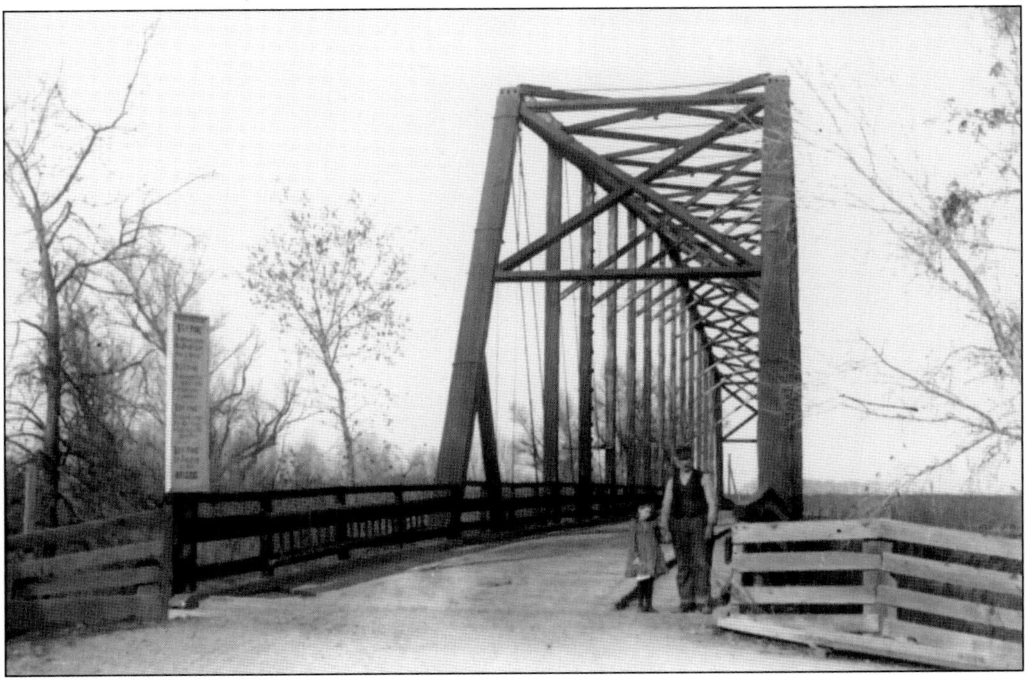

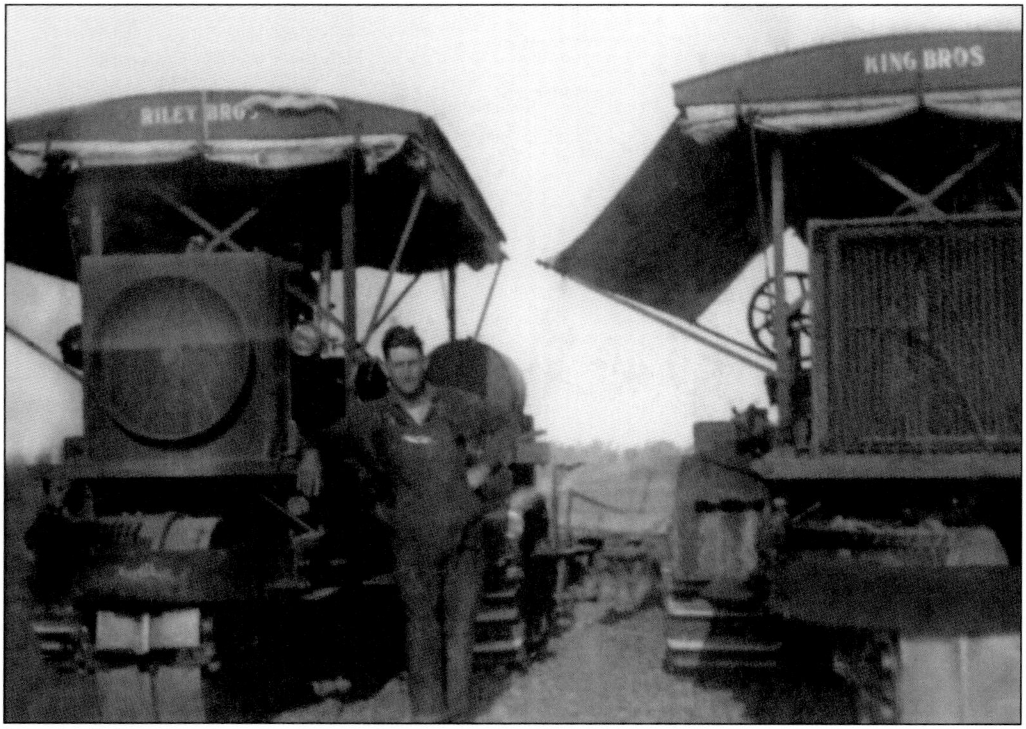

On the left is a Holt 60 tractor pulling a Harris combine owned by the Riley brothers. On the right is a Holt 75 tractor pulling a Holt combine owned by the King brothers. (Courtesy of Warren Riley.)

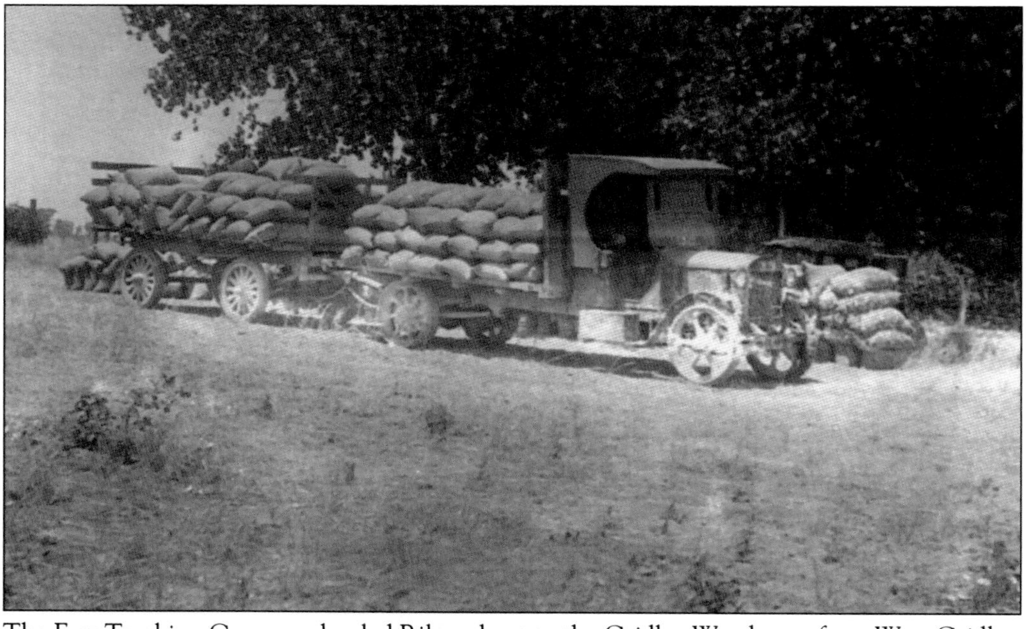

The Farr Trucking Company hauled Riley wheat to the Gridley Warehouse from West Gridley. The Riley and King brothers ranched west of Gridley. Wheat was an important commodity in the Gridley area. (Courtesy of Warren Riley.)

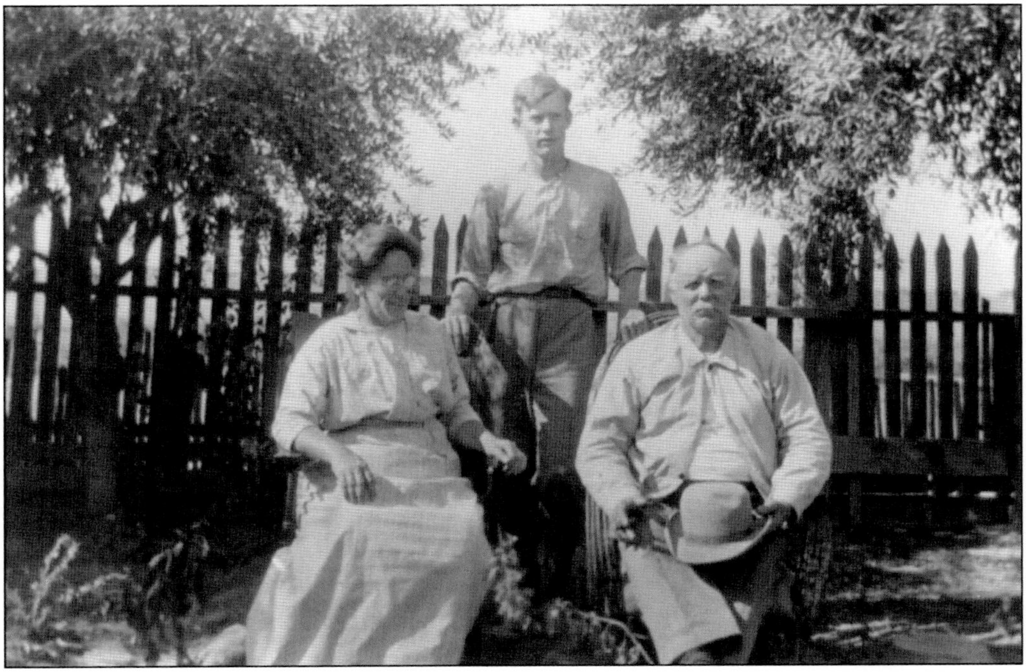

One of the leading grain and dairy men in the county, David Humphrey Evans settled in Gridley in 1883. After leasing 320 acres from Helen Gridley, which he sowed to grain, he began to farm. After prosperity followed him four successive seasons, Evans bought his leased property and raised wheat and barley on a large scale. He served two terms as a Butte County supervisor, and his influence and experience brought about good, reliable roads. Evans was a student of problems connected with the development of the state; experience gave him discernment, and his judgment was sought out. He is pictured below at his home with his wife, Etha, and children William, David, and Sarah. Pictured above are, from left to right, Sarah Elizabeth Evans, William Evans, and David Humphrey Evans. (Both, courtesy of the David Evans family.)

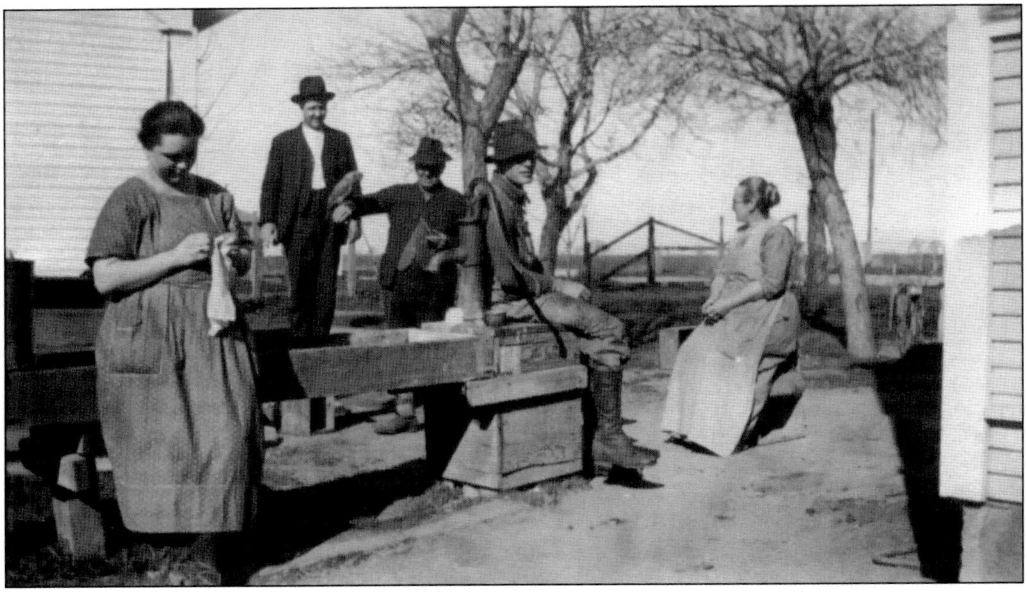

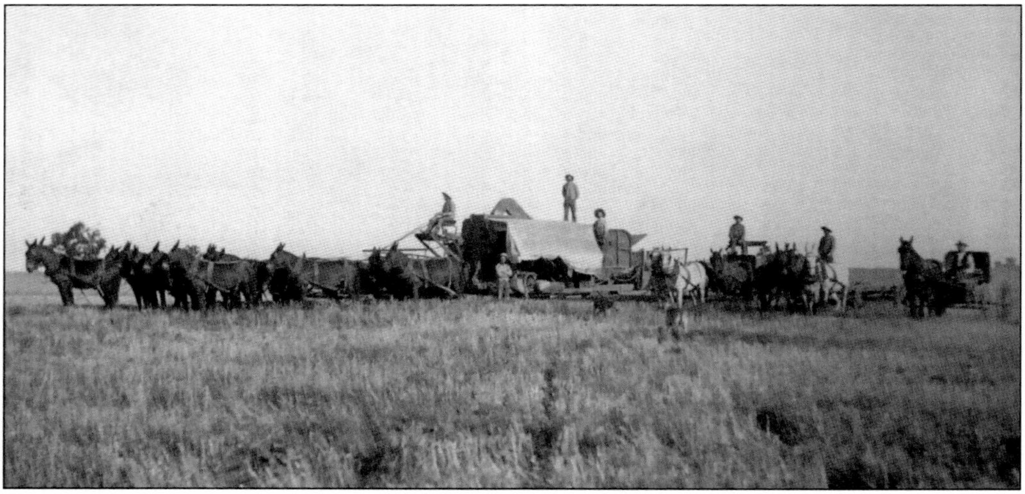

Washington Dunn Barker came to California from Shelbyville, Missouri. Pictured here is his harvest crew in 1888, with his wife, Catherine Gilstrap Barker, with a baby in a carriage (at far right) out for a visit. (Courtesy of the Barker and Cassady families.)

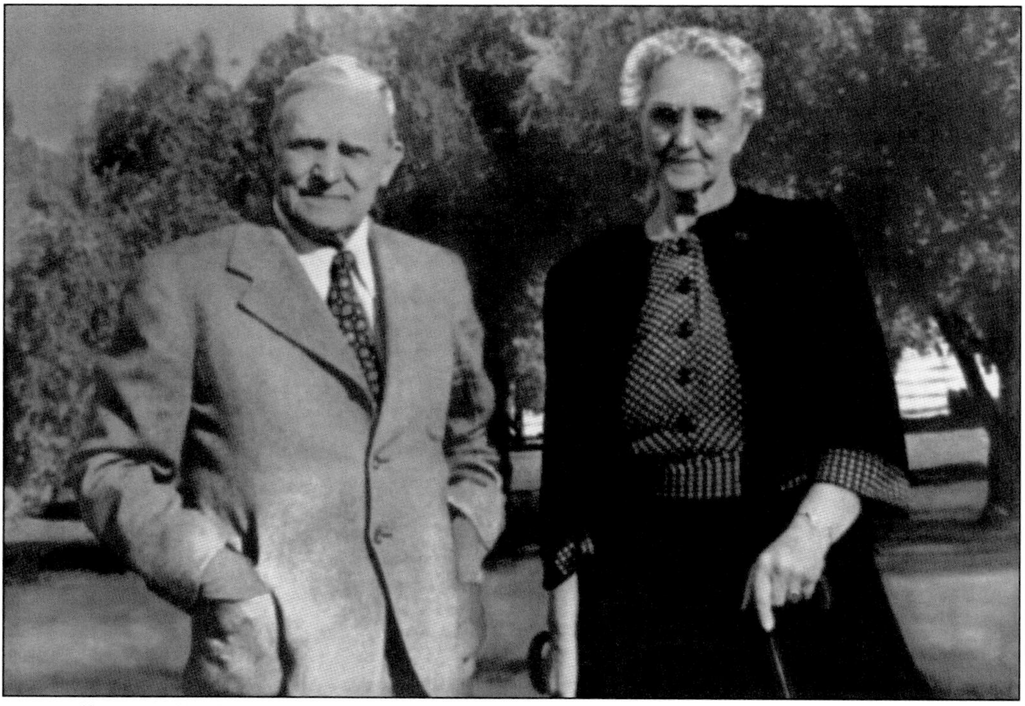

Maxmillian Paul Schohr was born in Germany and came to America in 1904. He and his wife, Elna Elizabeth Browning, inherited the 8,000-acre Browning Ranch west of Gridley after the death of her father, pioneer John William Browning. They farmed commercial rice and raised cattle in the same manner as Browning. (Courtesy of Barbara Spurgeon Stohlman.)

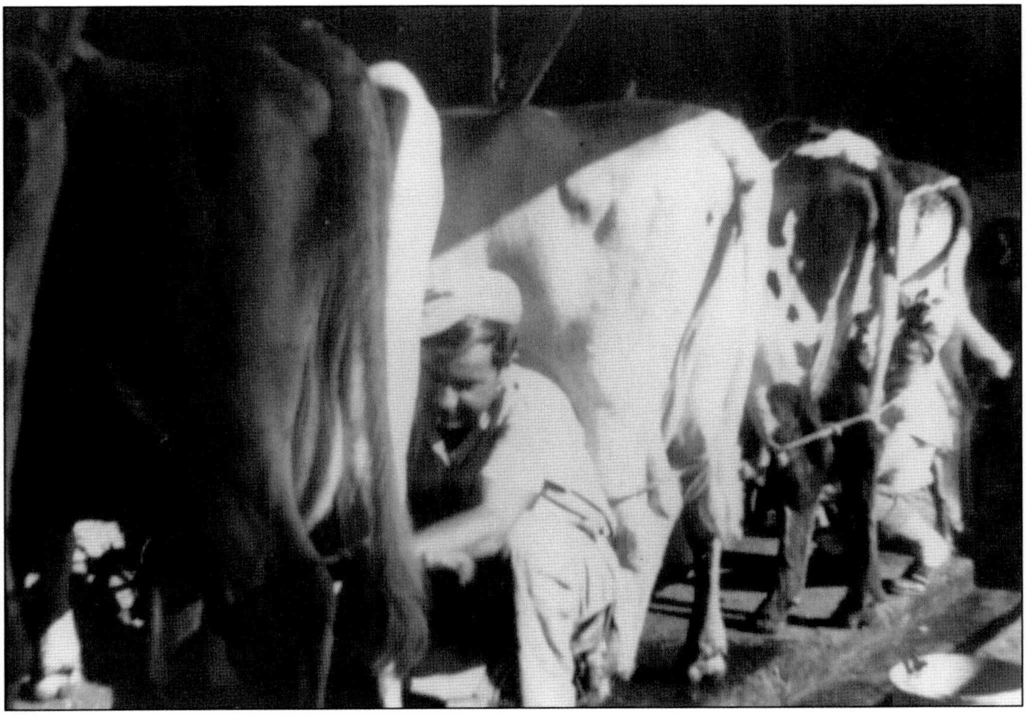

Alfonso "Al" Costa was born in Gridley in 1918 to Manuel and Maria Costa. He was one of five children. Costa was a lifelong resident, and after returning from the Army service in World War II, he was a dairy farmer for 40 years. Here Al is milking his cows and working in the field the old-fashioned way. (Both, courtesy of the Alfonso Costa family.)

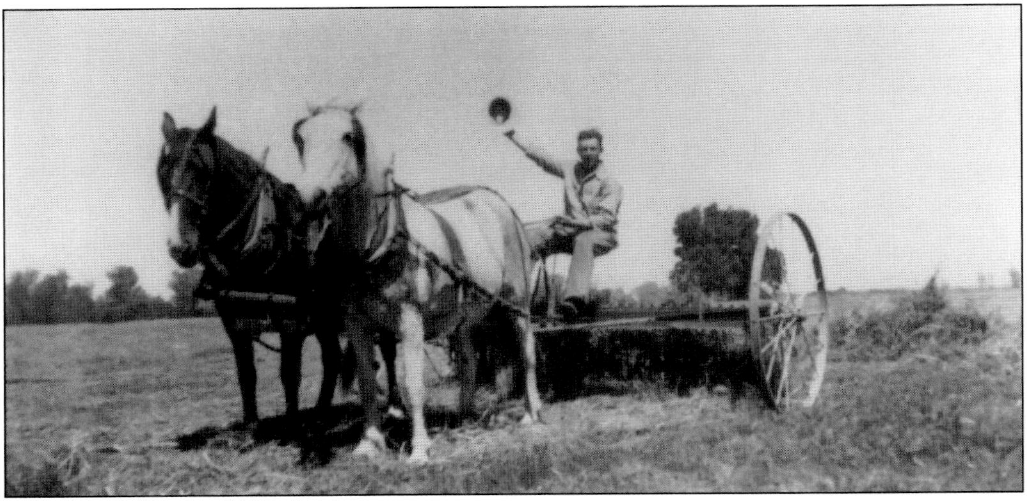

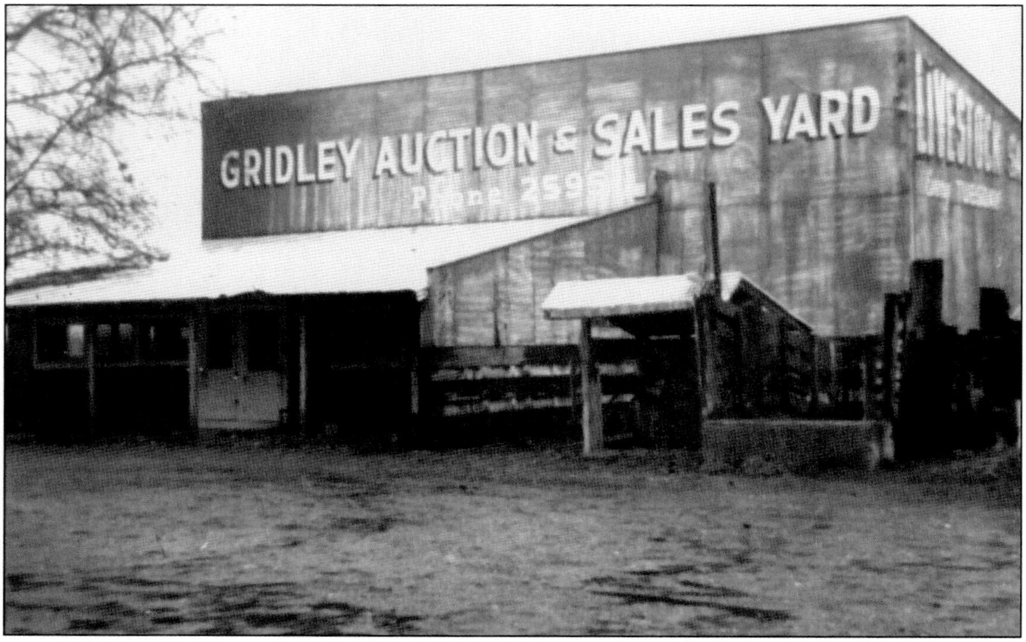

Gridley Auction & Sales Yard on Ord Ranch Road was the place for locals to purchase their livestock. Earl Carnes was the owner-auctioneer along with Ben Wedin as auctioneer. (Courtesy of the *Gridley Herald*.)

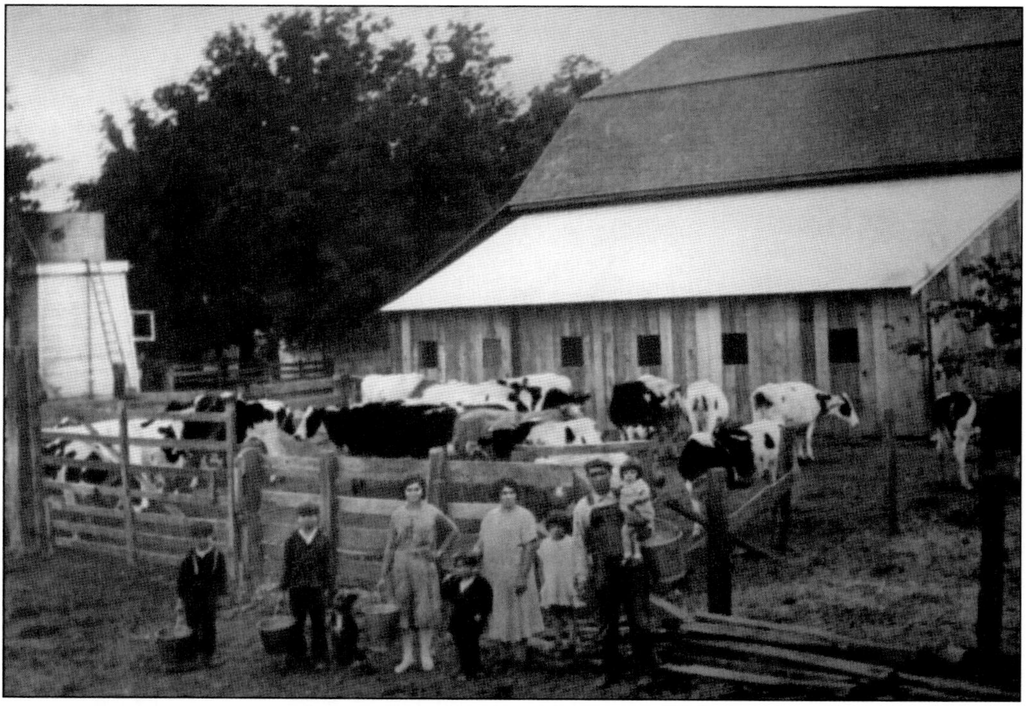

Pictured here is the Azevedo Dairy. Dairying in the first decades of the 20th century meant production of milk, from which cream was separated and sold to a local creamery for the manufacture of butter. It was the main source of livelihood, and dairymen were paid based on the butterfat content. (Courtesy of the Azevedo family.)

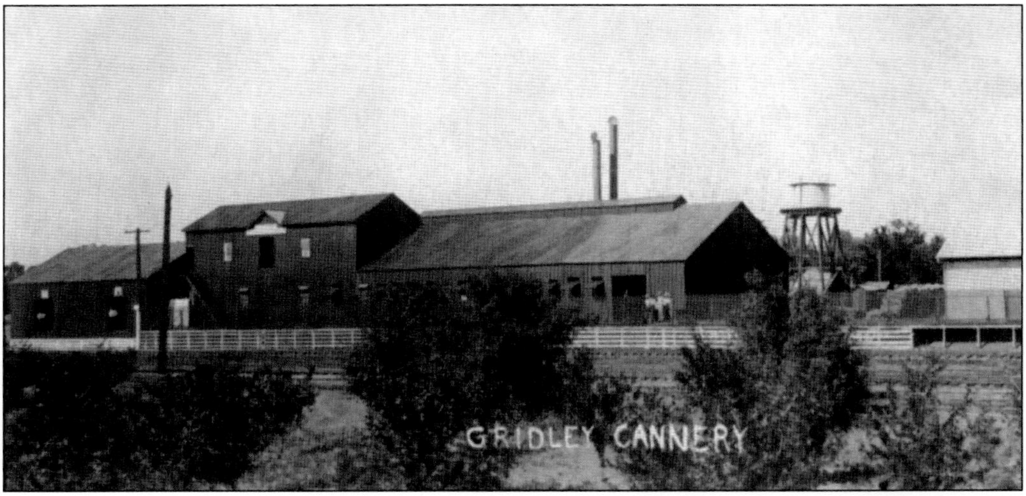

Marion Biggs, US congressman, advanced agriculture in February 1883 by planting 400 fruit trees. On this, the *Herald* speculated, "If every rancher in the neighborhood would do the same, it will not be long before our town would possess a fruit cannery." The construction of Gridley Community Cannery in 1896, in time for peach harvest, was a singular event in town. This cannery eventually became Hunt Brothers. (Courtesy of the Gridley Museum.)

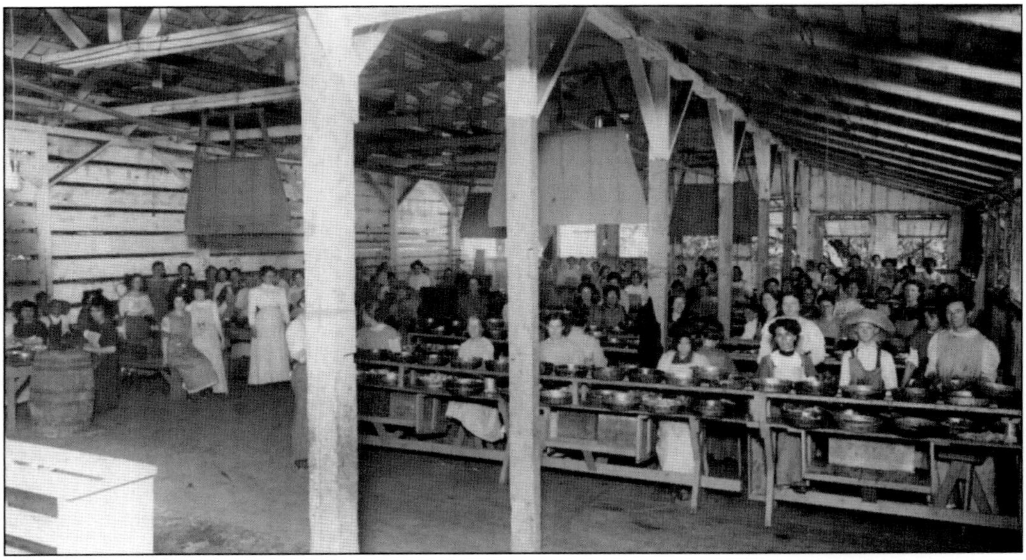

Pictured here sometime before 1900 at the original Hunt Cannery in Gridley, more than 100 Gridley area ladies prepare peaches for canning. The cannery became the forerunner of an industry that grew prodigiously over the years. The primitive methods pictured here have long since given way to improvements that finally led to the Libby, McNeil and Libby Plant in Gridley being one of the most productive in the nation. (Courtesy of the *Gridley Herald*.)

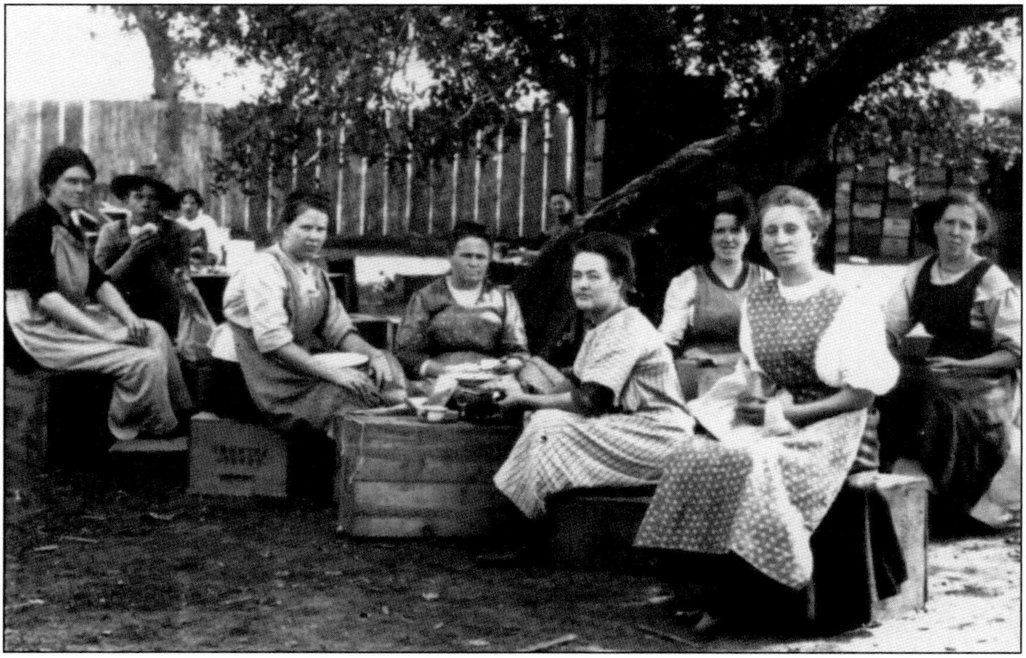

These people are on a lunch break from work at the Hunt Brothers Cannery around 1916 or 1917. Hunt Brothers built a cannery in Gridley to take advantage of the new method of preserving fruits and vegetables. Shown here are Flossie Soeth, Louisa Borrowman, Lola and Lucille Tolley, Zoe Cole, and Winnie Smith Borrowman. (Courtesy of the Gridley Museum.)

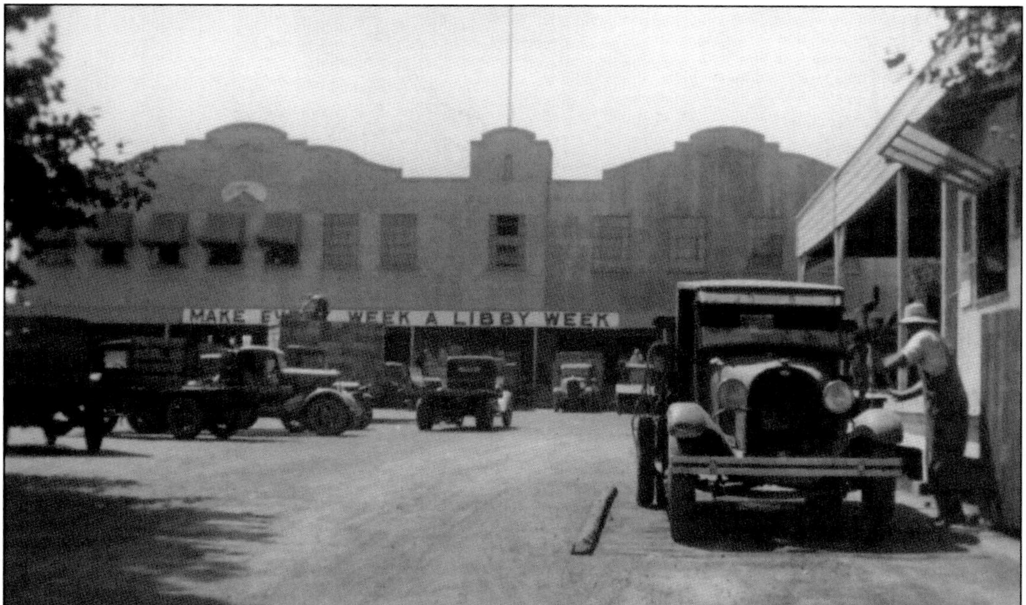

With a population of less than 1,000, Gridley became the center of mechanized industry in the upper Sacramento Valley. As the cannery grew, it became the property of Libby, McNeil and Libby, eventually employing 1,500 people working two full shifts. The slogan on the building reads, "Make Every Week a Libby Week." In 1920, it became necessary to build a new plant. This was the largest peach cannery in the world. (Courtesy of the Gridley Museum.)

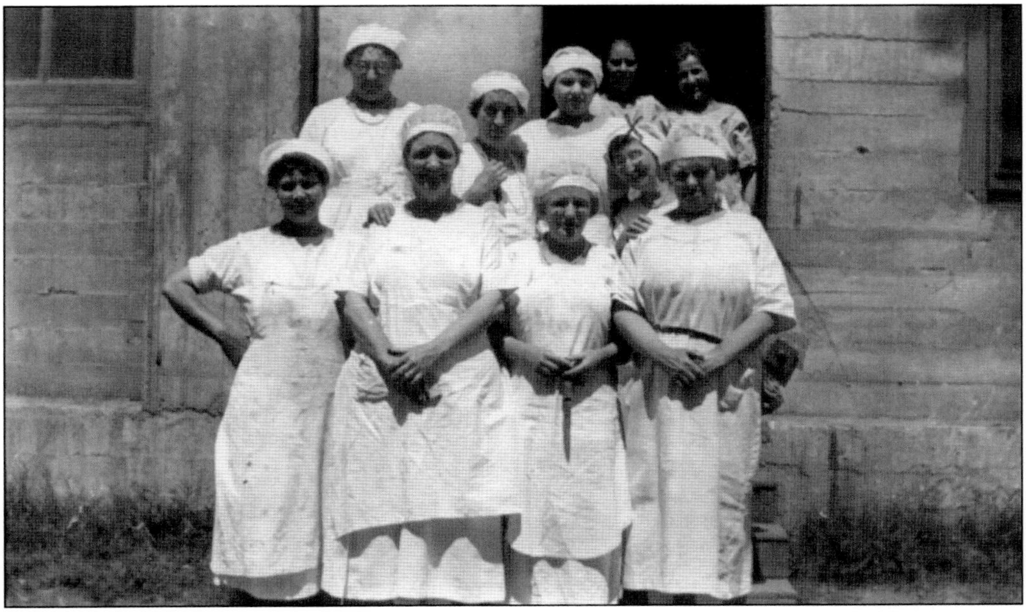

Ladies working at the cannery wore all white garments. It was common to see them in the community shopping after a long day's work canning peaches. There was on-site child care for some of the children of these workers. There also were cabins for some of the seasonal workers as well. Some of the children ate in the cafeteria with their mothers. The Libby McNeill and Libby Cannery is pictured below. (Both, courtesy of the Gridley Museum.)

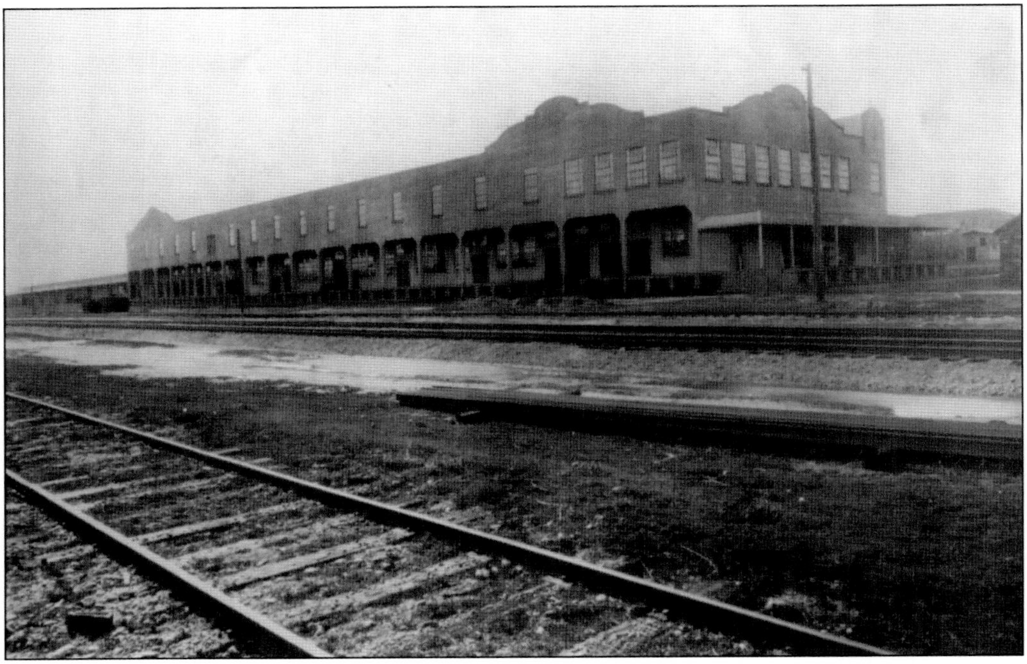

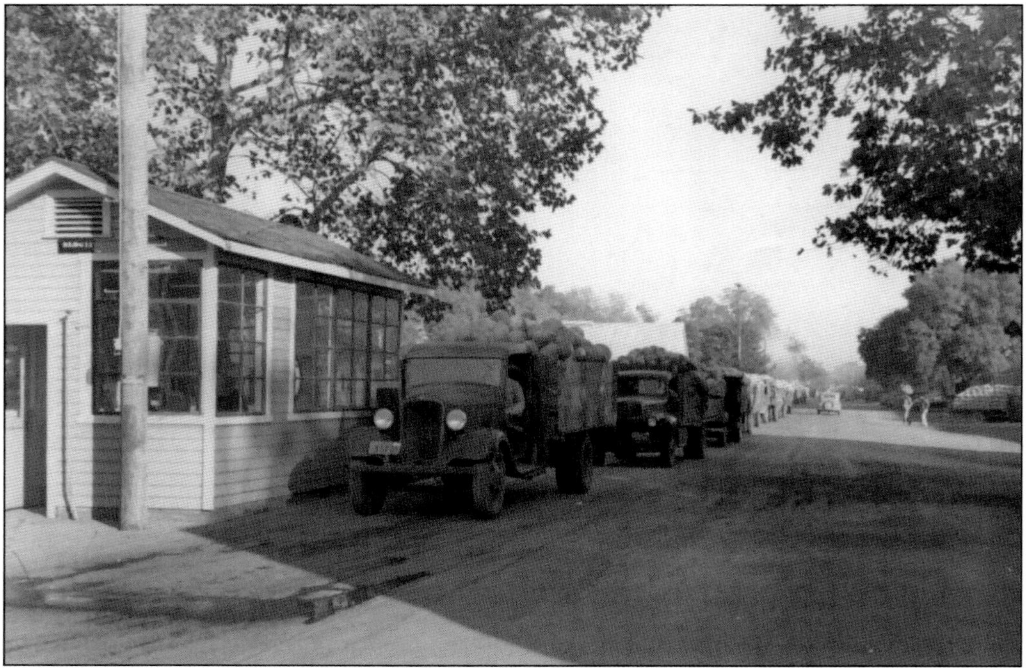

Pictured above are trucks loaded with pumpkins. When the cannery decided to put in pumpkin-canning equipment, the production of pumpkins increased dramatically in the valley. The largest peach-packing plant in California also became the only pumpkin-packing plant in the state. Gridley-packed pumpkin was distributed all over the West Coast, as far east as Denver and as far south as El Paso. The operation poured millions of dollars into the Gridley economy each year, and the products found their way to almost every part of the world. The cannery picnic brought shouts from the crowds, which once watched Gridley's baseball team defeat Oroville 39-18. The footraces, other competitions, and the groaning tables are all a part of the past now. Pictured below is the Libby McNeill and Libby Cannery. (Above, courtesy of the Gridley Museum; below, courtesy of Warren Riley.)

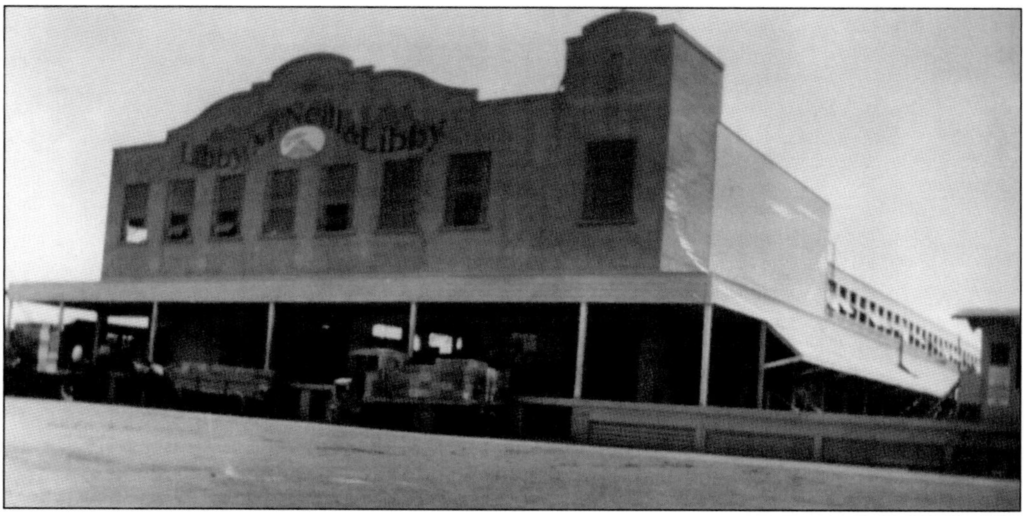

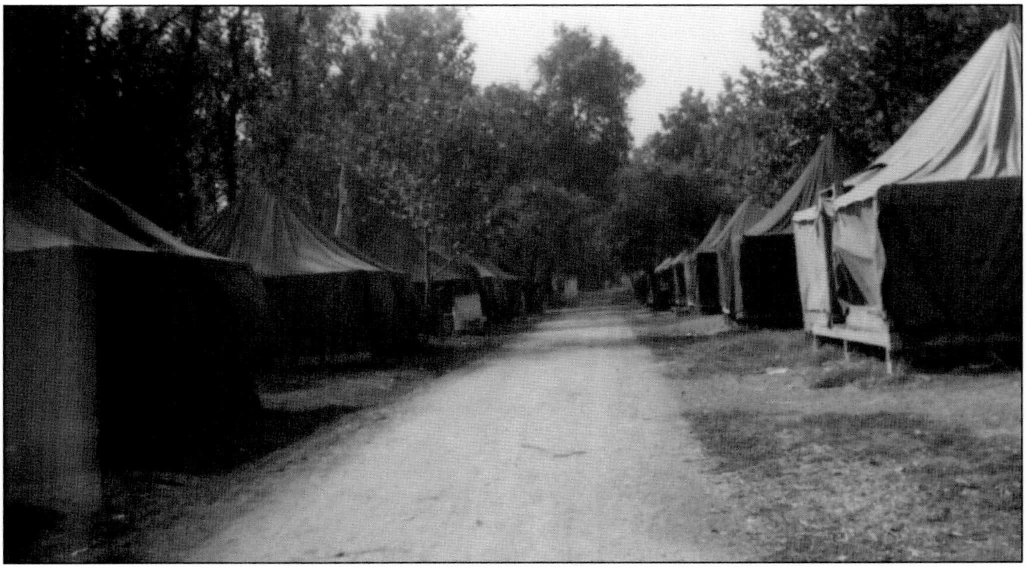

The Gridley farm labor camp was one of dozens of labor camps in California that were developed and managed by the Department of Agriculture through the Farm Security Administration between 1938 and 1942 in areas where migrant farm workers congregated. The Gridley camp was likely a squatter camp with farm workers and their families living in makeshift shelters and in their automobiles. A camp like this was featured in John Steinbeck's novel *The Grapes of Wrath*. In October 1937, Steinbeck went to the Central Valley and met with Tom Collins at his new camp in Gridley. While living in Gridley to write his novel, the two agreed to go out and work in the fields. He documented the plight and struggles of the workers as well as their entertainment. This camp existed prior to government involvement and was maintained and managed by the residents. (Both, courtesy of the California Farm Security Administration.)

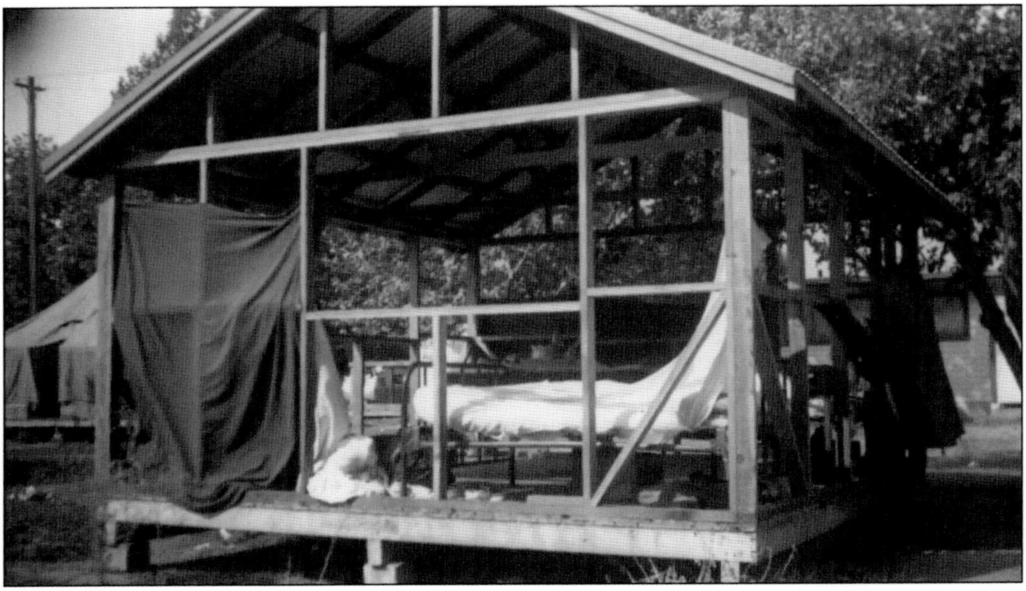

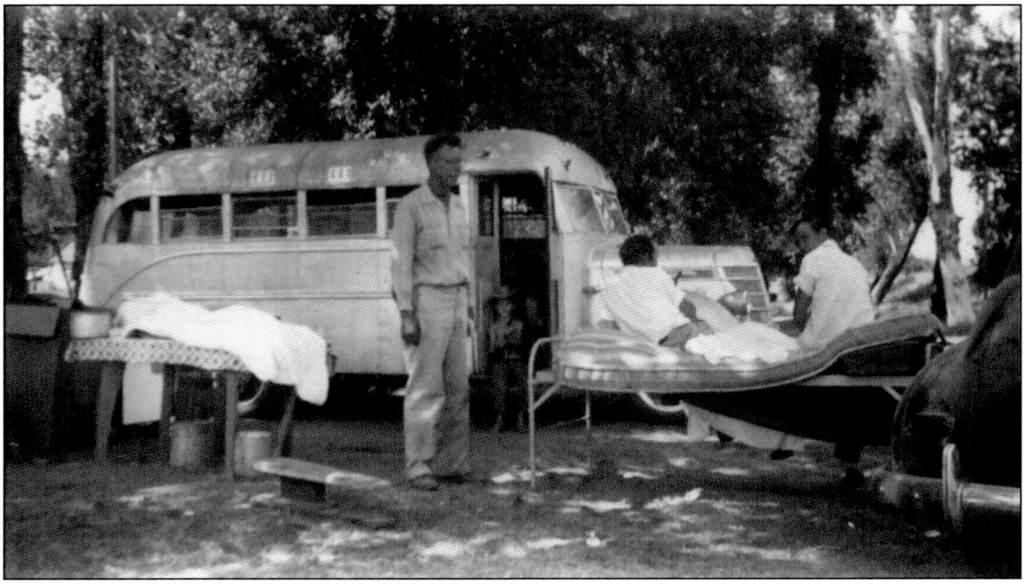

The Gridley farm labor camp was set on a nearly flat site on East Gridley Road, which forms the north boundary of the site. The Feather River borders it to the east, and Kirk Road forms the west boundary. The Gridley camp was one of the dozens in California at which migrant farm workers congregated. Housing consisted of basic shelters made by various means, including construction debris, vehicles, tents, and campers. (Both, courtesy of the California Farm Security Administration.)

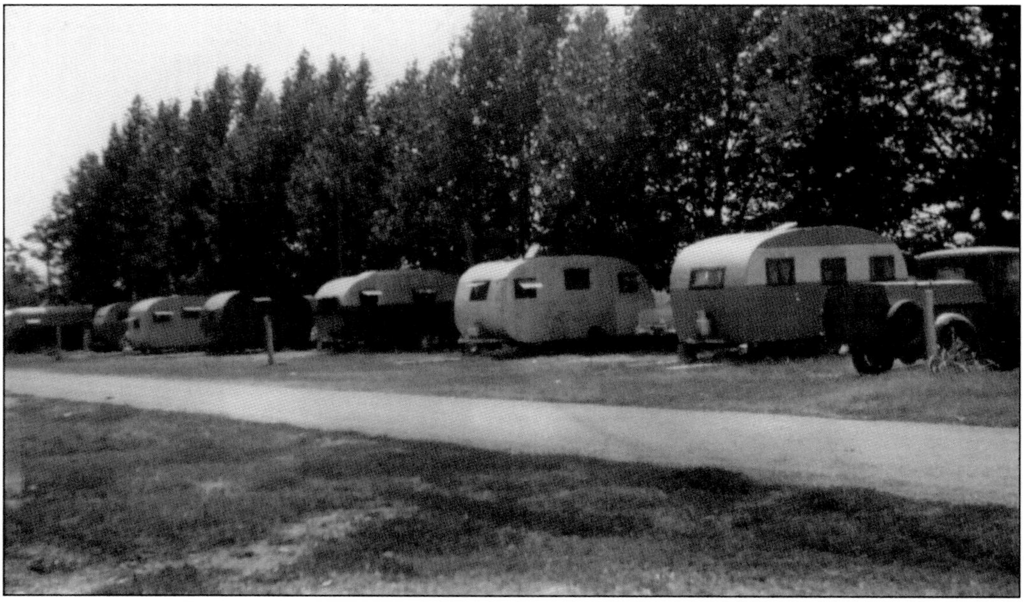

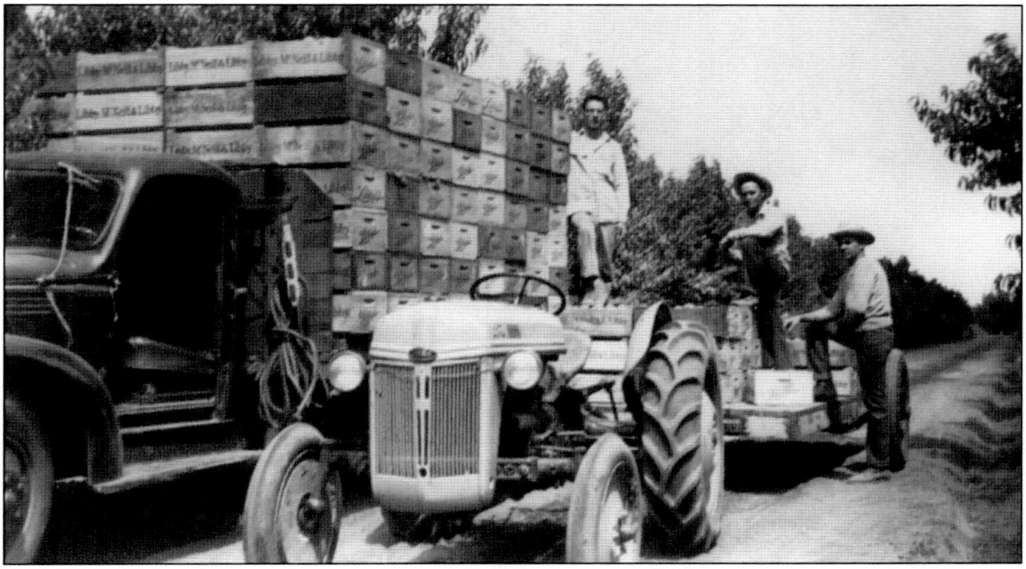

This photograph shows a Chambers family peach harvest. The fruit was picked by hand, put into lug boxes, and stacked in between the rows of trees for the tractor and trailer to retrieve. They would bring them out of the orchard and load them by hand onto the bed of the truck. From left to right are Robert Kirch, Elliot Penrose "EP" Chambers, and Morgan Chambers. (Courtesy of Morgan Chambers.)

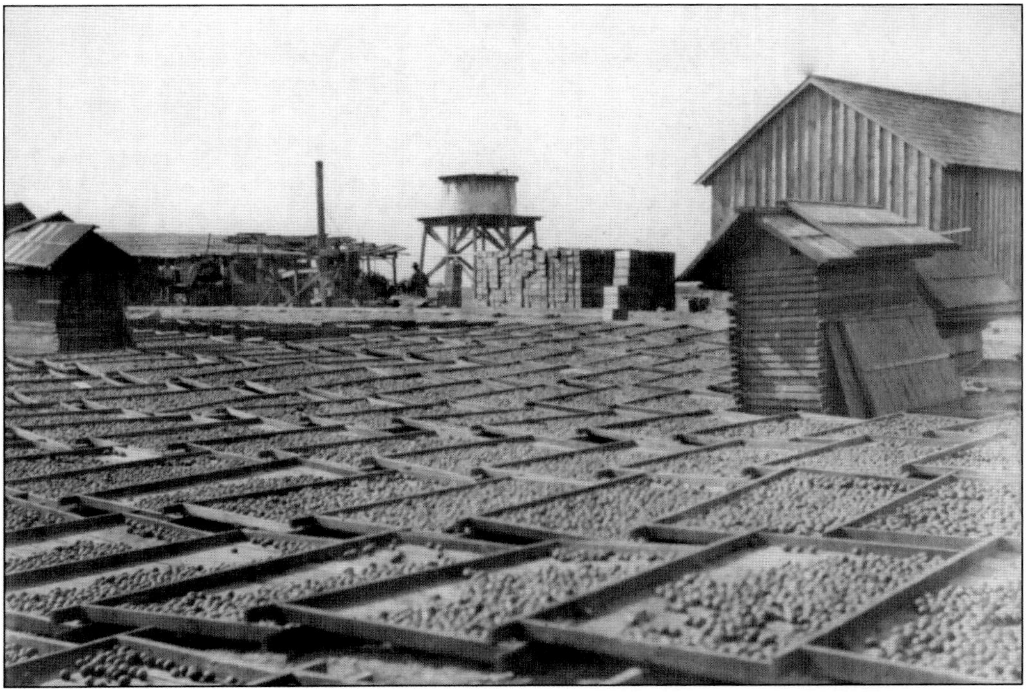

Before there were dehydrators, solar heat was used to dry prunes. In Gridley, prunes were plentiful and could be dried in the sun even in winter months. The fruit was usually knocked to the ground with a long pole and then picked up by hand, put into a bucket, and poured into a lug box. The boxes were stacked in the orchard to be picked up for processing to be dried. (Courtesy of the *Gridley Herald*.)

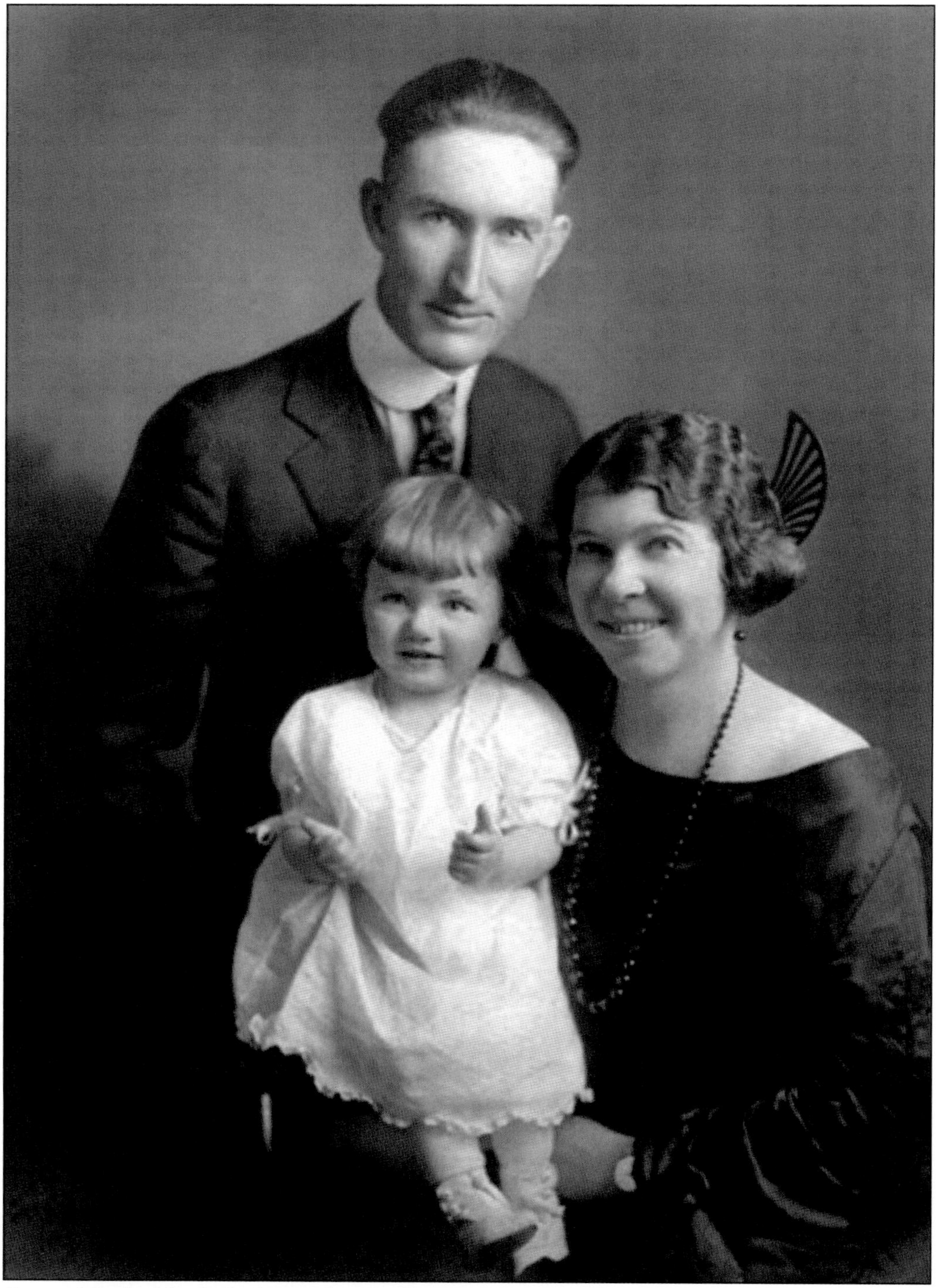

Otis and Birdie Vanderford moved to Gridley in 1924. Otis and his brother Carl formed a farming partnership with George Adams west of Gridley. Even though Otis was a rice farmer, he was fascinated by airplanes and got his pilot's license. He would use any excuse to fly over his property. The family included daughter Thelma. After being widowed, Birdie continued to be active in the family's farming. (Courtesy of Jon Moss.)

Five

SERVICES

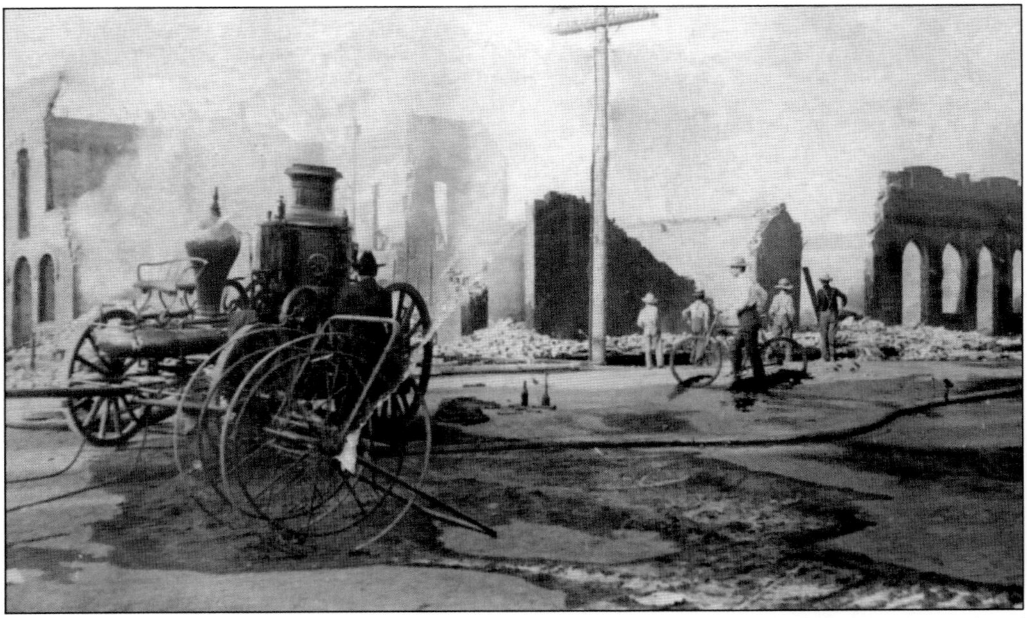

Much of the original Stone Block was reduced to rubble by the fire that broke out the night of July 9, 1905, and devastated the block between Virginia and Kentucky Streets. This view looks southwest toward ruins that were left by the blaze, which consumed the property. The fire got out of hand when the town's steam pumper was unable to pump water due to hardened valves. (Courtesy of the *Gridley Herald*.)

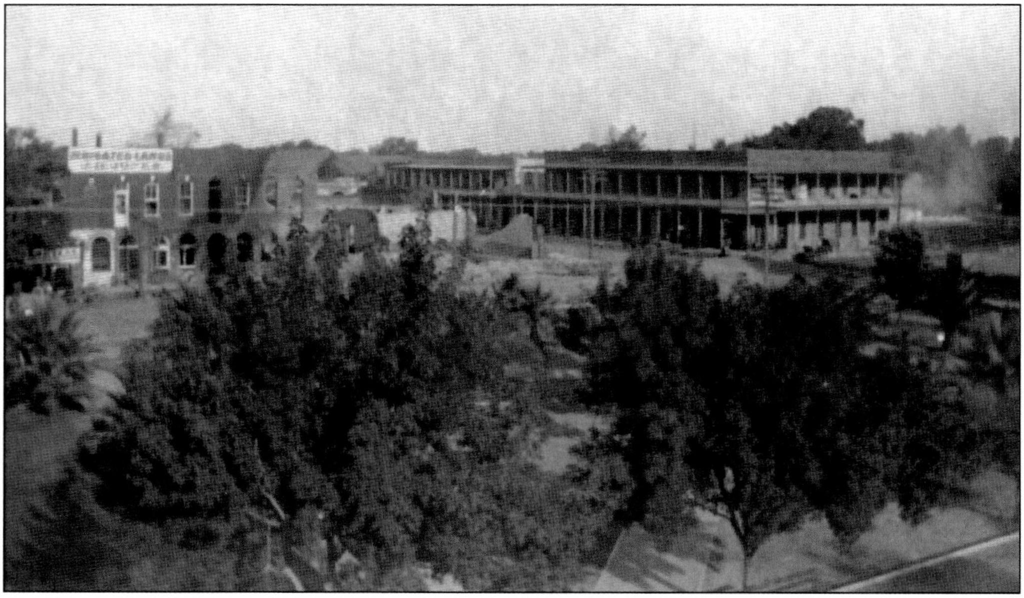

Gridley's worst business district fire reduced much of the Stone Block to blackened rubble and destroyed several other brick buildings as well. That blaze consumed structures, fixtures, equipment, and stocks of merchandise worth $100,000. Only about half of the loss was covered by insurance. Gridley's Amoskeag steam pumper was brought to the scene promptly enough. However, there was a long delay before it could put water on the fire. The steamer was positioned to draw water from the fire well at Hazel and Virginia Streets, but it could not pump a drop there. Engineer Jesse Porter had it moved down Hazel Street to the Kentucky Street intersection but was unable to pump there either. It was then realized that the fault was all in the engine. The steam pumper's valves had "baked" while being stored in the hot sun for two weeks. (Both, courtesy of Butte County Historical Society.)

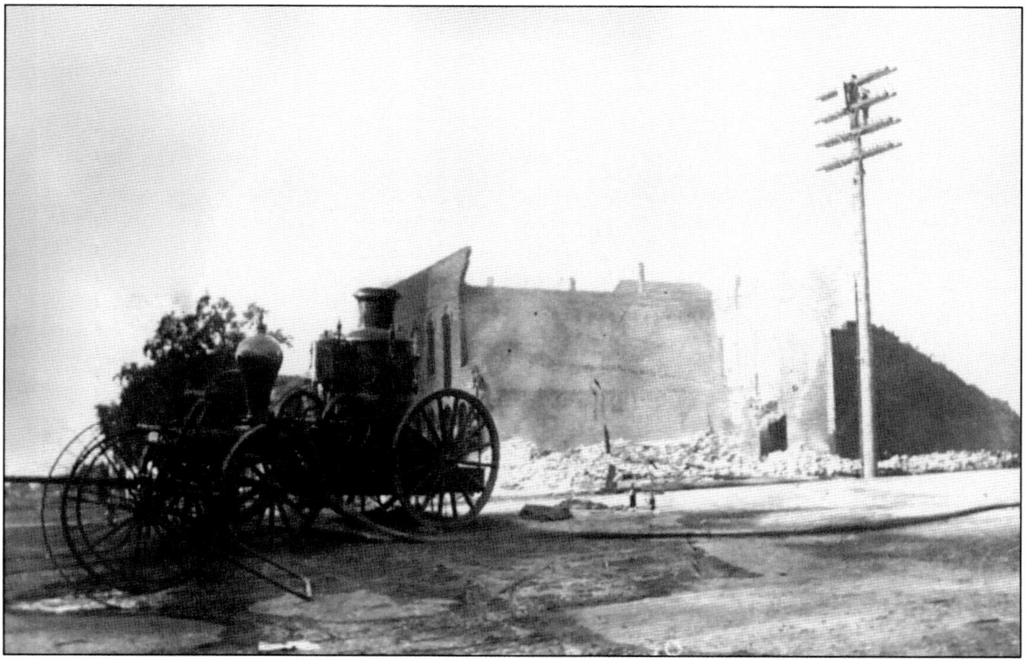

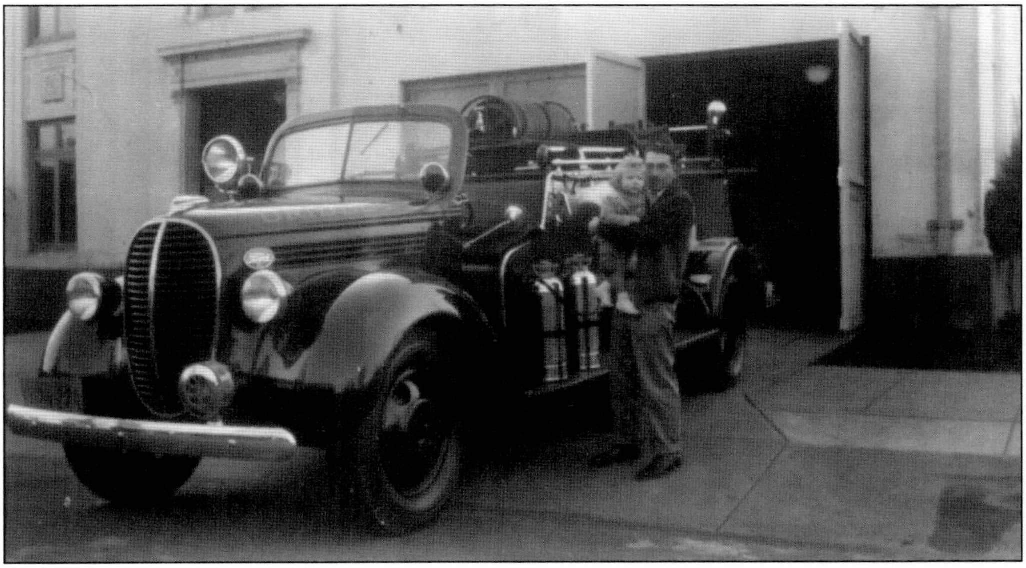

Loreto Antonio Panecaldo Jr. is pictured above at the fire station on Kentucky Street with the city's pumper and the LaFrance that was purchased in 1922 and driven from San Francisco in February 1923. It had a pumping capacity of 600 gallons per minute and was of the modern type used by Chico and Marysville Fire Departments. The addition of the equipment placed Gridley's firefighting facilities on a par with those of any city of its size in the state. The purchase price was $10,250 and the city trustees were of the opinion it would reduce the insurance rates by 10 percent, giving them a savings that in three years would pay for the purchase of the engine. Panecaldo is pictured second from left at right. (Both, courtesy of Howard Hamman.)

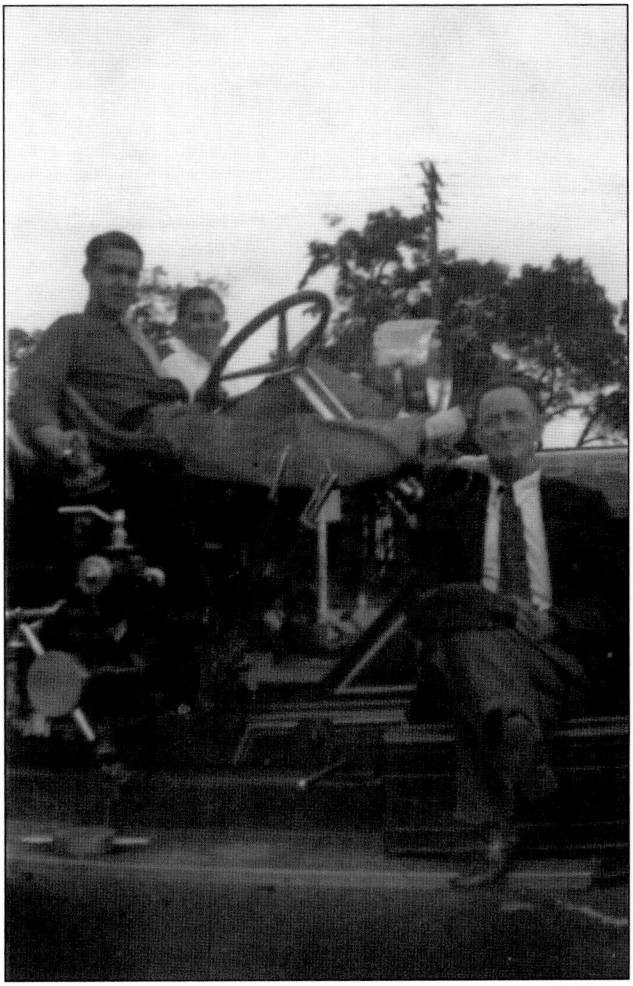

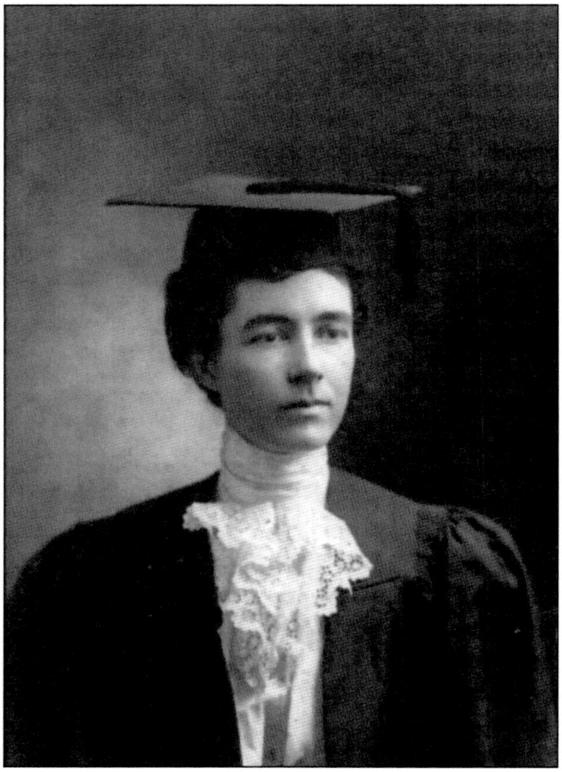

Birdine and William King, son and daughter of Michael Jason King, grew up in Gridley and went to Northwestern College in Chicago. Both studied dentistry and practiced in Gridley. William married and stayed longer than his sister Birdine, who moved her practice to Los Angeles and never married. She came back to fill in for her brother at vacation time. (Both, courtesy of Evelyn King Briggs.)

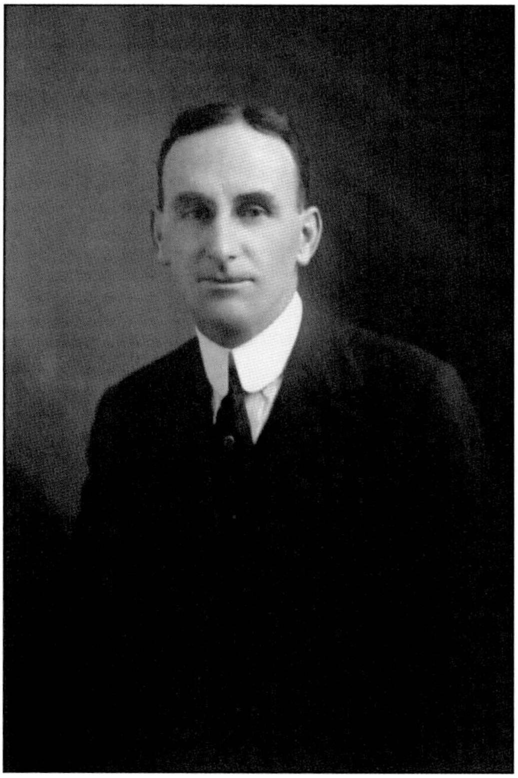

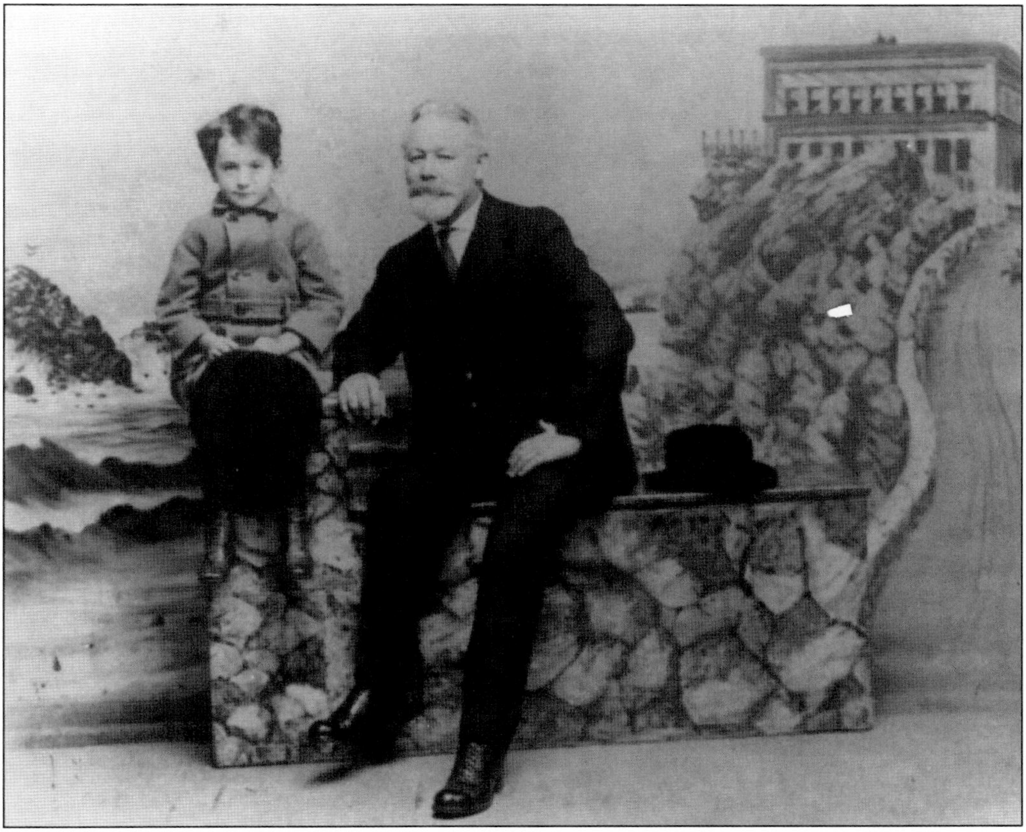

Dr. William Sebastian Lavy was born in Wheatland, California, and taught school in Yuba and Sutter Counties before he attended medical school. He married Eleanor Lear (right) in 1906 and moved to Gridley after the San Francisco earthquake. They settled on Park Street and raised two sons, William Jr. (right) and Lyell. Lavy was a practicing physician for over 40 years and served as the medical examiner in Gridley and Butte County and was called the "Dean of Physicians." Many times he was "paid in kind" for his services. He often mixed his own medicines and remedies for his patients. (Both, courtesy of Barbara Spurgeon Stohlman.)

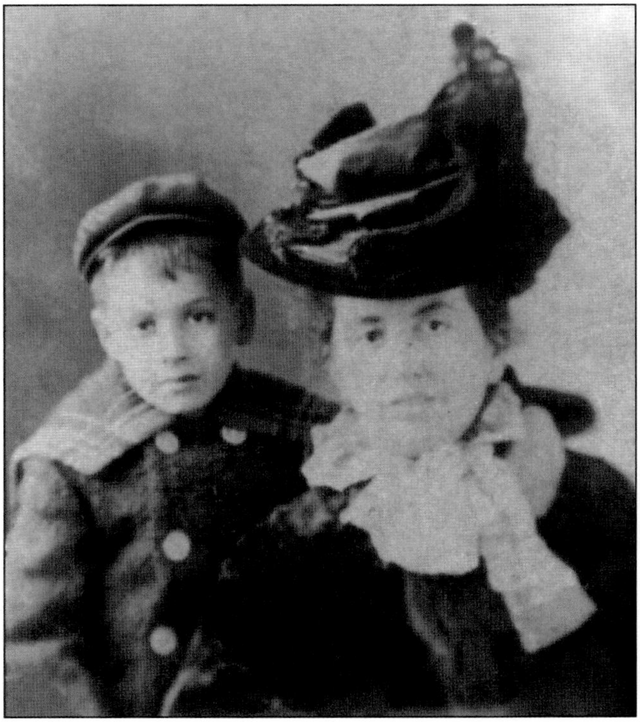

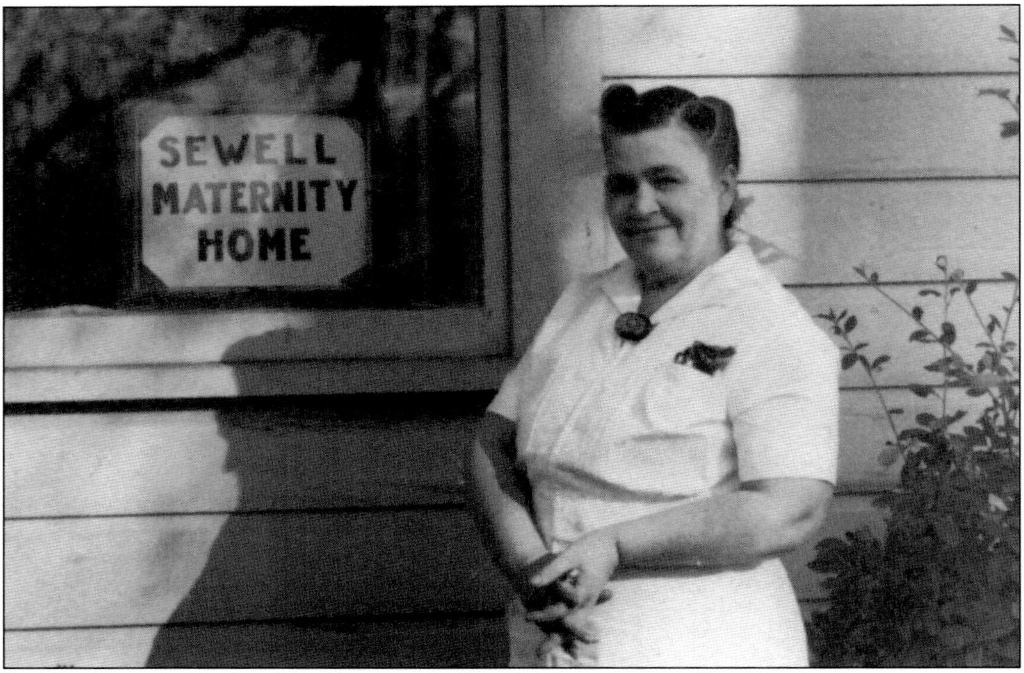

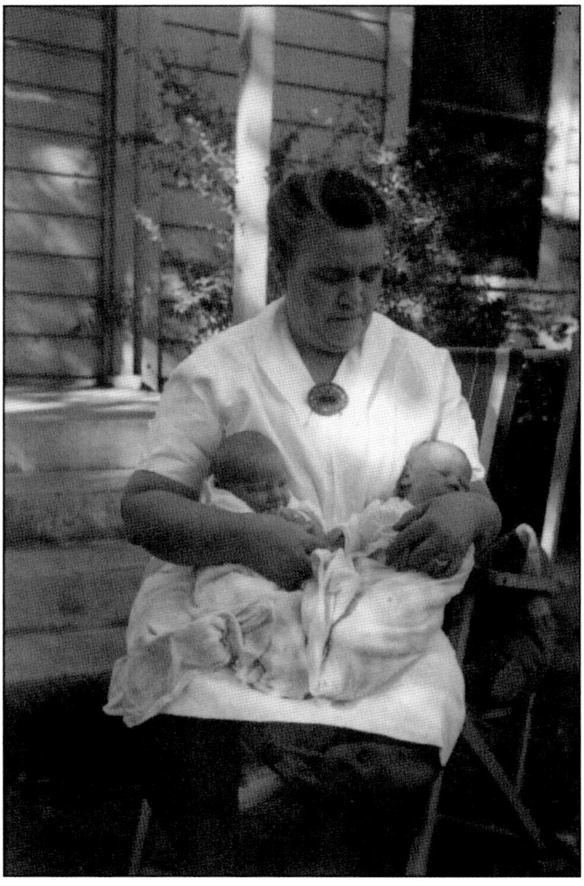

As there was no hospital in Gridley, under the encouragement of Doctor Freudenthal, Lola Bessie Sewell opened a maternity home at 740 Vermont Street in 1935. The closest hospitals were either in Chico or Oroville. This maternity home was originally a three-bedroom house that was turned into a three-bed delivery and post-partum facility for mothers and babies. Mothers and babies usually stayed 10 days recuperating. In 1942, Lola married Otis Zumwalt and gave the home up to Cecil Huston, who ran it as the Stork Retreat in the old Burleson home on the south end of Kentucky Street until Biggs-Gridley Memorial Hospital was built in 1949. (Both, courtesy of the Gridley Museum.)

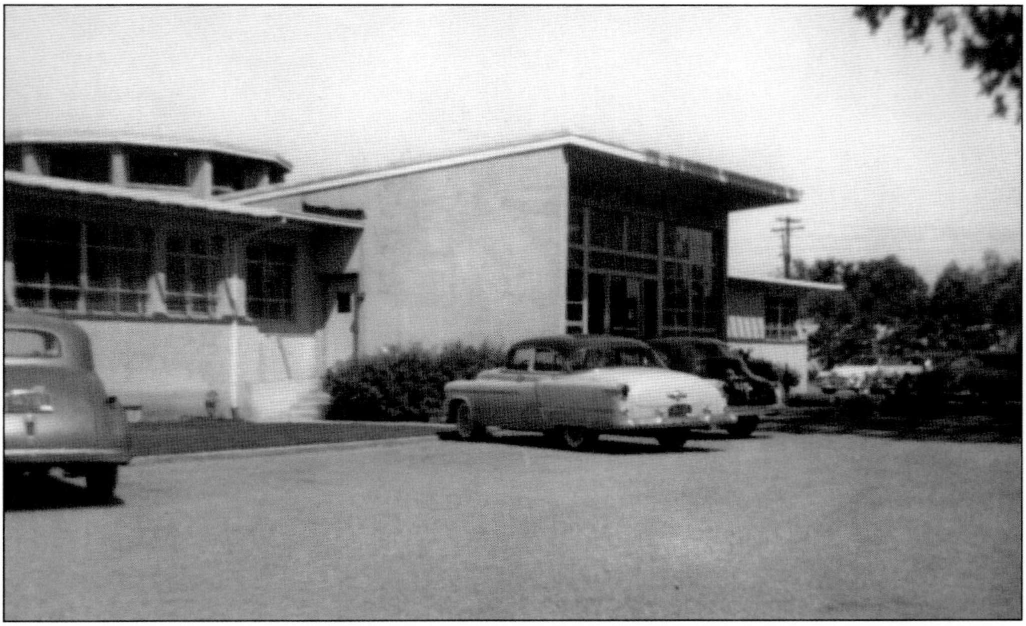

In 1945, the California Farm Bureau Federation made an agreement with an insurance company to provide accident and health insurance for its members either as individuals or as a farm center group when at least 80 percent of the members joined. A large number of active public-spirited people, willing to support work for community projects, decided to call a public meeting to publicize the need for a hospital. It was felt that $400,000 could be raised. The Biggs-Gridley Memorial Hospital became a model of how to get a hospital built without debt. The pledge drive was held throughout the Biggs, Gridley, Live Oak, and Richvale areas. Each donor who pledged $100 or more received voting privileges in the organization. Fundraising drives over the next two years raised enough money to build the hospital, which opened on June 10, 1949. (Both, courtesy of the Gridley Museum.)

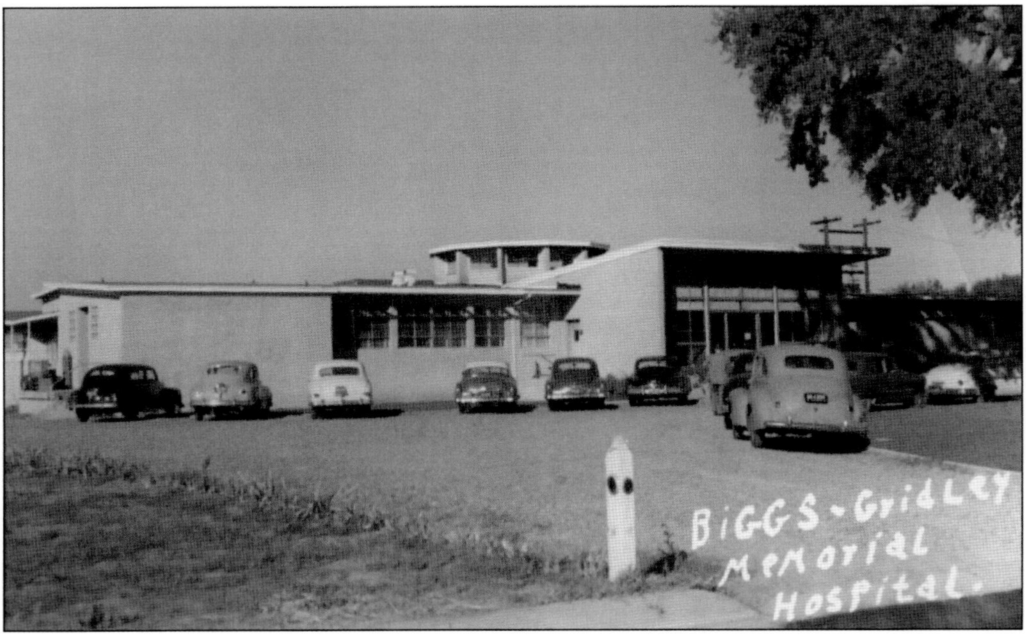

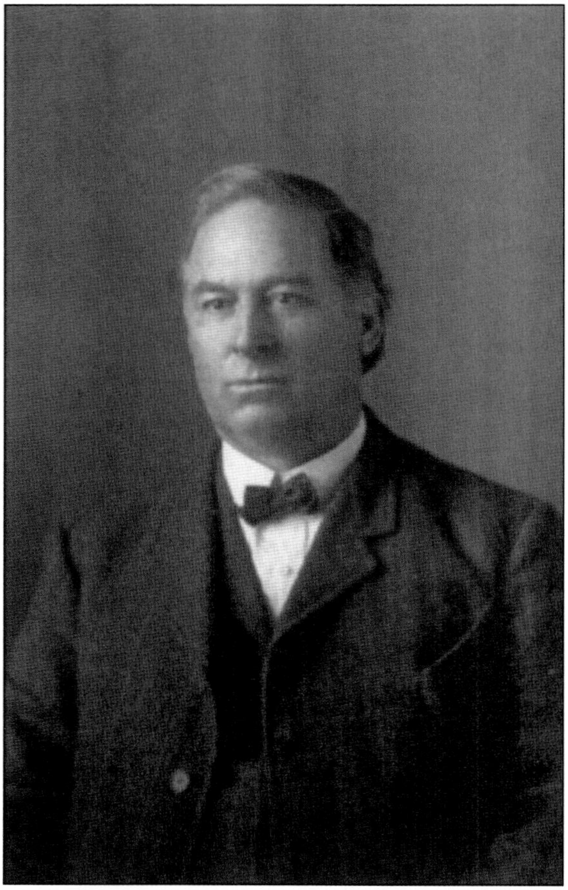

Lewis Quinton Thompson was a physician in Gridley practicing on Hazel Street. He was listed as practicing in the 1900 census, and was listed in the 1920 city directory. His wife's name was Thela. It is believed that he donated the deodar spruce trees for the city plaza, showing his civic generosity. (Courtesy of the Gridley Museum.)

No doctors are more honored than those known as country doctors. Dr. Leslie Frudenthal was worn out by his vigilance at bedsides, and strained by excessive demands, fell asleep at the wheel of his car. He died at a hospital in Oroville. He was highly revered by his patients. (Courtesy of the Gridley Museum.)

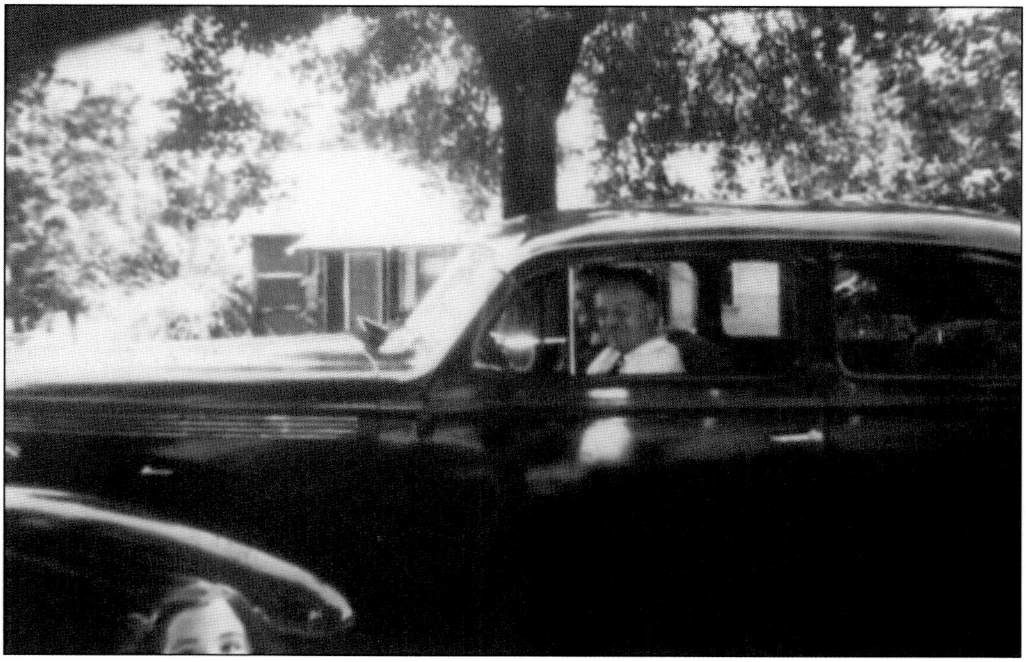

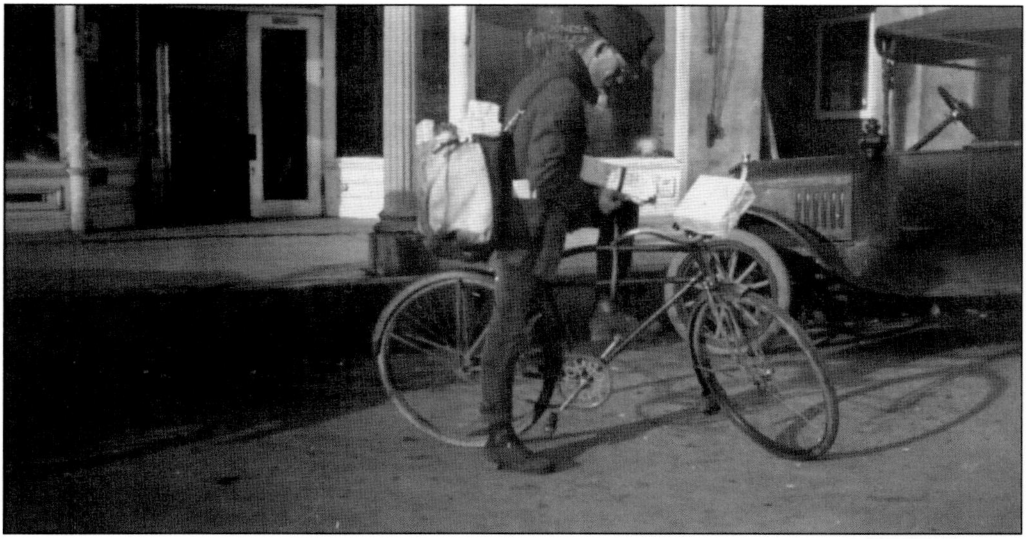

In June 1915, the *Gridley Herald* reported, "Postmaster Osborn has been informed by the department that the Gridley Post Office has been advanced to a second class rating due to the increase in business during the past year." While the news was gratifying to the people, it indicated that changes in service might not suit the patrons. The postmaster had to make changes to office hours, limiting them to 8:00 a.m. to 6:00 p.m. daily, and rural carriers would not be required to deliver mail on Sundays. Lee Green is seen above delivering mail on Christmas Day 1920 on a bicycle. Green is also pictured below between Coy Kofford and Walter Harkey after he retired. (Both, courtesy of the Gridley Museum.)

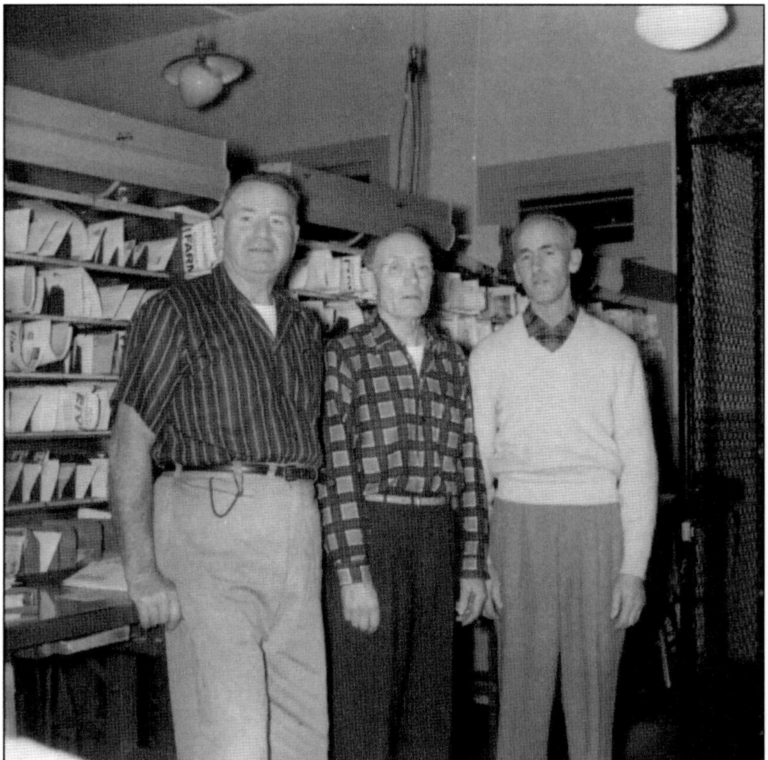

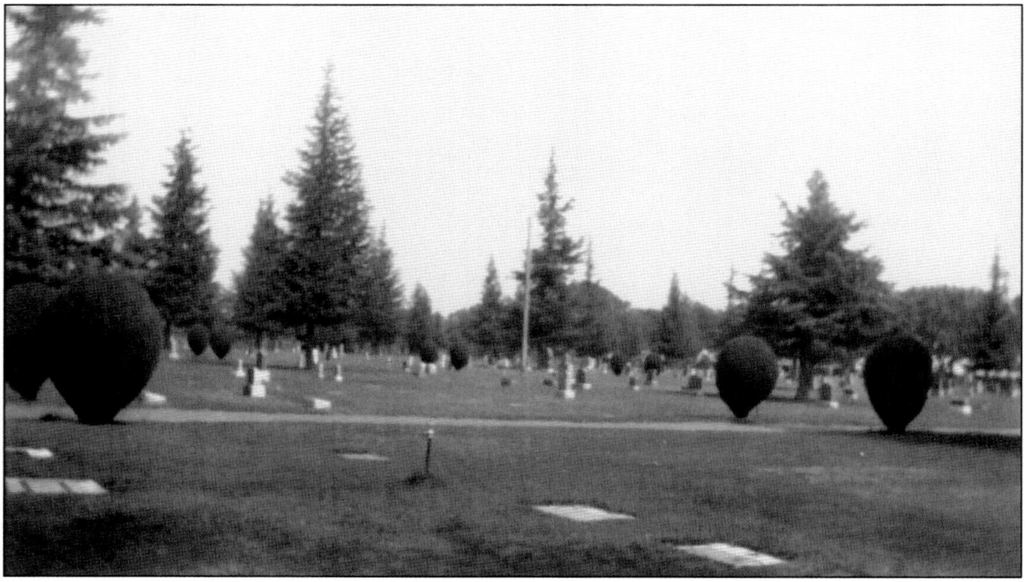

The sexton of the cemetery, John Wharton, was a hardworking, conscientious, and dedicated man who was never known to refuse to dig a grave regardless of wind, weather, or time of day or night. It seems people took advantage of him by failing to pay him for his labors. The Gridley-Biggs Cemetery is pictured here on an unknown date, but the deodar cedars are small. (Courtesy of the *Gridley Herald.*)

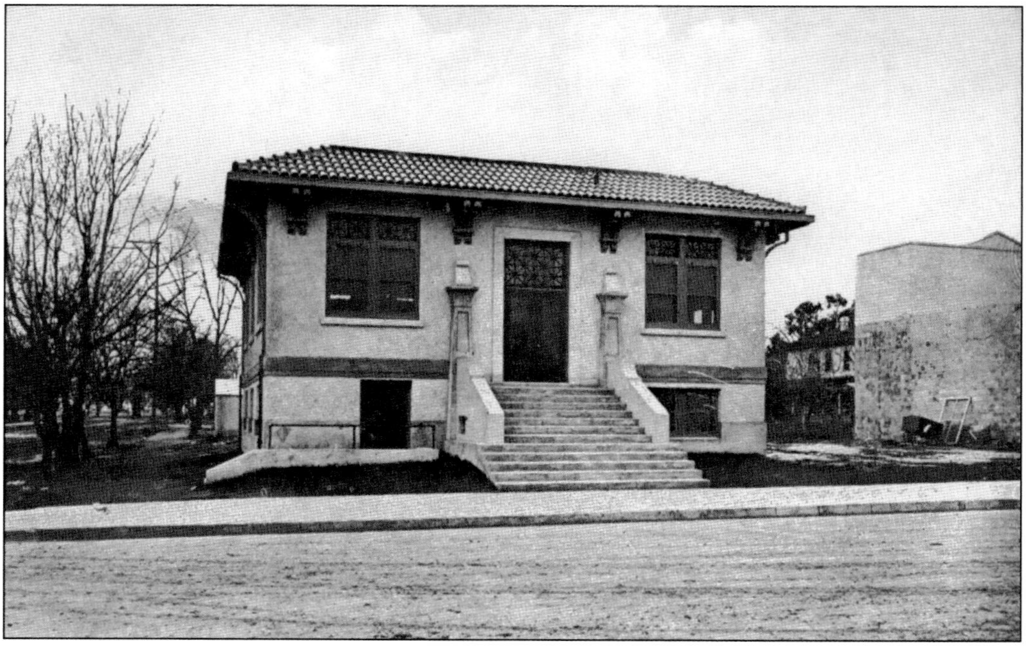

The Ladies Improvement launched its effort to establish a city library in 1906, with the club agreeing to pay $600 a year. In 1912, the club sought a grant of $8,000 from Andrew Carnegie to build the library. The notice for plans needed was signed by Malinda Shaeffer, club president. It was not until 1915 that Carnegie gave his approval and construction began. (Courtesy of the Gridley Museum.)

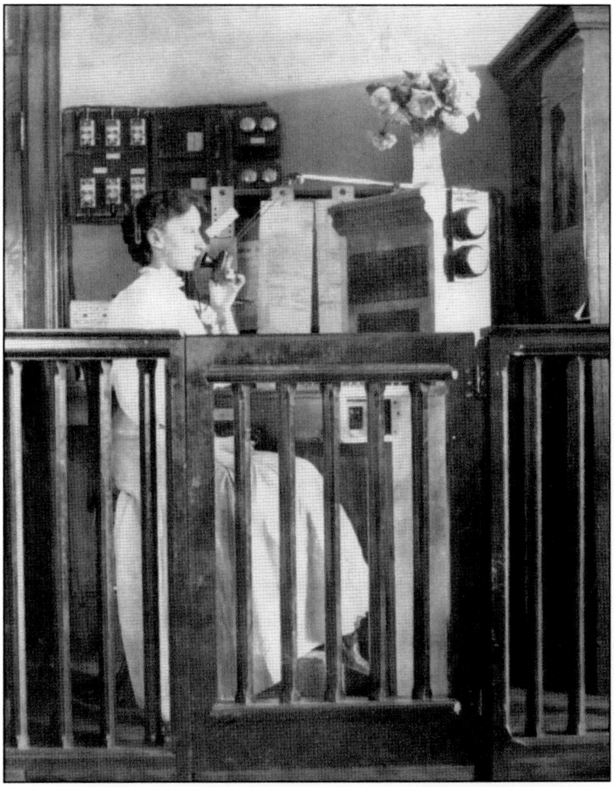

About 1900, telephone service, which had been sporadic at best in Gridley, became more widespread with the installation of this modern switchboard. The older folks flocked to the office to watch the workings of the board. The younger fellows swarmed into the place to watch the pretty operator at work. The woman pictured at right is believed to be Georgia Scribley, who manned the board until she was lured away to become someone's livewire. (Both, courtesy of the *Gridley Herald*.)

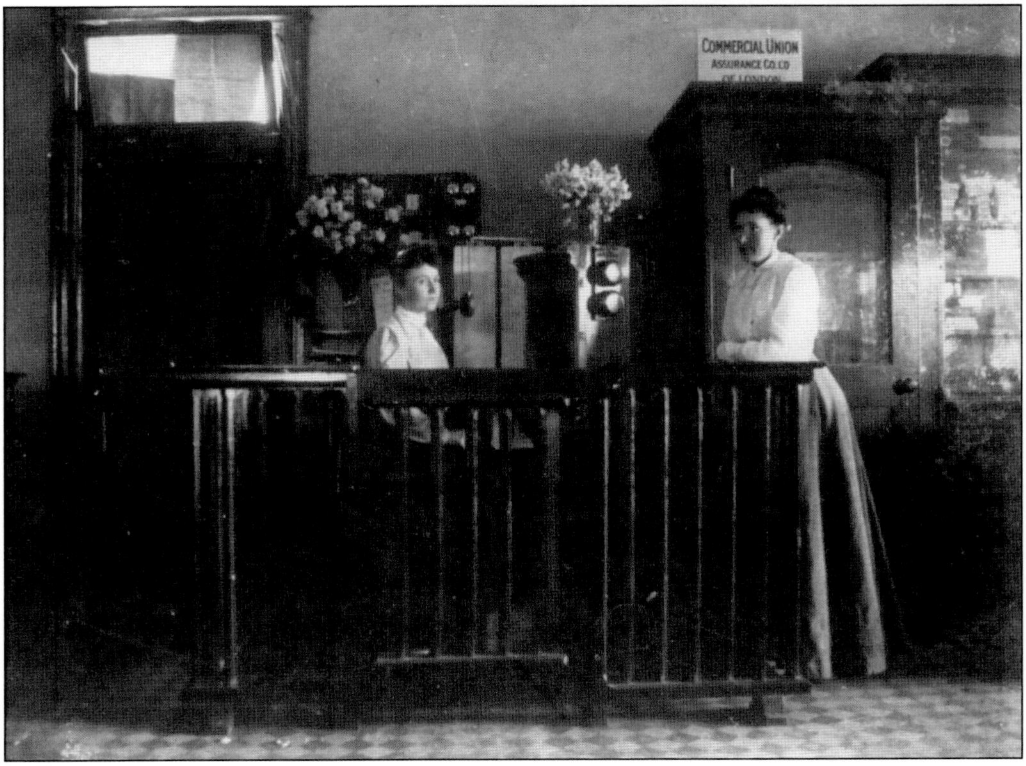

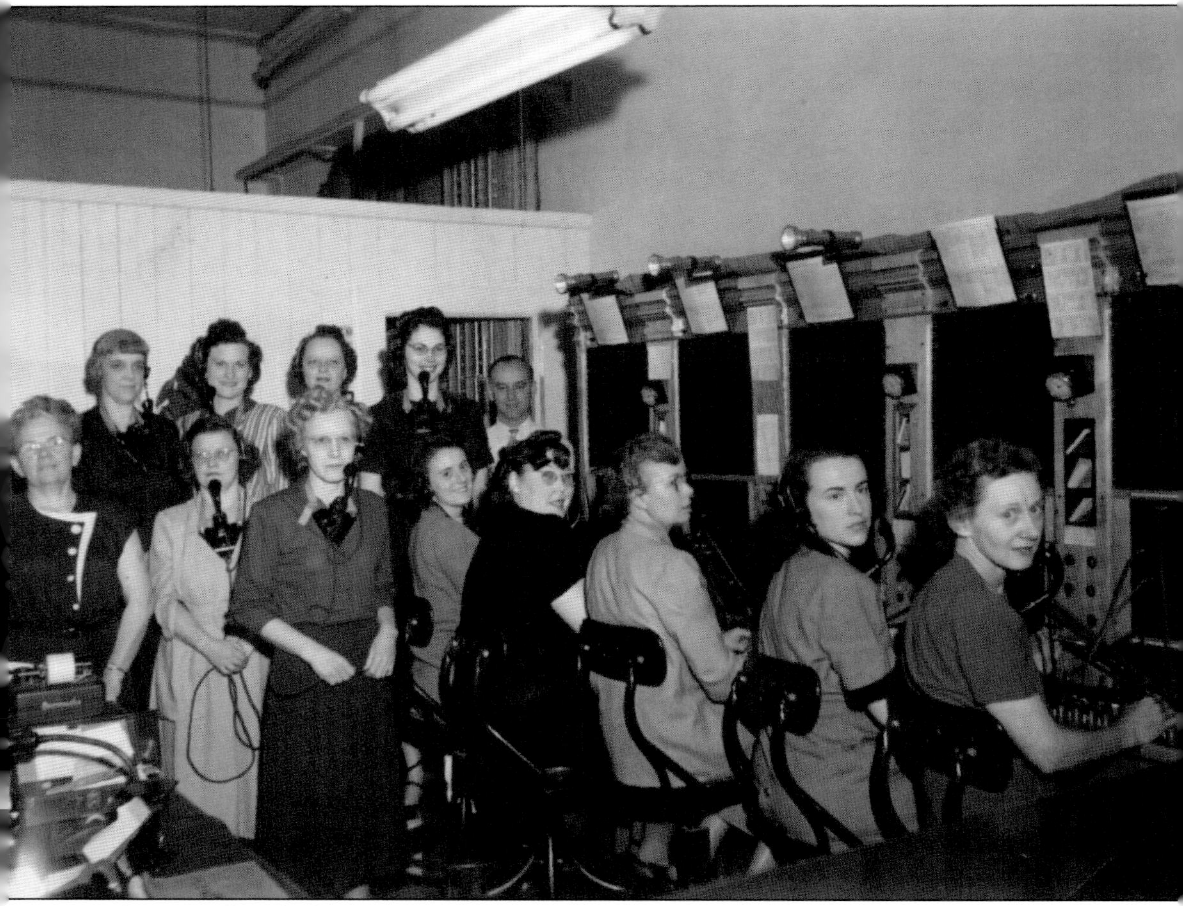

These are the telephone operators at the Gridley office. From left to right are (first row) Alta Ownby (supervisor), Catherine Edwards, Mary Morton Eunice Bull, Mercedes Hepworth, Ella DeVore, Jean Hale, and Bessie Grinell; (second row) Vivian Moon, Mary Davis, Bernice Jones or Leora Dunlap, Regina Deniz (wire chief), and Kyle Wilson. (Courtesy of the Gridley Museum.)

Six

Leisure Time

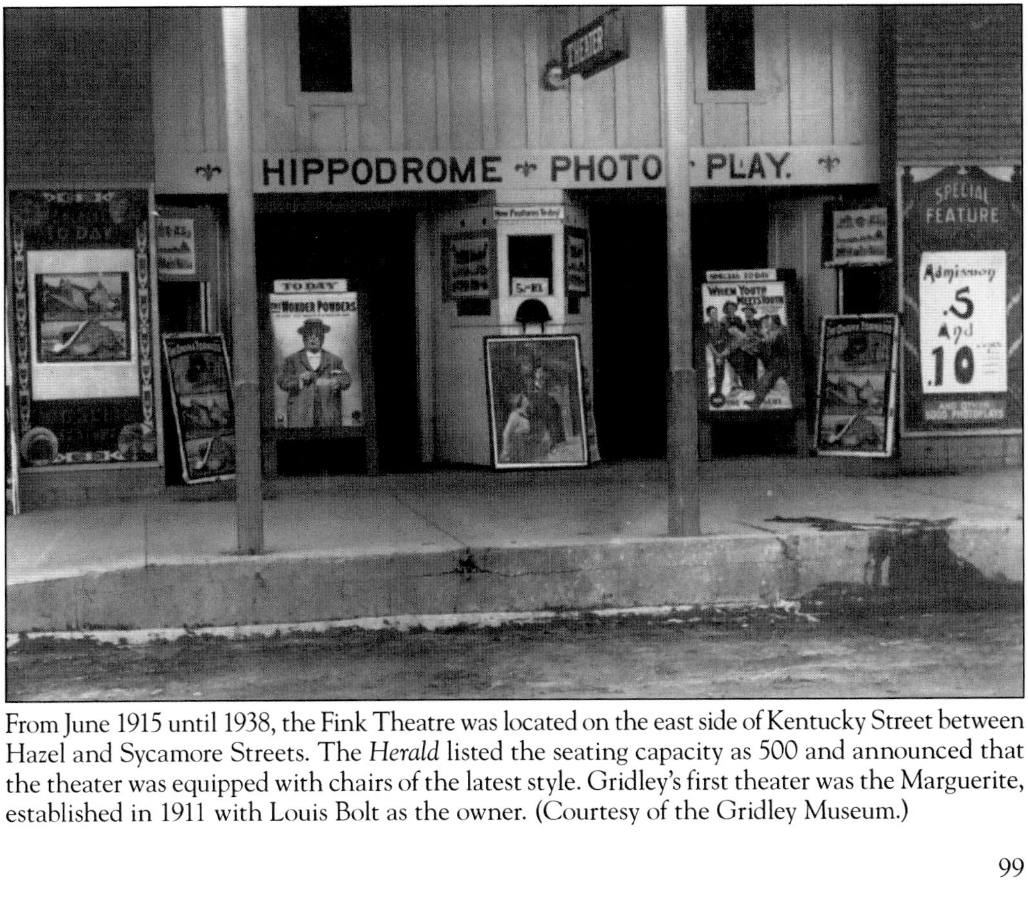

From June 1915 until 1938, the Fink Theatre was located on the east side of Kentucky Street between Hazel and Sycamore Streets. The *Herald* listed the seating capacity as 500 and announced that the theater was equipped with chairs of the latest style. Gridley's first theater was the Marguerite, established in 1911 with Louis Bolt as the owner. (Courtesy of the Gridley Museum.)

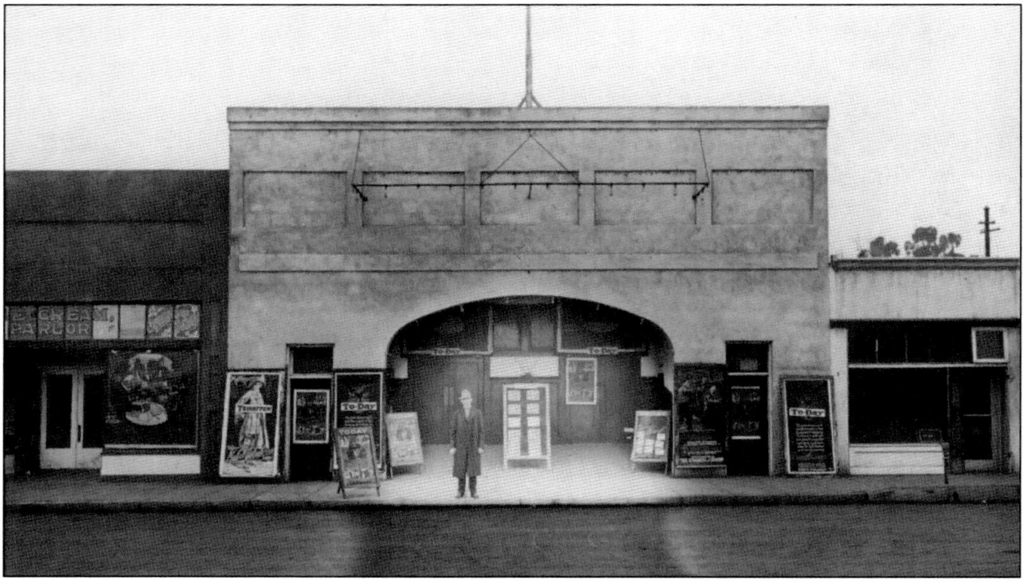

Fred Fink Sr. was the first man to run a successful moving-picture theater in Gridley. In 1911, he opened the Hippodrome Theatre, which operated until January 1, 1915, when he built the beautiful modern Fink Motion Picture Theatre. Fink was known as one of the best and most effective boosters of the fast-developing town. He always took the liveliest interest and a prominent part of the affairs of the town. His wife, Rosie Hamman Fink, was as popular as Fred. The thoroughly up-to-date structure, with all modern improvements including steam heat, showed all the best attractions. (Courtesy of the Gridley Museum.)

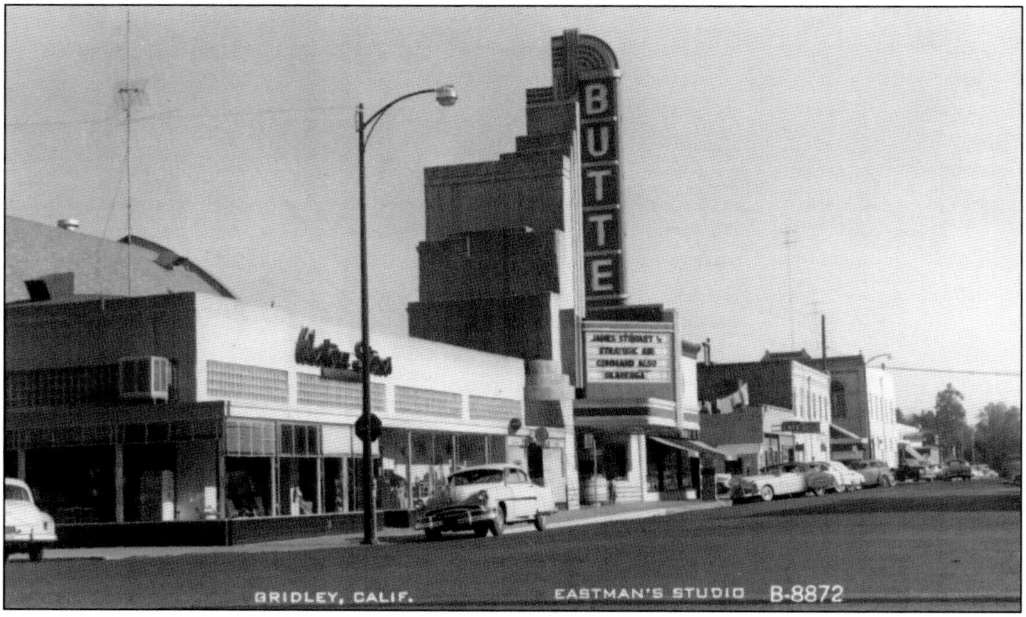

The Art Deco period is clearly reflected in the marquee and tower of the Butte Theater. The traditional sloping entrance floor was made of small blue and rust tiles. The octagonal ticket booth had etched glass panels and a small safe. This theater was constructed by Associated Theatrical Enterprises of San Francisco as part of a chain and played a vital part in downtown Gridley. (Courtesy of the Gridley Museum.)

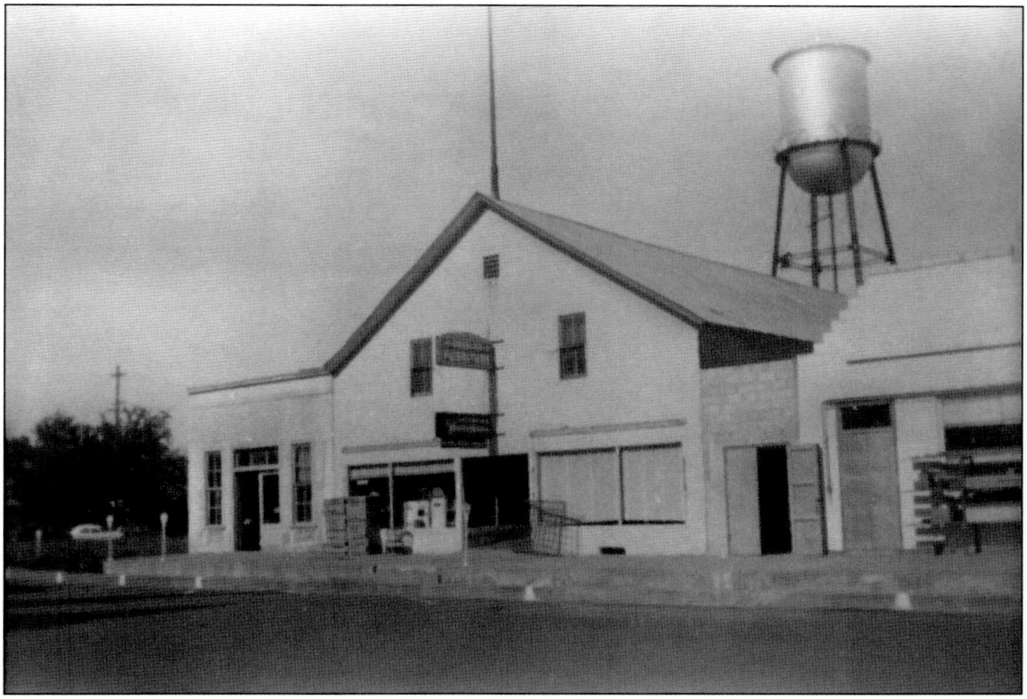

The *Gridley Herald* reported that contractors added new opera chairs to the Old Opera House in April 1915. The Reel California Girls from San Francisco came to perform in May 1915, including Irene Outtrim, who for some years was connected with the famous Alcazar Stock of San Francisco, along with Florence Young, a musical comedy artist. Admission for children was 10¢, adults 20¢, and reserved seats 30¢. (Courtesy of the Gridley Museum.)

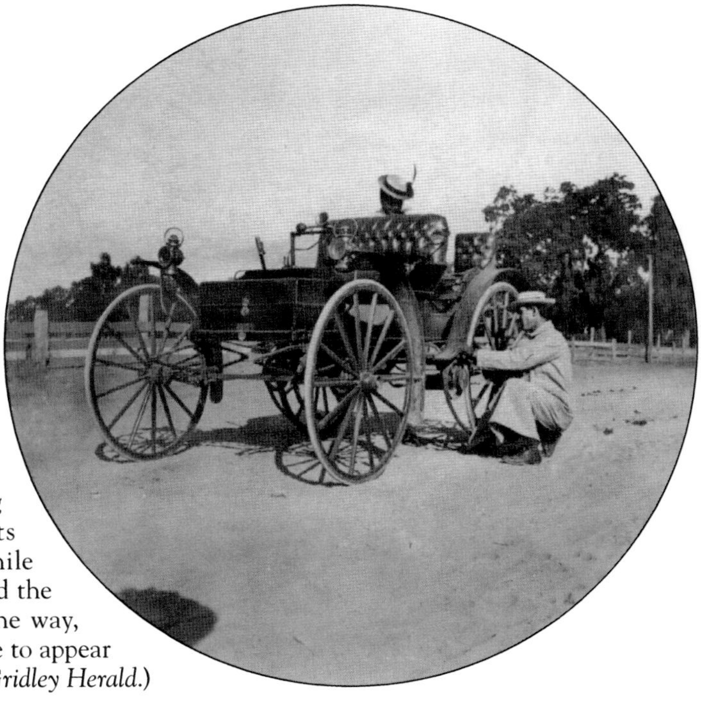

What started out to be a nice Sunday drive suffered a slight delay when Jim Fagan's Oldsmobile developed a bug back in 1906. Clara Tibbets sat in dignified patience while Jim fixed the contraption, and the drive continued. This, by the way, was the first horseless carriage to appear in Gridley. (Courtesy of the *Gridley Herald*.)

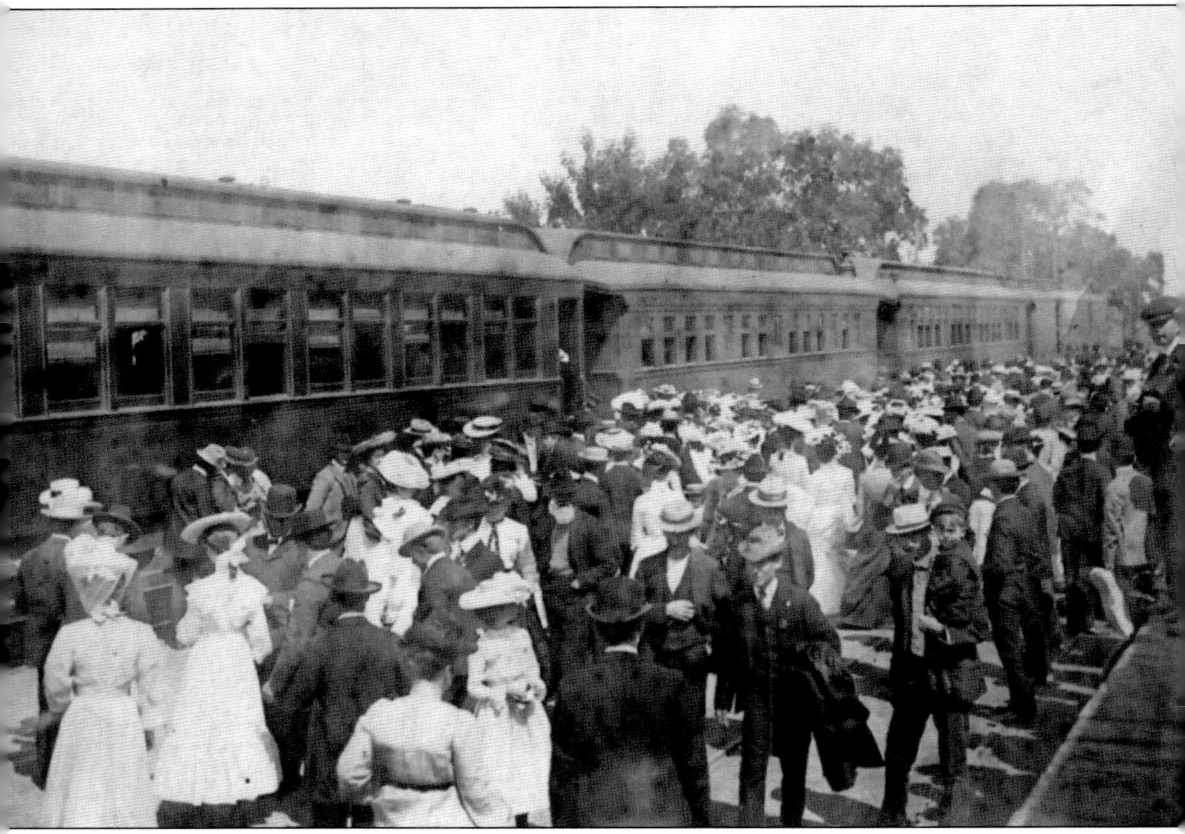

Before the state highway was built, most visitors to Gridley's annual picnic came to town by train instead of automobile. Later, Southern Pacific ran special trains from Gridley to Sacramento to the south and Chico to the north. Other times, the railroad added extra cars to its regular passenger trains to accommodate the crowds. This scene shows the arrival of one of the special trains at the Gridley Depot. (Courtesy of the Gridley Museum.)

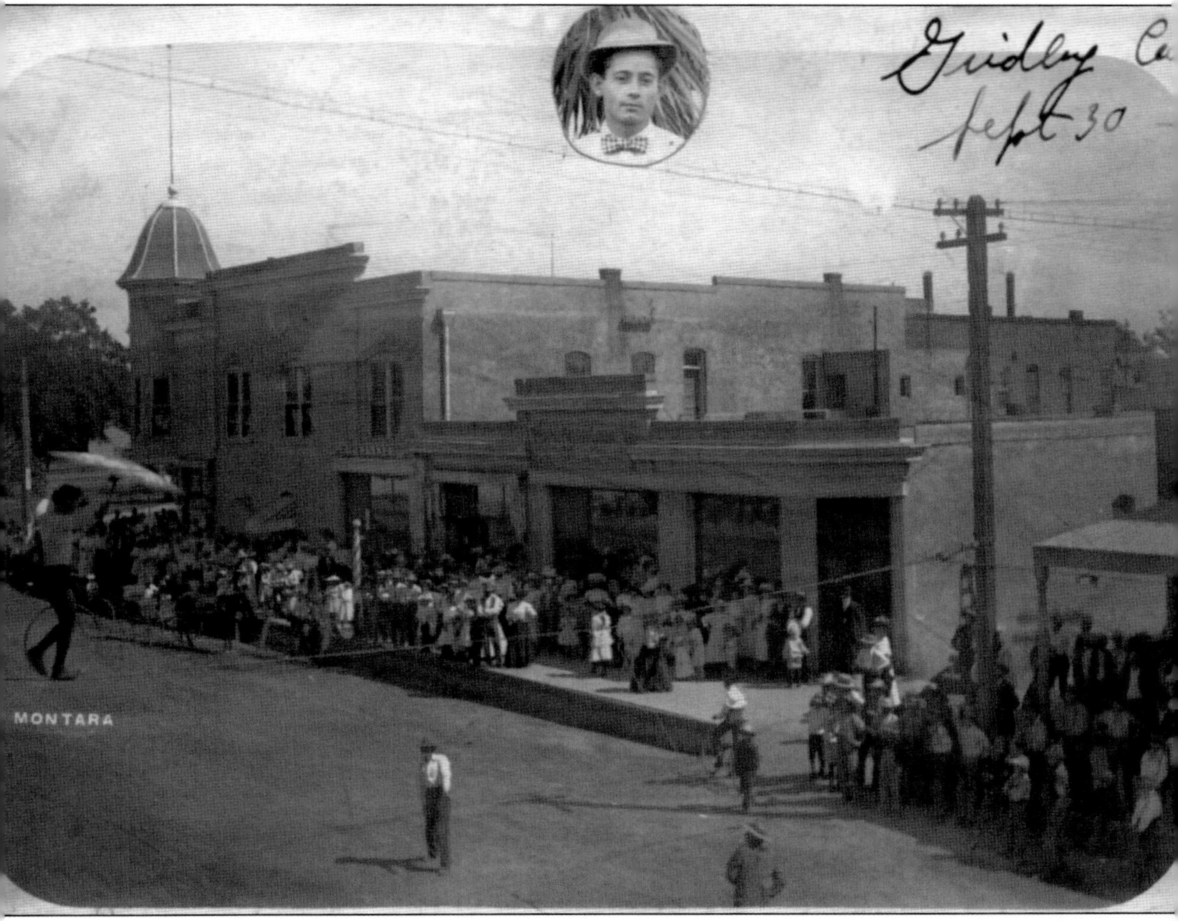

Ralph Bolt, from Oroville, who billed himself as "Montana, The King of the Air," entertained a crowed of Gridleyans on September 30, 1908. Bolt traveled from town to town putting on his wire-walking exhibitions. Merchants helped to underwrite the performance, and other contributions were obtained by passing the hat. This photograph of one of his performances was taken on Hazel Street before the Rideout Bank was built. The Stone Block is in the background. (Courtesy of the *Gridley Herald*.)

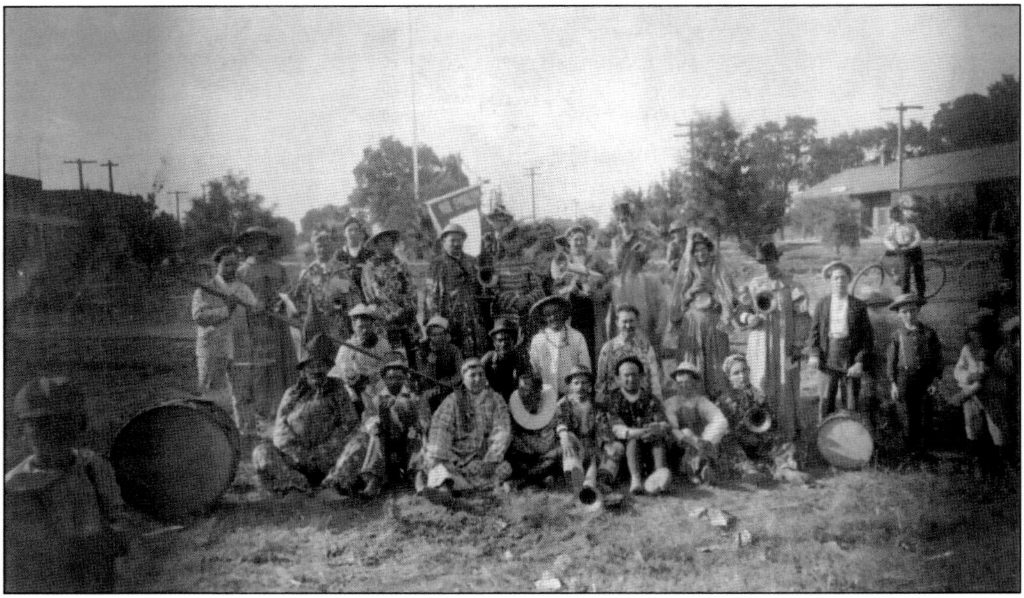

This Gridley band scoured the entire town to find these costumes when they were told they were to play for a masquerade ball back in 1900. Then, when they got to the city park (which was mighty young then), they learned that the ball was not going to be held after all. The day was not lost though; instead, they had this portrait taken. (Courtesy of the *Gridley Herald*.)

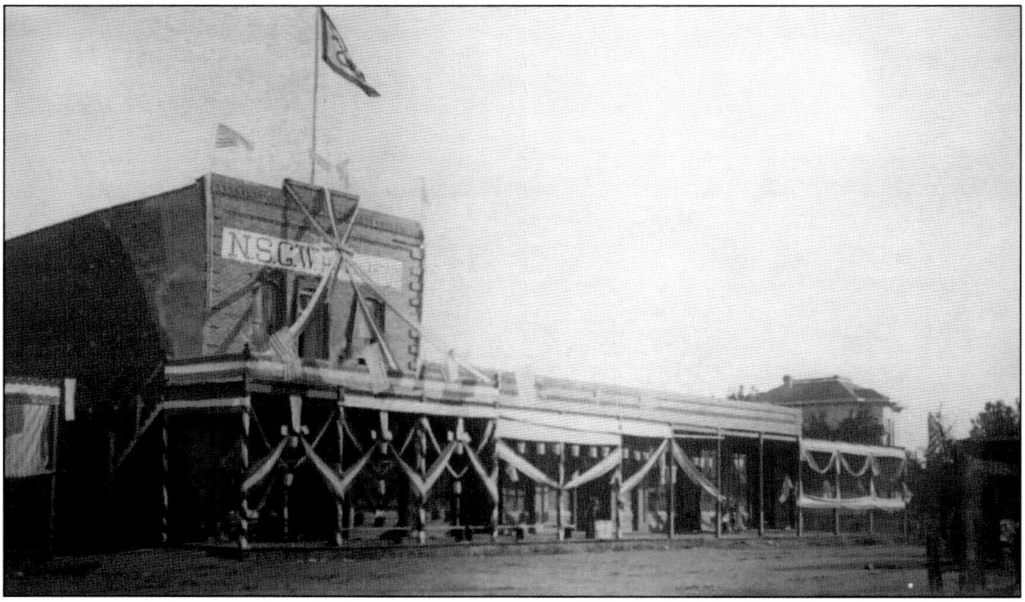

This group of brick store buildings on the south side of Hazel Street east of Ohio Street was named for its owner, Jacob Schorr. The Native Sons of the Golden West was holding a meeting in the Odd Fellows Hall, which occupied the second story of the building next to the alley. Schorr's first brick block on this site was erected in 1883. It was destroyed by fire in 1891. (Courtesy of the *Gridley Herald*.)

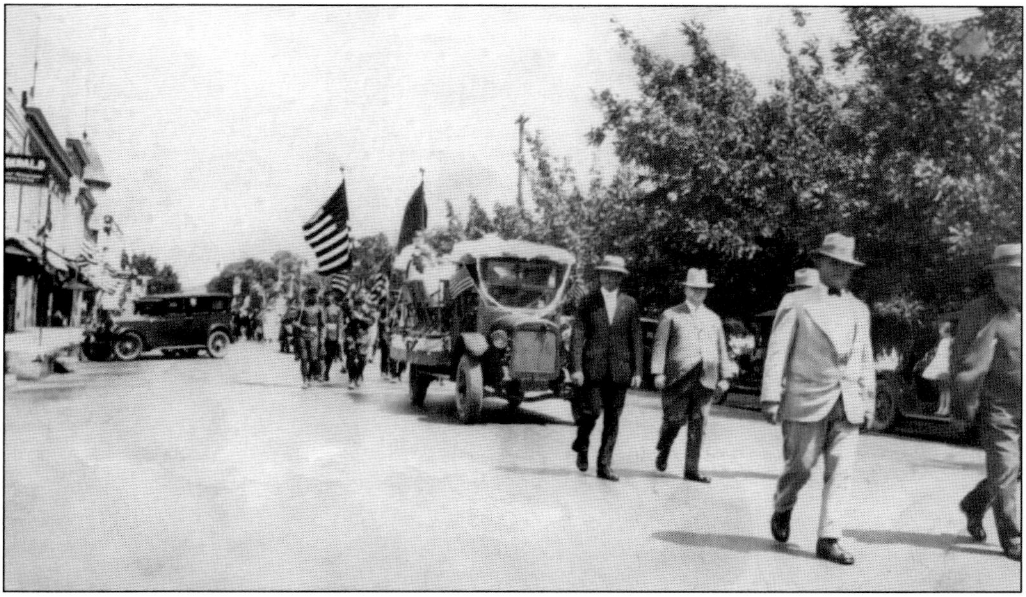

During the 1920s and 1930s, Gridley held an annual Memorial Day parade, honoring all the veterans of wars past. People were reminded not to forget the veterans and to decorate the graves of those who had passed on. Civil War veterans led these parades. (Courtesy of the *Gridley Herald*.)

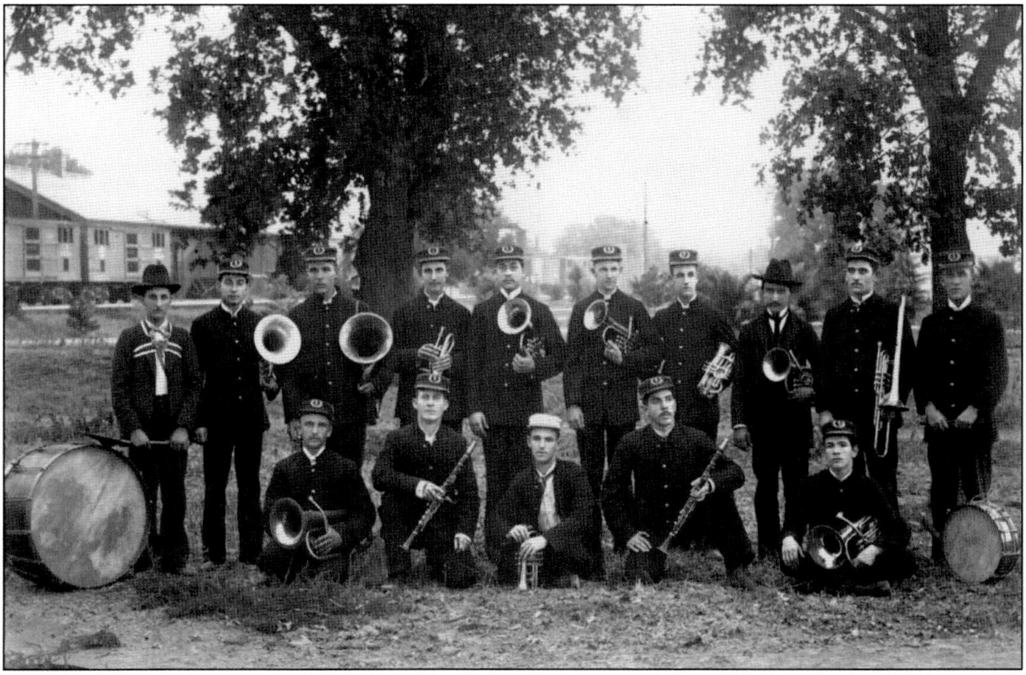

The Gridley City Brass Band is pictured here in 1898 at the railroad depot in Young City Park. From left to right are (first row) Billie Robbins, Tom Horner, Bill Lilly, Albert Norman, and Johnnie Vermillien; (second row) L. Young, A.M. Miller, R.O. Schellenger, C.V. Green, Abe Gile, Southard Simpson, Claude Lilly, Max Peters, Hank Nulls, and Claude Rogers. (Courtesy of the *Gridley Herald*.)

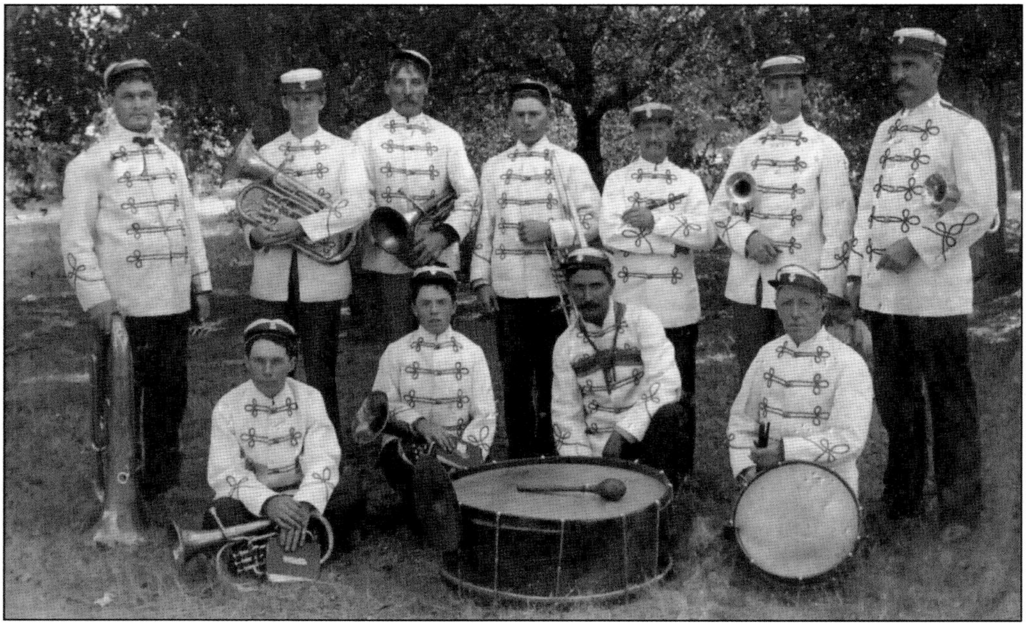

Gridley residents combined a spirit of intense patriotism with a strong desire for entertainment to organize their Fourth of July celebration. In 1881, Gridley's celebration was the biggest event in all of Butte County and therefore attracted residents from every corner of Butte. An astounding 2,000 people showed up for the festivities. On this day, the event got off to a noisy start at exactly one minute after midnight. That is when the first cannon fired, as a signal to let fly with the firecrackers. At 9:25 a.m., the grand parade formed on Virginia Street facing south, led by the colorful Gridley Brass Band and featuring Emily Taylor as the Goddess of Liberty and Clara Marshall as the Goddess of Justice. (Both, courtesy of the *Gridley Herald*.)

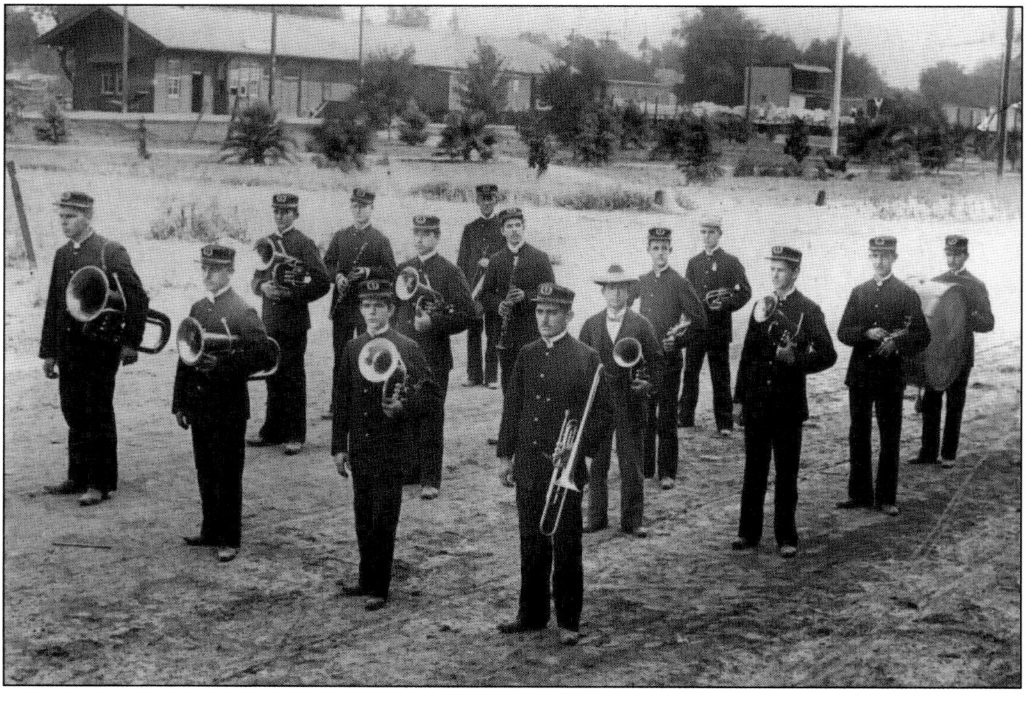

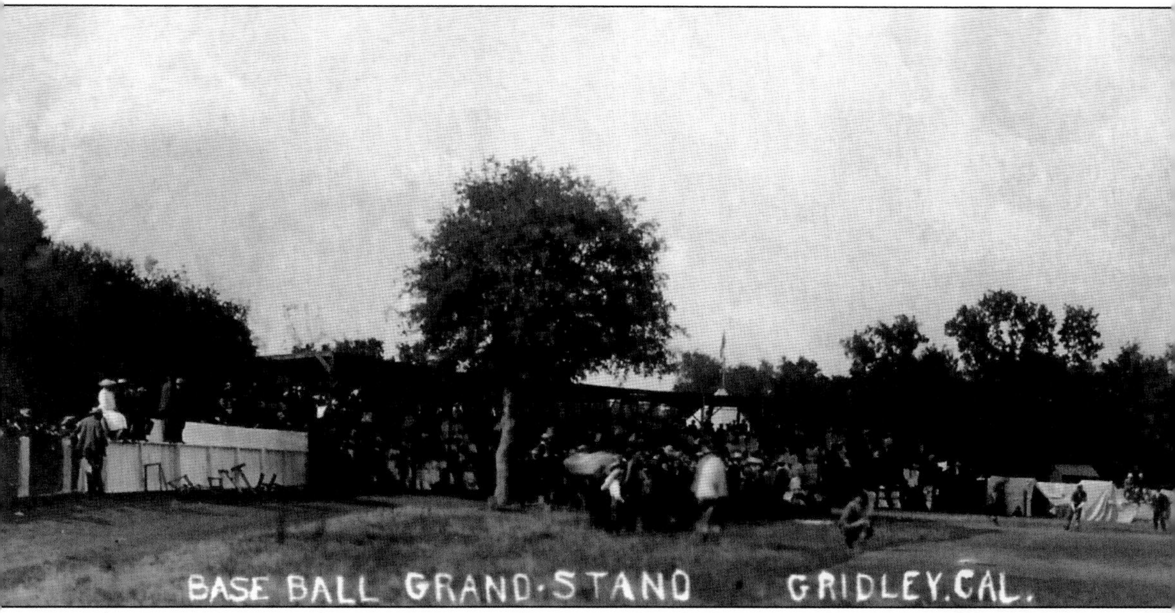

Each year at the annual cannery picnic, there were baseball games, like this one on June 22, 1907. There was a baseball diamond near the cannery that was used for recreation for cannery workers, and eventually, a town team like the Normans. There is no information on how the team got its name, but it has been reported that John Franklin Shaeffer only hired people to work for him who could play a good game of baseball; he was a huge fan of the game. (Courtesy of the *Gridley Herald*.)

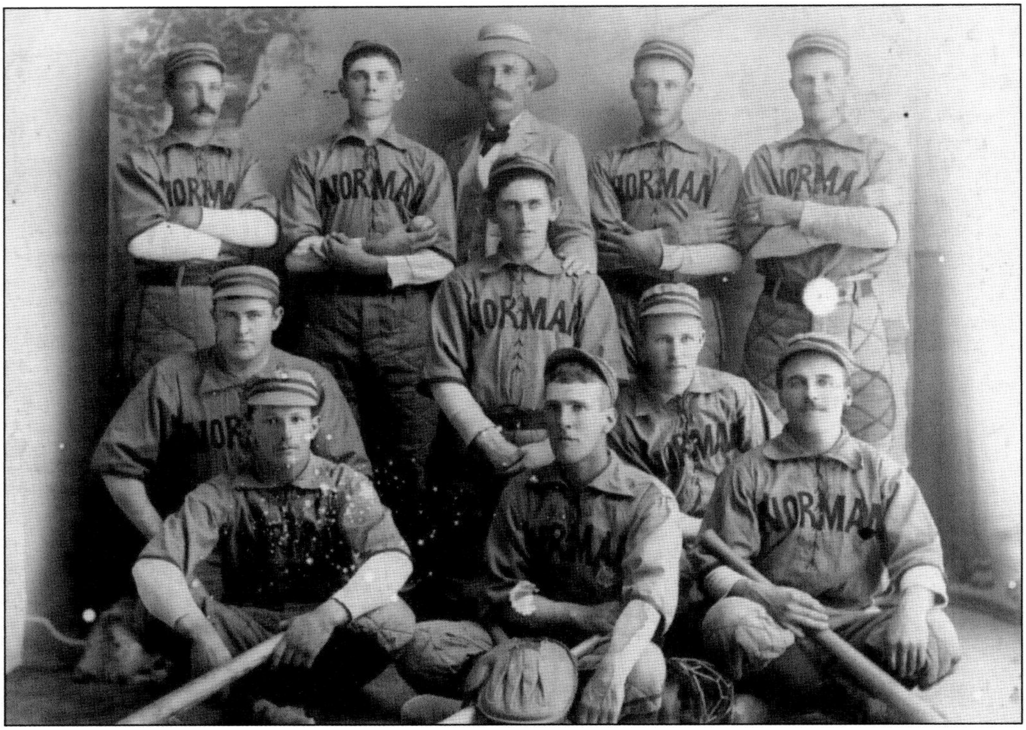

The Norman baseball team was a town team that played other town teams. Players pictured are, from left to right, (first row) Sewell Young (fielder), Lee Winters (second baseman), and Mike Jarvis (fielder); (second row) ? Humble (first base), Hank Mills (fielder), and Ed Sooy (fielder); (third row) Harry Young (short stop), Ed Wells (pitcher), John Shaeffer (manager), and Eugene Young (third base). (Courtesy of the Gridley Museum.)

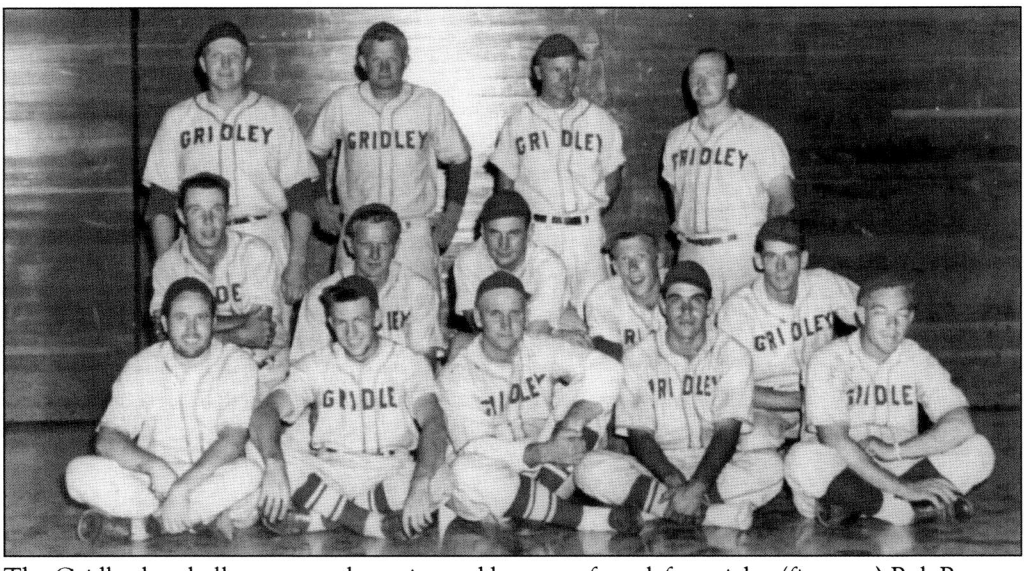

The Gridley baseball team members pictured here are, from left to right, (first row) Bob Bassett, unidentified, Walter Little, Lou Morton, and John Adams; (second row) Marvin Cassady, George Doering, unidentified, George Peekema, and Bill McMurtry; (third row) Dean Hogeboom, Ben Doering, Buzz McFarland, and coach Raymond Roberts. (Courtesy of the Gridley Museum.)

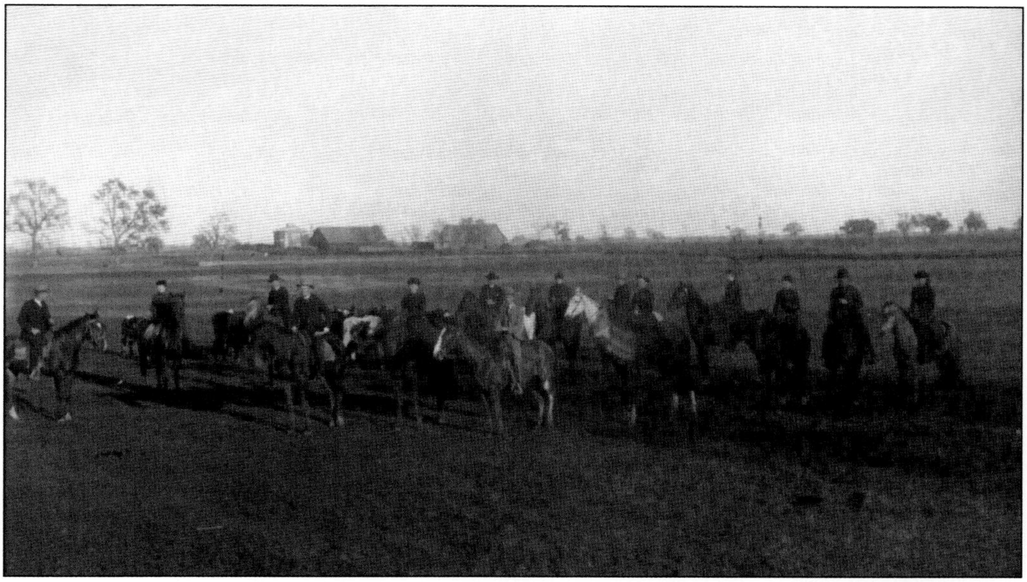

The horses outnumbered the cows when this photograph was taken on the Fagan Ranch in 1884. Actually, these fellers and their ladies (riding sidesaddle), were gathered together before setting out on a sociable ride through the countryside, which was plentiful around Gridley in those days. (Courtesy of the *Gridley Herald*.)

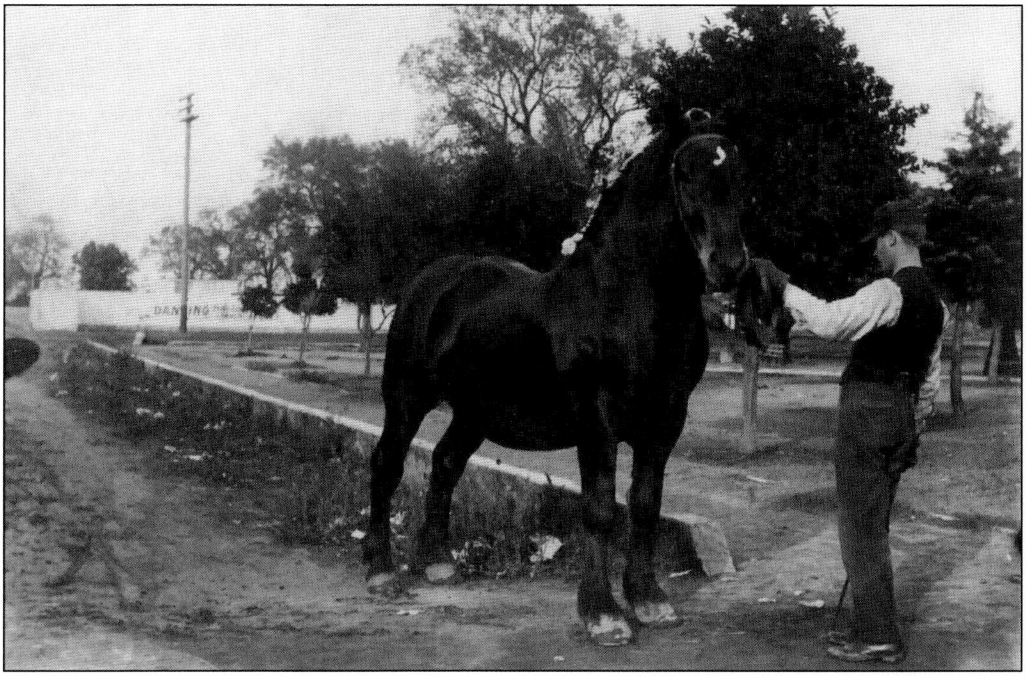

The cannery picnic always had a dance that was held in the open-air dance pavilion. It was located on the corner of Hazel and Virginia Streets, seen here in the background. Although the focus of this photograph is on this fine specimen of a horse and its owner, the pavilion was a landmark for the town. The park is visible on the right. (Courtesy of Butte County Historical Society.)

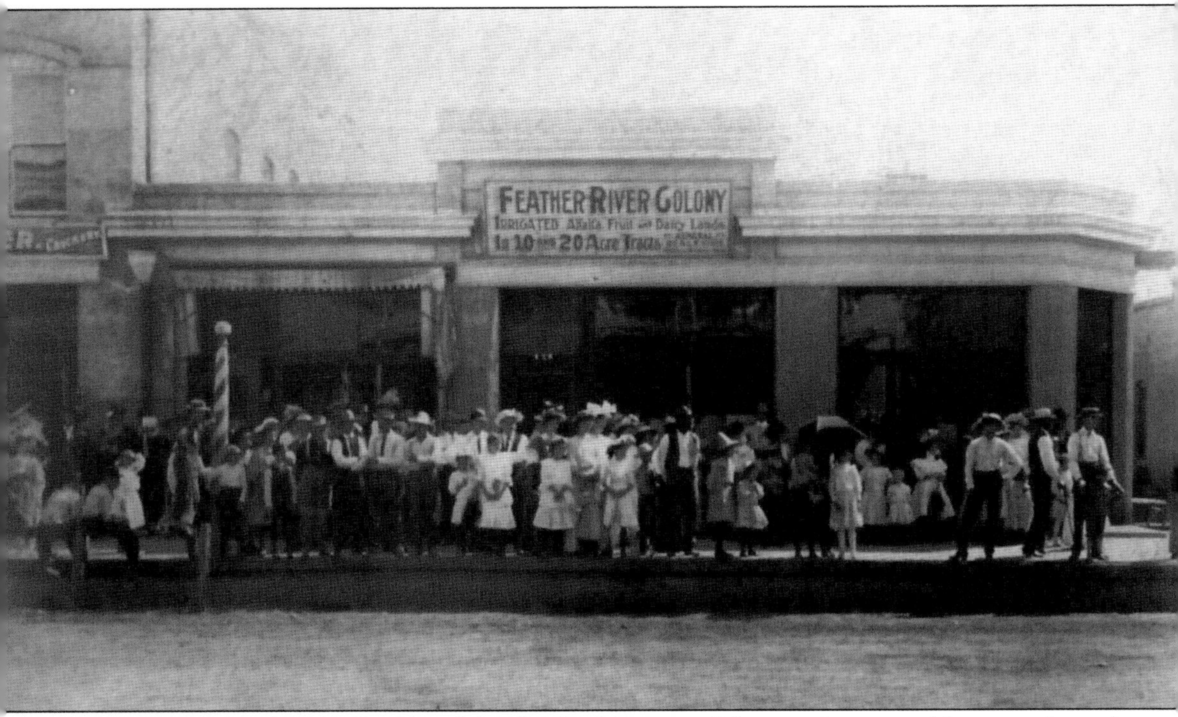

The townspeople came out for all kinds of celebrations. The people pictured here are dressed up in their finery, waiting for the parade to begin. The marquee on the building behind them advertises the Feather River Colony. (Courtesy of Butte County Historical Society.)

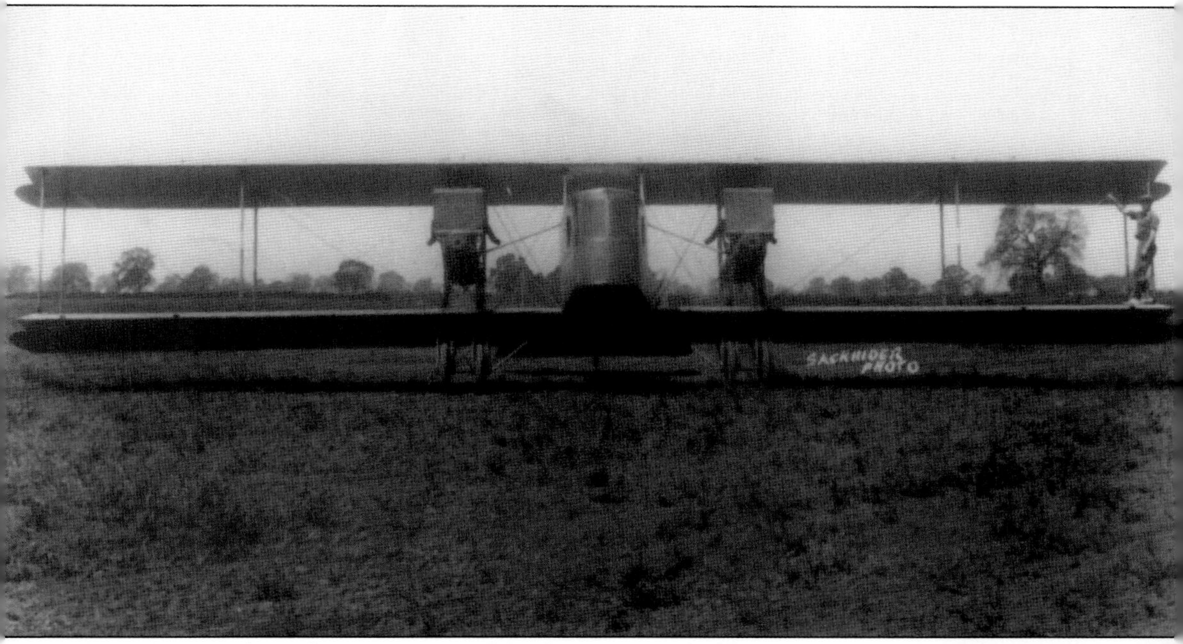

This is the famed *Friesley Falcon*, one of the forerunners of today's modern airliners. The *Falcon* was built in Gridley and financed mainly by local capital. It had a brief but spectacular life. More than 17,000 persons flocked to the Dan Corcoran Ranch at Biggs on April 17, 1921, to see the inaugural flight of this aircraft. Military aircraft from Mather Field and famous fliers Capt. Eddie Rickenbacker and Capt. Reed Chambers were on hand to watch the successful launching of the huge plane. On August 21, 1921, the Marysville baseball team became the first team to use an airplane to travel to a game. The Marysville team used the Falcon to fly to Woodland for a game on a Sunday afternoon. (Courtesy of the Gridley Museum.)

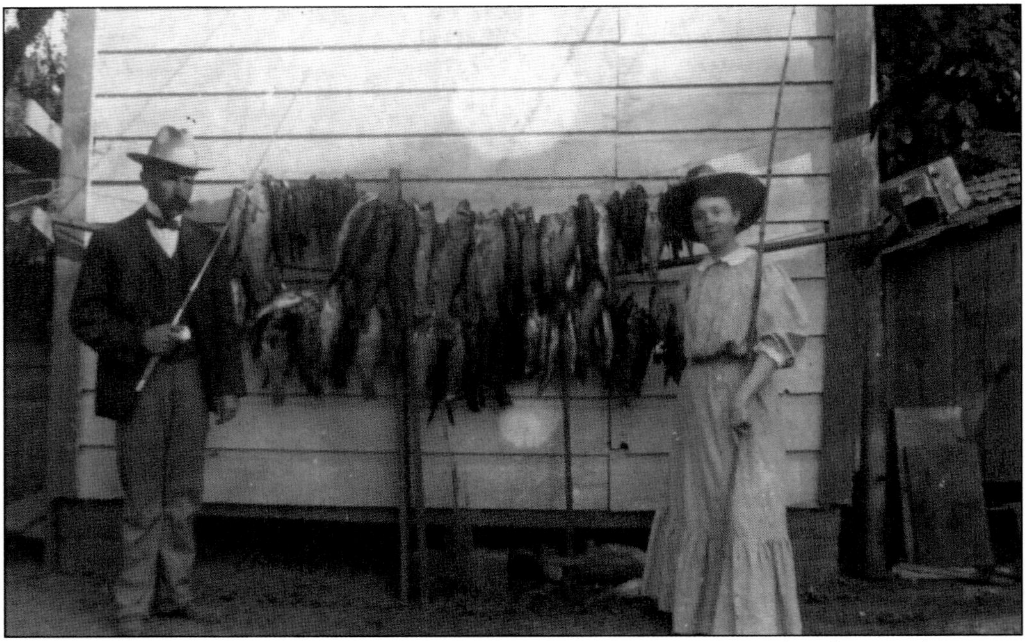

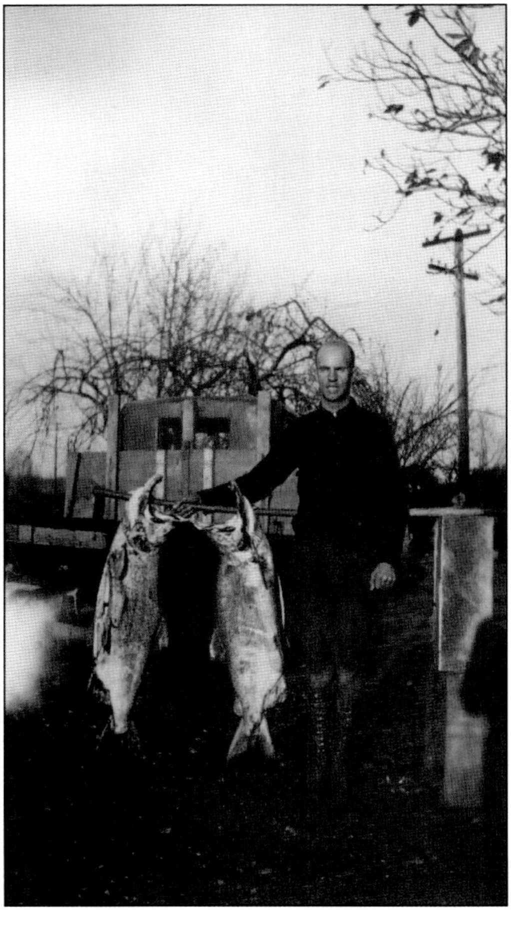

"Good Fishing" read a headline in the *Gridley Herald* on March 8, 1883. "A party returned from fishing in the Sacramento River, and the fishing is good in the Feather. The catch numbered 467 fish weighing over 600 pounds. The biggest catch was a salmon at 19 pounds. The largest catfish was 13 pounds." The couple pictured is unidentified. (Courtesy of the *Gridley Herald*.)

This image shows young Arthur Carlin with his catch of fish pulled from his favorite fishing hole before he headed out to his tractor on the family farm. (Courtesy of Gary Carlin.)

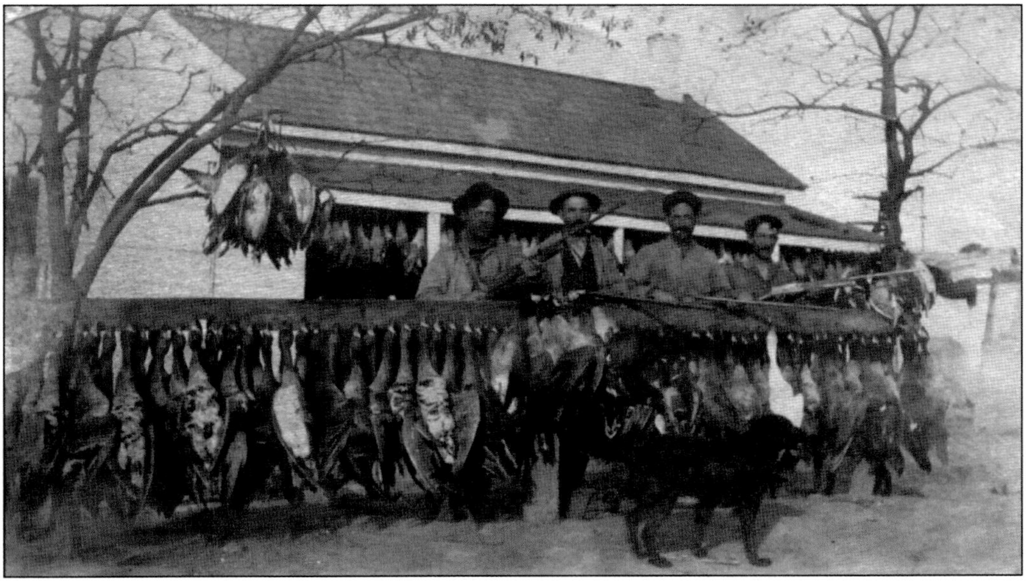

The King brothers are pictured here around 1918 on the King Ranch nine miles west of Gridley. Above are, from left to right, Lee King, Louie King, Thomas King, and Edward King. Below, from left to right are Lee King, Tom King, and Louie King. The brothers hunted professionally, raised cattle and mules, and farmed wheat and rice on their 1,700-acre ranch. There were six sons in this family and five daughters. Their parents were Michael Jason and Alice Ryan King. Their brother John Francis moved into town and owned a grocery store, and another brother, William, became a dentist. (Both, courtesy of Evelyn King Briggs.)

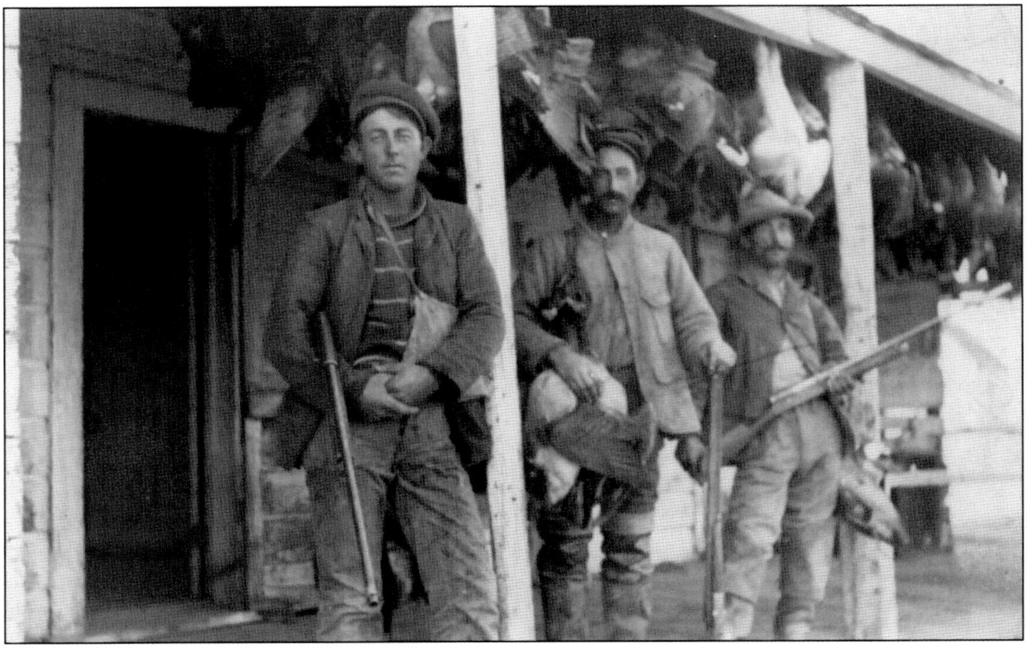

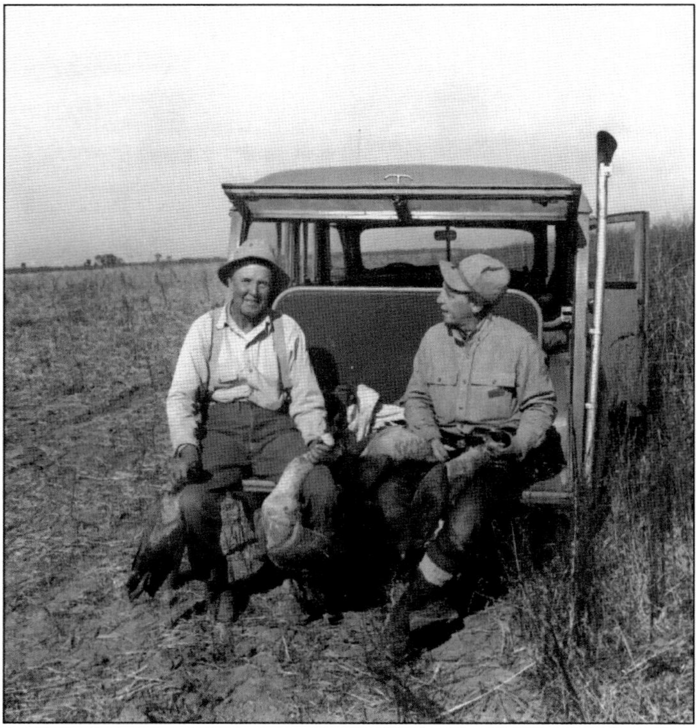

Frank Carlisle Hackett operated the Gridley Goose Club from 1940 to the 1970s. He was the first waterfowl hunting guide in Butte County. Hackett could call birds using nothing but his vocal chords and mouth. Celebrities like Bing Crosby and football player Leo Nomelini used him as their guide in Gridley. Later, Hackett developed poor vision and had difficulty walking, but with help into a blind, he could still call birds. (Courtesy of Joseph Viscuso.)

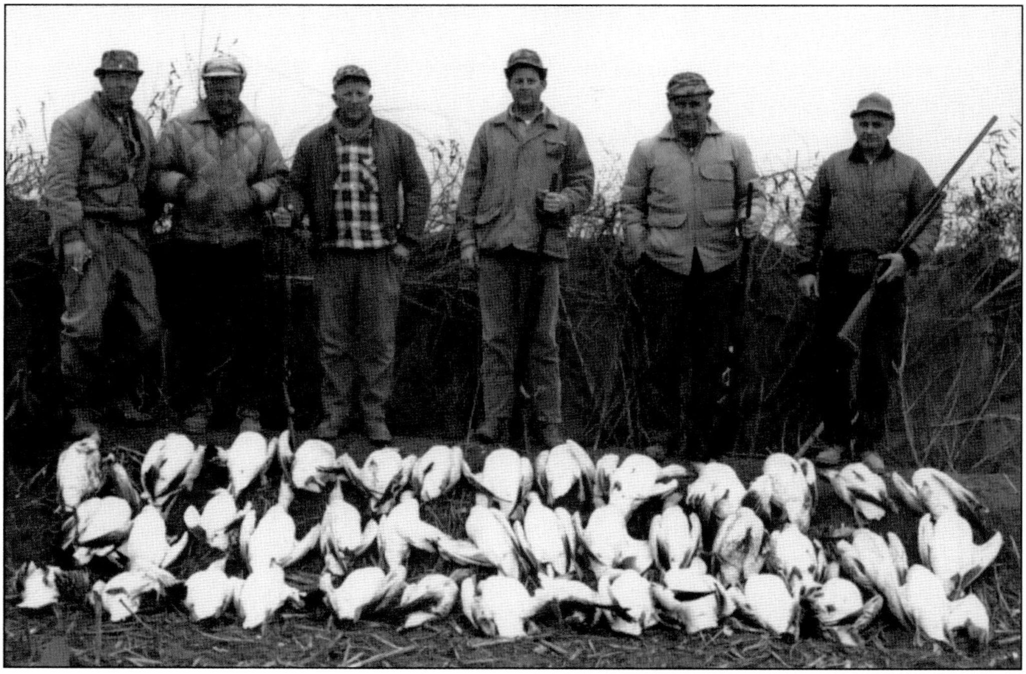

One of California's most active gun clubs was purchased by the State of California in 1931 at a cost of $51 per acre for the purpose of establishing a waterfowl refuge. Two miles north of the Sutter-Buttes, Gray Lodge started with 2,540 acres for ducks and geese to escape from hunters. This was the first wildlife refuge established in the Sacramento Valley, and it was maintained as a complete sanctuary from 1931 through 1952. (Courtesy of Joseph Viscuso.)

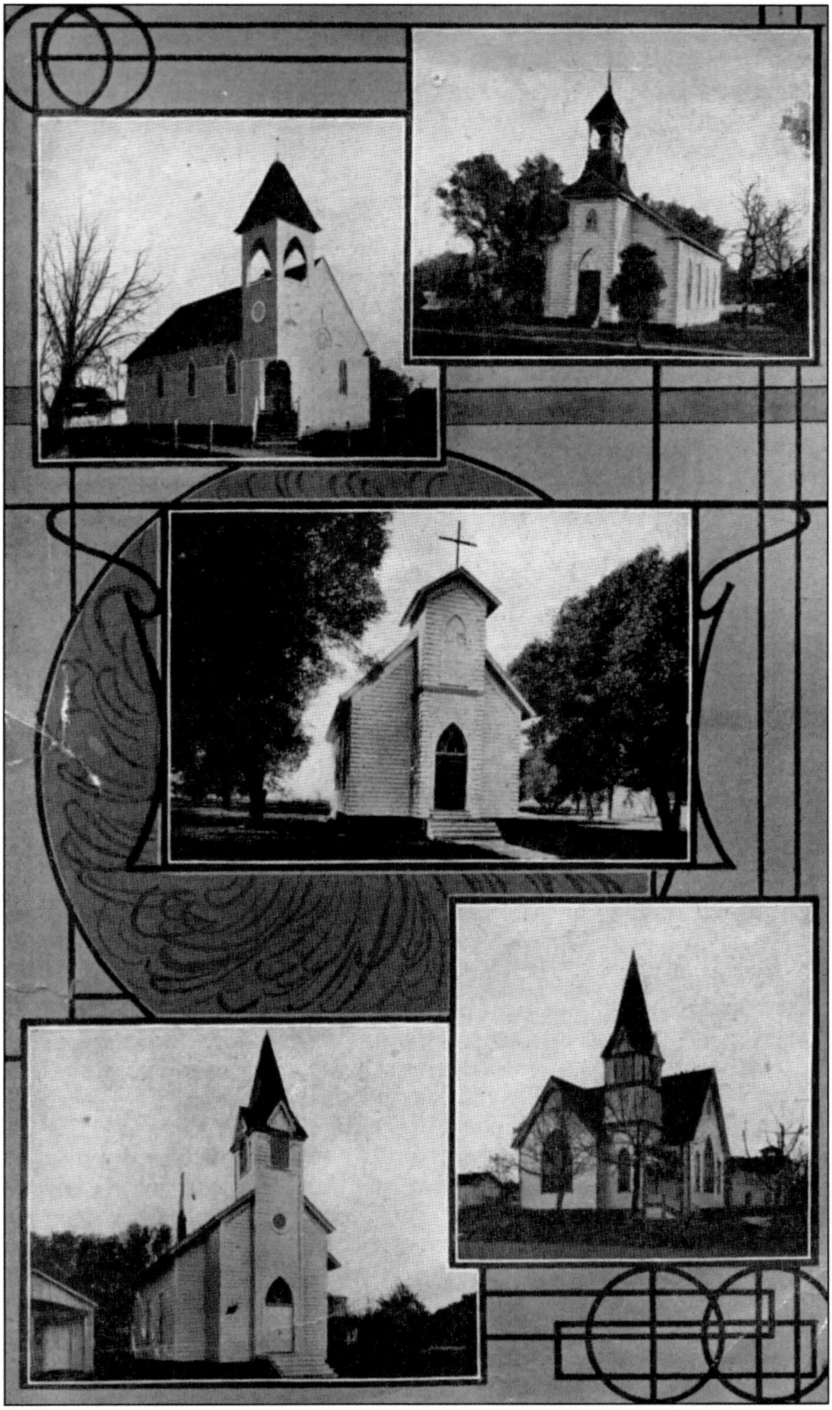

Churches of all denominations were represented in Gridley. In 1905, there were five church buildings in town. In rural districts, services were held in schoolhouses and other buildings. The houses of worship pictured here are the Christian church and United Brethren Church at top, the Catholic church at center, and the Methodist-Episcopal church and Presbyterian church at bottom. (Courtesy of the Gridley Museum.)

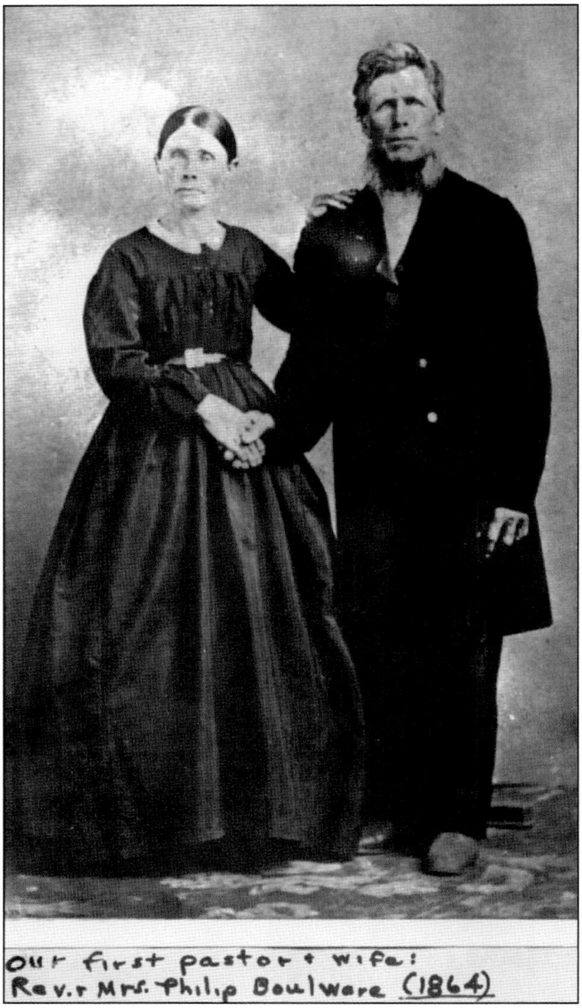

United Brethren Church began in 1884 where the cemetery now stands, known as North Live Oak before Gridley became a reality. Services were held at a tree stump and then in tents. Founder Philip Boulware built the first edifice there. The church was deeded 40 acres from John Keppel and John Hurburt in September 1865 within the city limits. In 1912, Biggs Methodist Church alternated services with Gridley Methodist-Episcopal Church; the name had changed to Evangelical United Brethren Church. Some of the first families to become members were the Boulwares, Sligars, and Davises. Pictured at left are the Boulwares; below is the then-new church building. (Both, courtesy of the United Methodist Church of Gridley.)

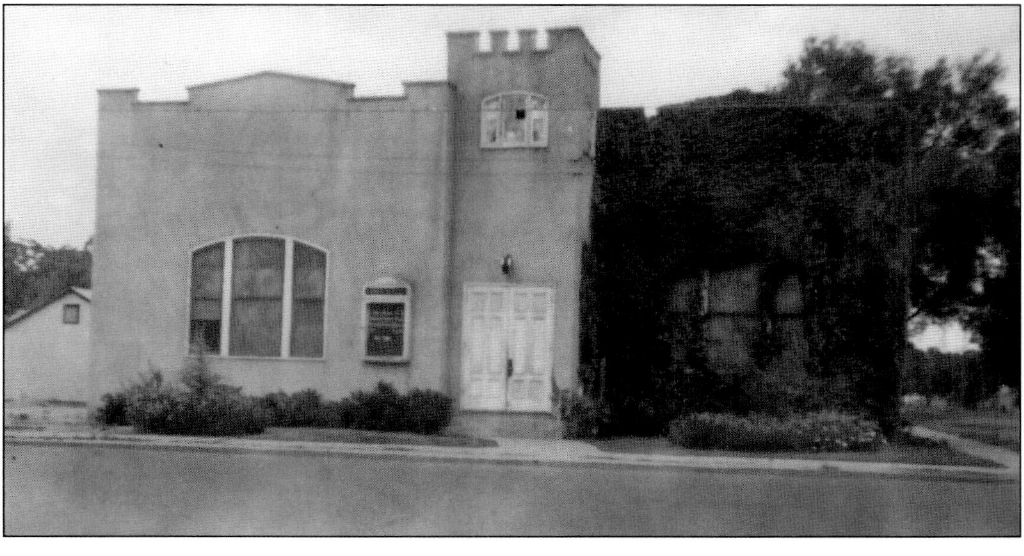

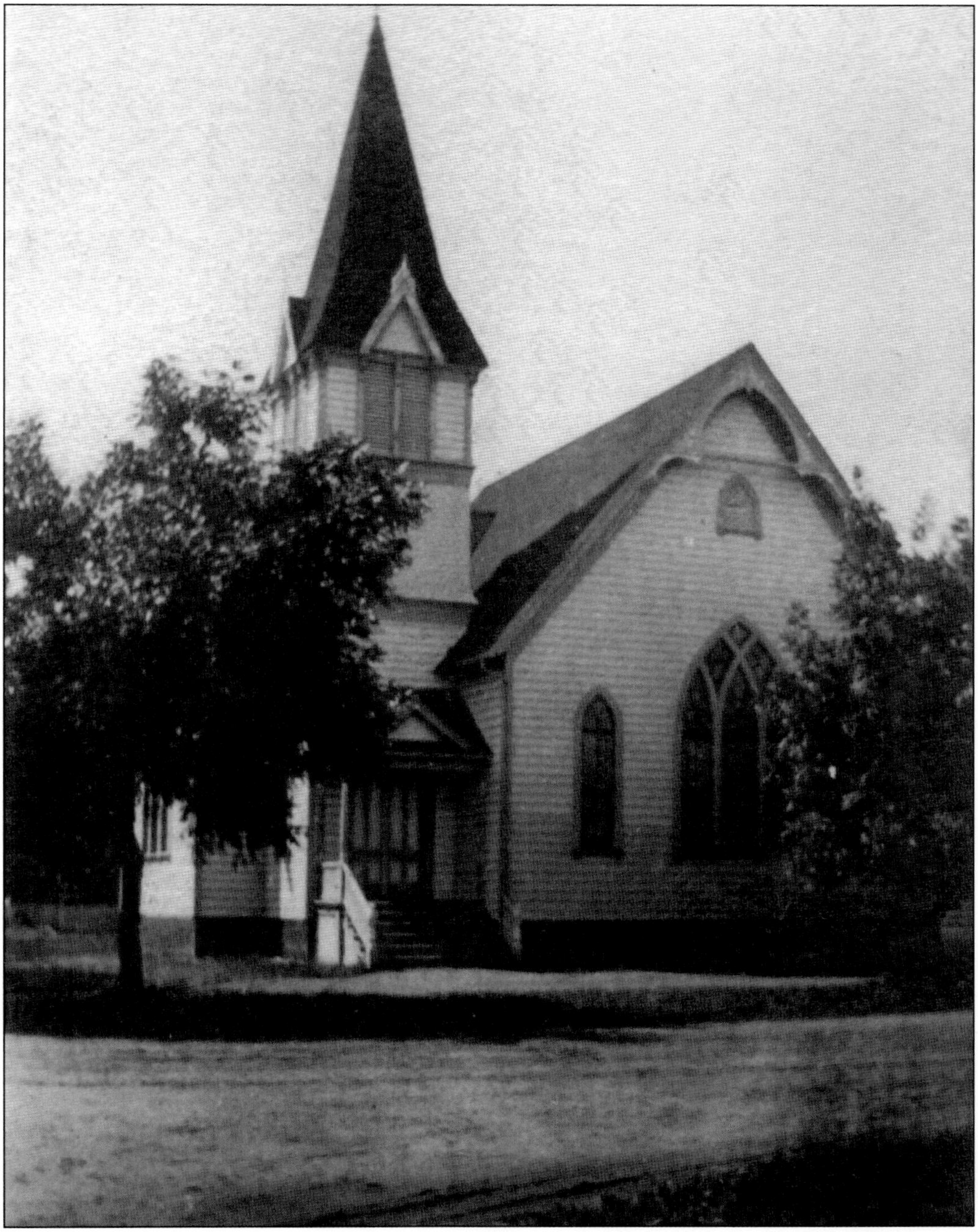

The lot for the Presbyterian church was donated by the Central Pacific Railroad Company, and John Bidwell donated $100. The building was dedicated on November 23, 1884. On August 23, 1891, fire spread from a house next door, and the building was destroyed. In 1892, the main part of the church was rebuilt. Due to slow growth, from October 1916 to December 1917, the church was closed. The Reverend Marcus Coen passed through Gridley and saw the boarded-up church. He had a feeling this was the place God had sent him. For several years, he supported his family by delivering the mail. Everywhere he delivered, he invited people to church. He did not blackmail them but made it clear that if they wanted their mail on time, they might want to come to church. By 1927, there were 188 members. (Courtesy of the Gridley Museum)

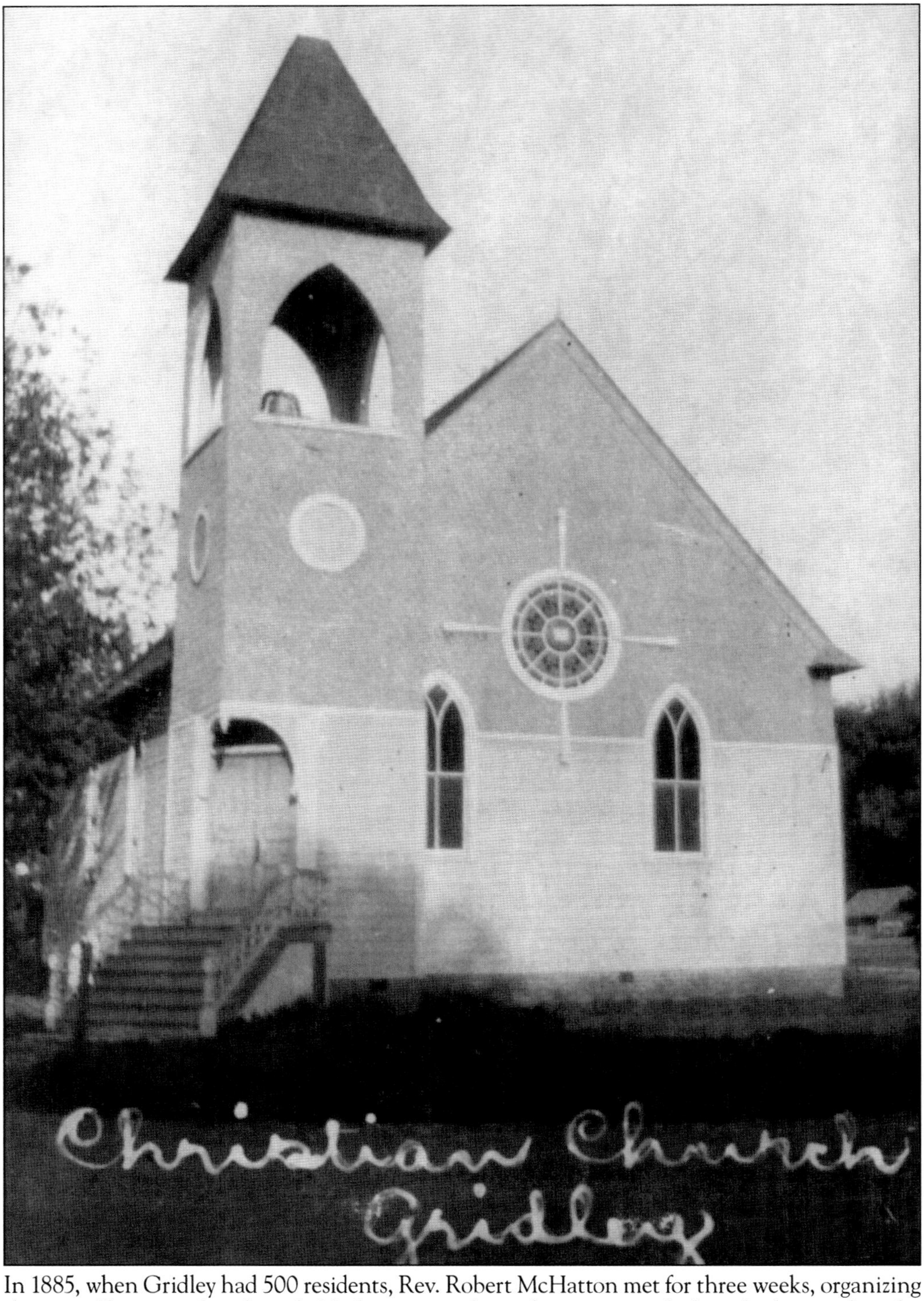

In 1885, when Gridley had 500 residents, Rev. Robert McHatton met for three weeks, organizing the new Christian church with 28 charter members, the majority of whom he baptized in the Feather River. They continued meeting in a one-story frame building on the corner of Ohio and Hazel Streets that became known as Christian Hall and was used until the present building was erected in 1900. (Courtesy of the *Gridley Herald*.)

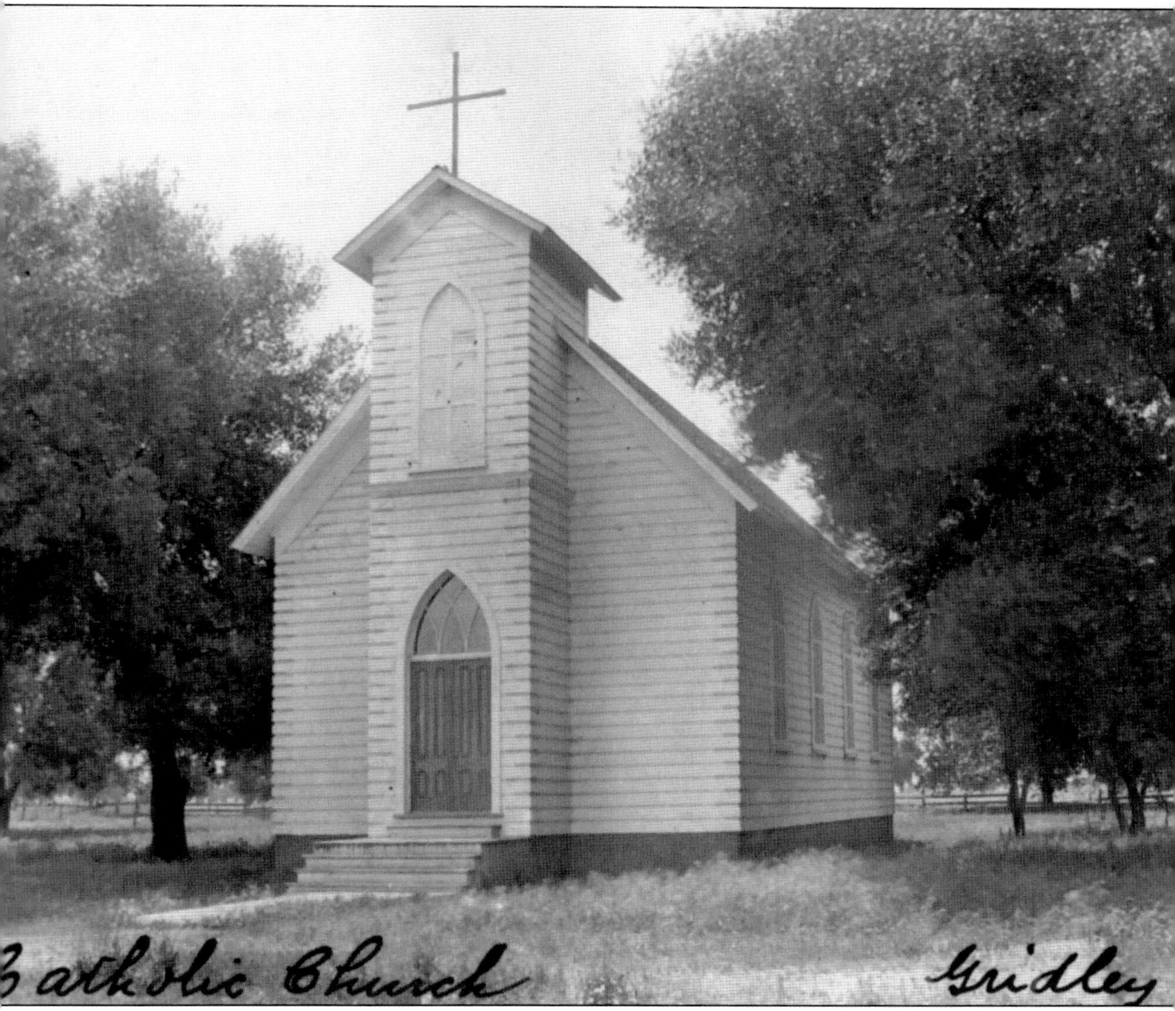

This Catholic church was dedicated on November 11, 1882, with Rev. Bishop O'Connor officiating. The building was on Ohio Street between Sycamore and Magnolia Streets. In later years, after the new church was built, it was used by the school district for the McKinley School pupils. (Courtesy of the Gridley Museum.)

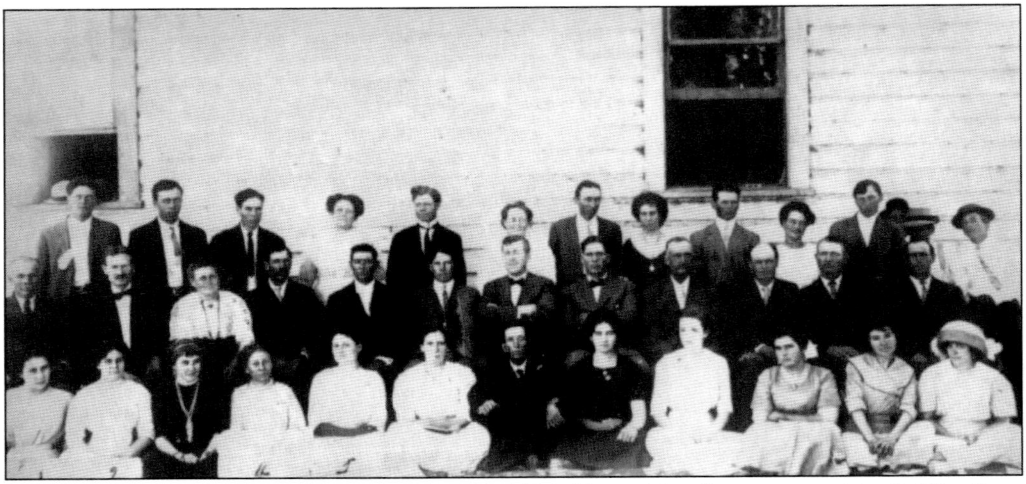

The *Gridley Herald* reported on November 22, 1906, "Latter-Day Saints arrived in Gridley from Rexburg, Idaho." The first Mormon settlers bought farms southwest of Gridley and began farming. They held their first sacrament meeting on December 10, 1906. Pictured above are, from left to right, (first row) Vida Sheppard, Ada Wilcox, Orlean Barrow, Mary Cole, Katie Price, Lucille Tolley, George Cole, Lillian Farr, Hazel Taylor, Edith Johnson, Mattie Black, and Clara Dewsnup; (second row) Frank Little, ? Herman, Emma Losser, unidentified, Frank Dewsnup, George Miller, and Joseph Robinson; (third row) Grover Cameron, Charles Swan, Melvin Richins, ? Hansen, Frank Terry, Lydia Barrow, Albert Hansen, Zoe Cole, David Smith, Winnie Smith, Jasper Cole, Raymond Quigley, and Albert Barrow. The church, built on the corner of Sycamore and Vermont Streets in 1912, cost $12,000 and sat 1,000 persons. George Tolley was in charge of the construction. (Both, courtesy of the Gridley Museum.)

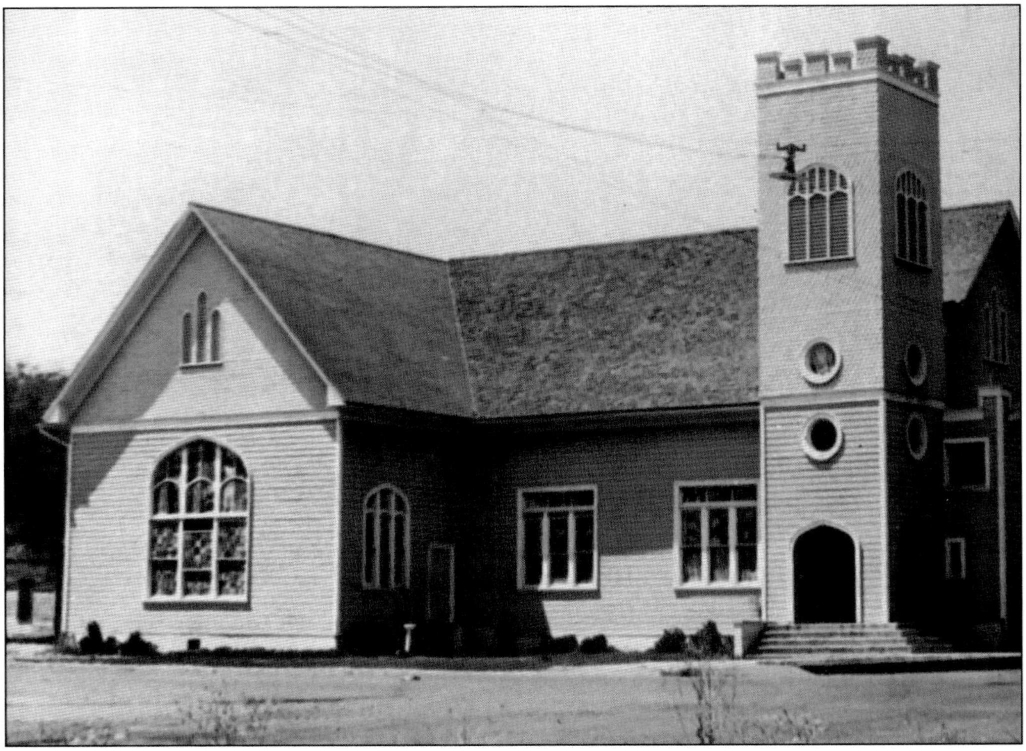

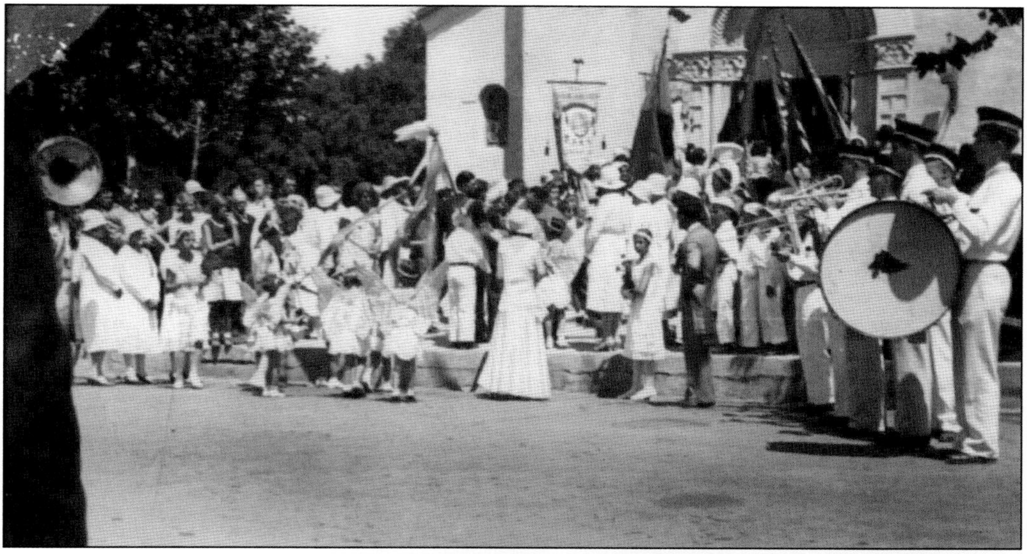

For the first 40 years of the 20th century, the Portuguese people were the most numerous of any immigrant population in Butte County. Among the fraternal and religious societies the Portuguese brought to the community is the Holy Trinity Association. The festa in Gridley, better known as the Portuguese Picnic, has a history of over 100 years. This celebration is observed with barbecues, parades, a little grappa, and dancing the chamarrita. Along with the traditional sopa and beef, unleavened sweet bread and potato salad are always served. The young lady at right is Mary Vierra Fawns, depicting Queen Isabel. (Both, courtesy of the Gridley Museum.)

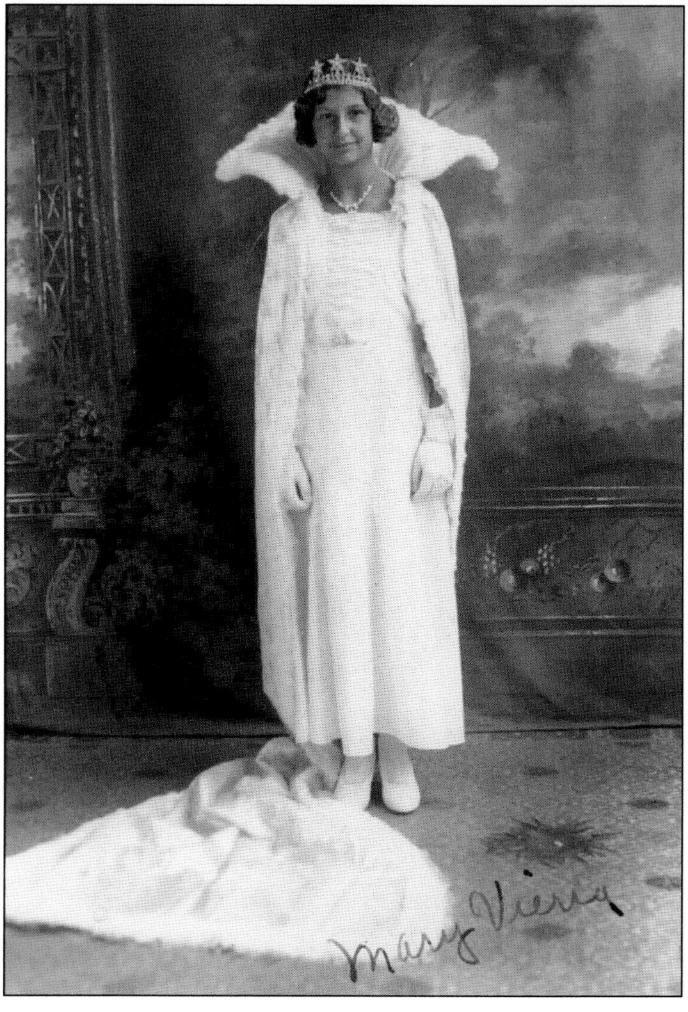

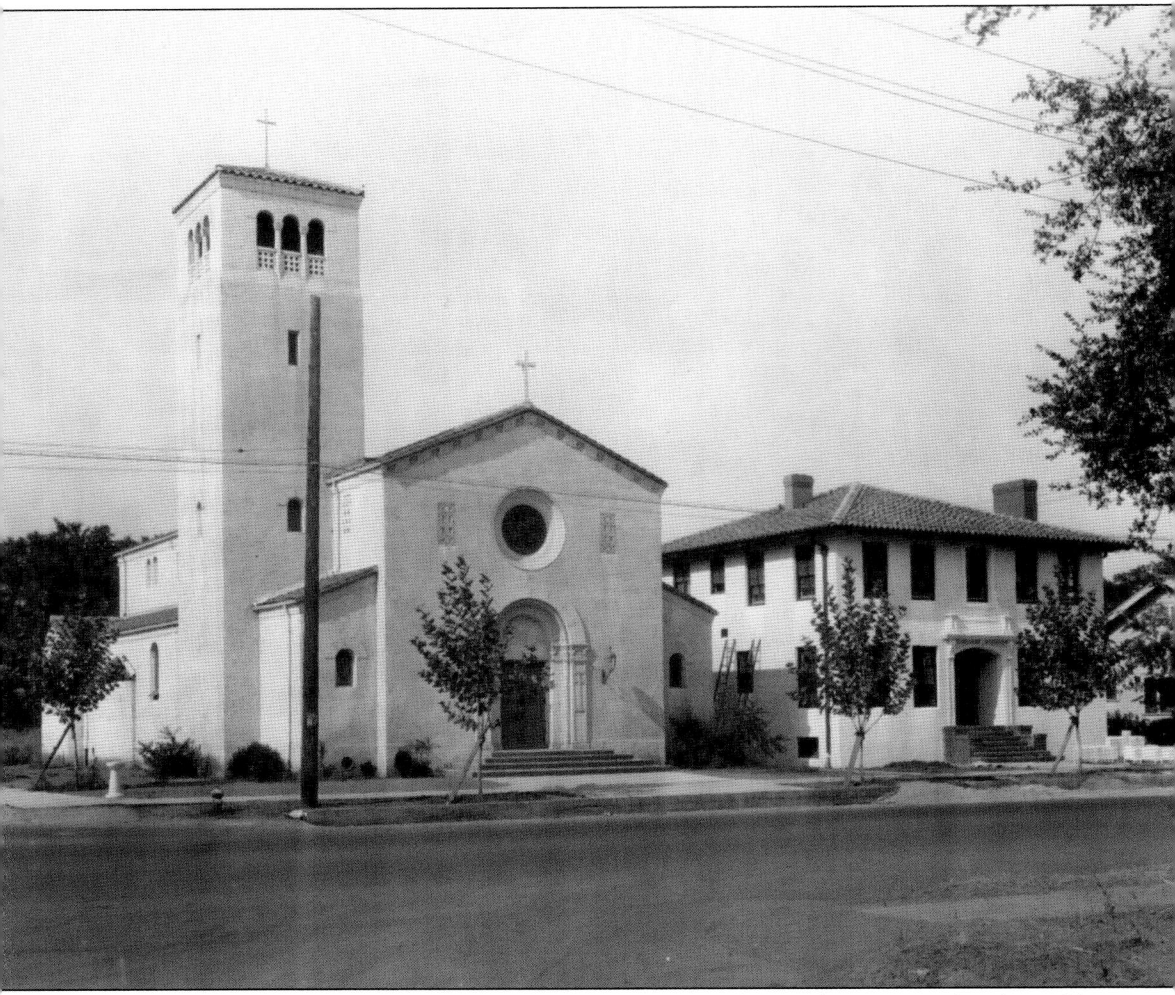

In 1929, Sacred Heart Catholic Church was built, replacing the smaller mission church on Ohio Street. It is in a Spanish style with beautiful stained-glass windows in memoriam of different family members. The debt of this church was paid off by potluck suppers, parties, and the fall festival held every year, as the collection plates did not quite provide enough funds. (Courtesy of the Gridley Museum.)

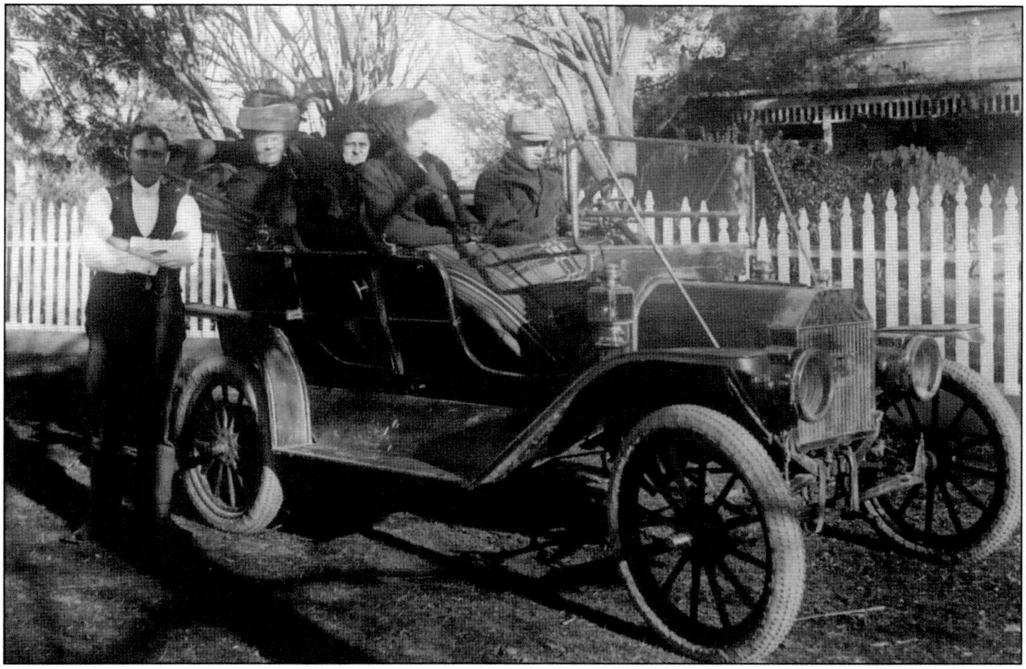

John Franklin Shaeffer served as the president of the Business Men's Association and was one of the substantial citizens of Butte County's thriving center of diversified farming, its largest grain grower, an indefatigable development worker, and a man who was identified with progress in that section for four decades. He had the first Ford dealerships in Gridley. He is show here standing beside his Ford with his wife and friends. (Courtesy of Tyrone Shaeffer.)

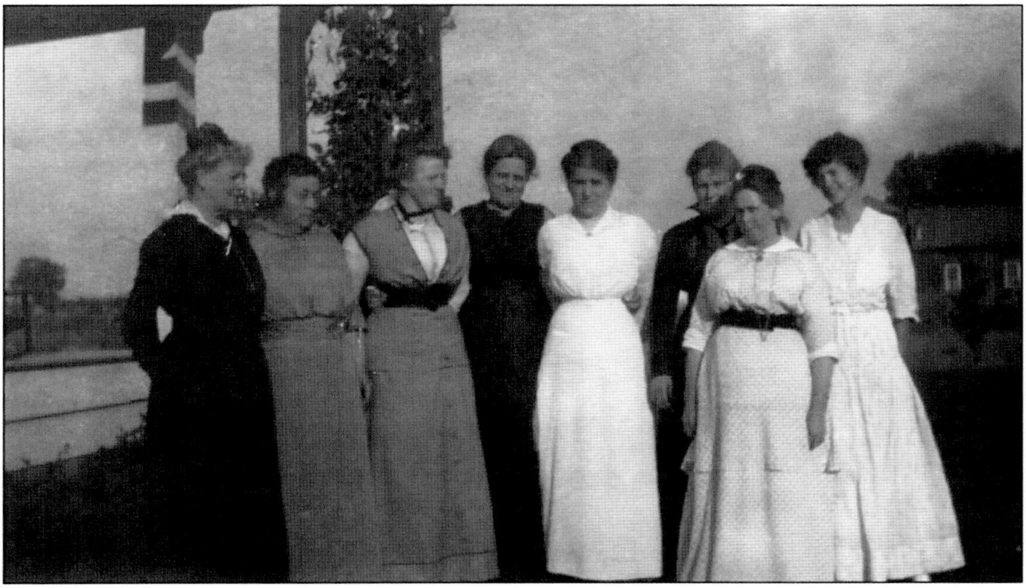

Women may not have had the vote, but that did not keep them from contributing to the development of the community. This was true in Gridley, where the organization known as the Ladies Improvement Club had a hand in several important projects, including construction of the municipal swimming pool. The most notable of the club's accomplishments was the establishment of the city library. (Courtesy of Tyrone Shaeffer.)

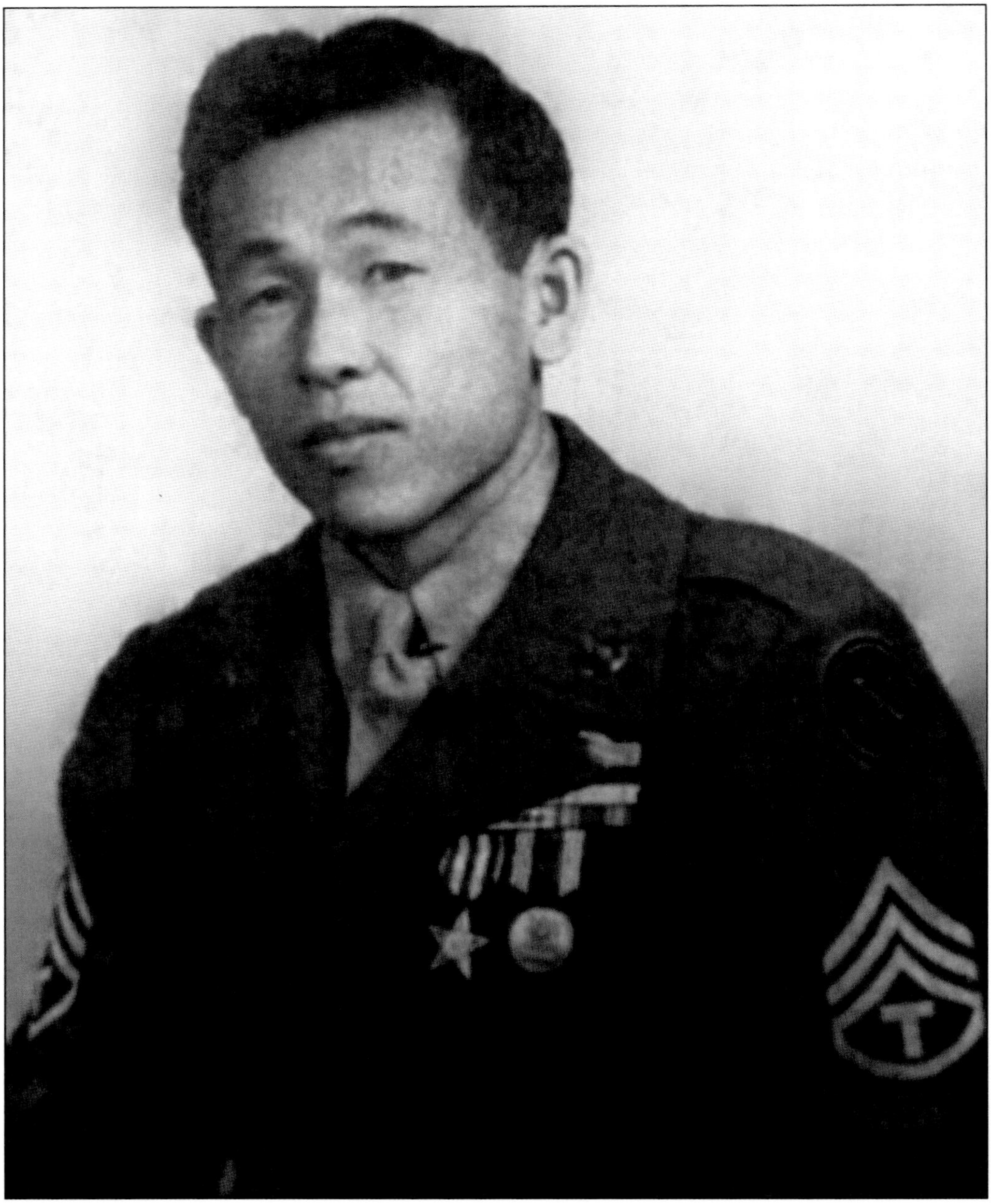

A Silver Star was awarded by the commanding general of the 27th Infantry Division to Shigeo Tanimoto for gallantry in action at Saipan on July 17, 1944. Tanimoto acted as an interpreter for an infantry regiment and voluntarily led a party of troops, including six Japanese civilians in custody, from a cave to safety. Prior to this act, he had assisted in removing six civilians from a ledge by swimming across a turbulent pool. (Courtesy of the Tanimoto family.)

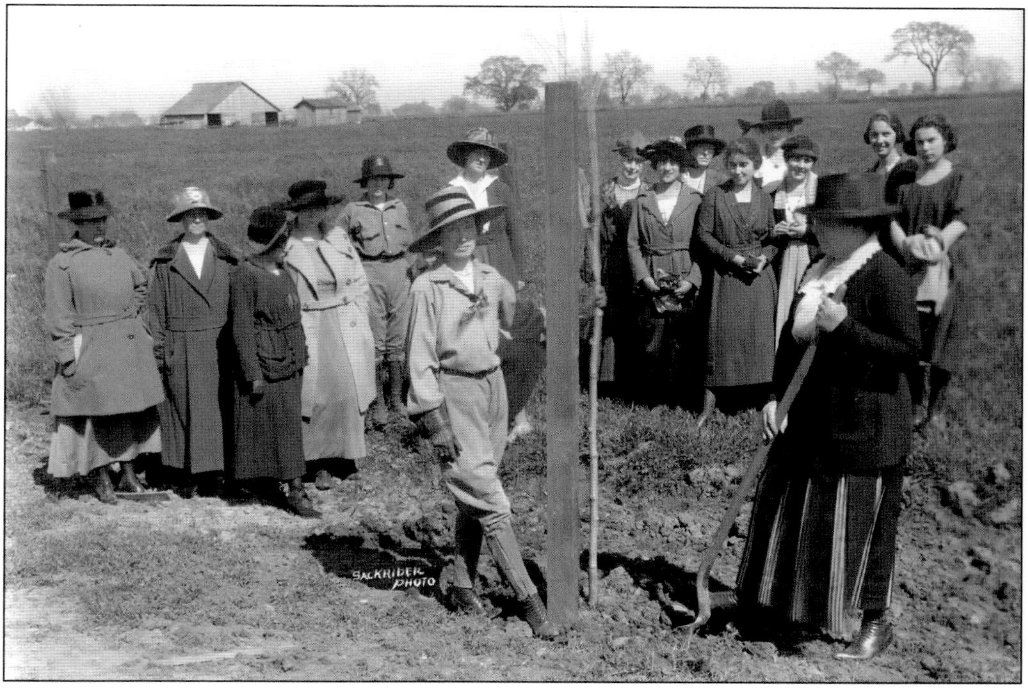

The Women's Improvement Club of Gridley spearheaded a planting of Oriental trees on the highway north and south of Gridley. This planting on March 7, 1921, resulted in a half holiday declared by every business, as well as farmers. People from the community congregated along the highway at noon. Martha Wickman, president of the club, is pictured at front right with the shovel. (Courtesy of the Gridley Museum.)

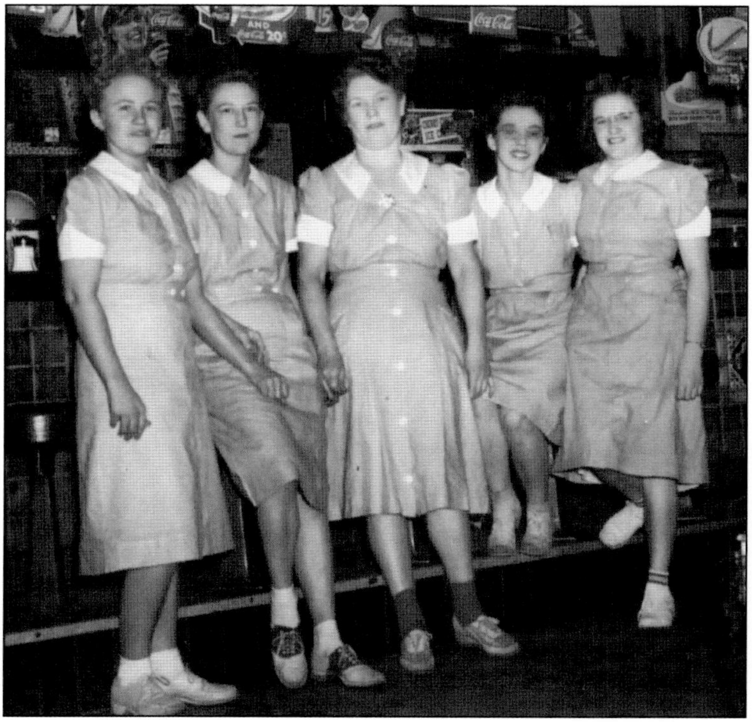

Pictured here in 1941 is the soda fountain at the Gridley Pharmacy. These fountains were popular lunch stops for merchants. They had sandwiches and ice cream, milkshakes, and sodas. The waitresses all wore uniforms, and the only one identified here is second from the left: Alice Vierra. Fred Schoen was the proprietor. (Courtesy of the *Gridley Herald*.)

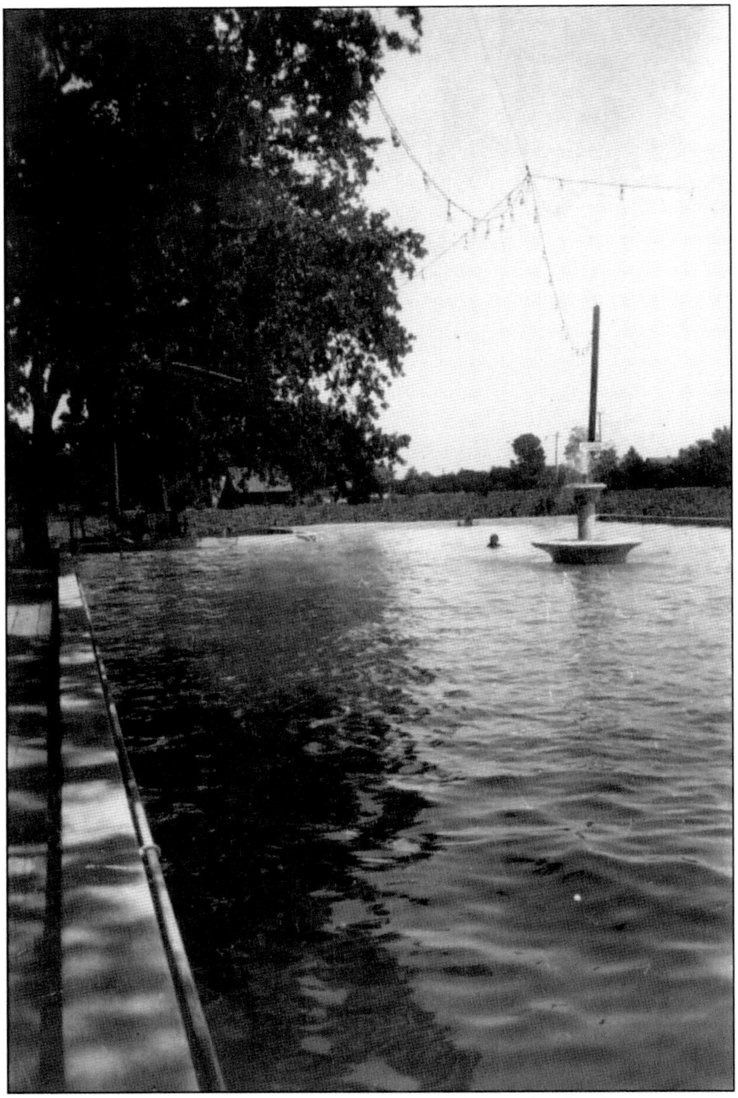

A cool dip on a hot day was an activity for the entire family. The Gridley Community Swimming Pool was a great place to cool off in the scorching summer heat. Although this pool, situated in the city municipal park, was not filtered, it was drained two times a week and refilled with cold refreshing water. The pool was another project of the Ladies' Improvement Club. It originally had a fountain in the middle and a diving board at the west end. (Both, courtesy of the *Gridley Herald*.)

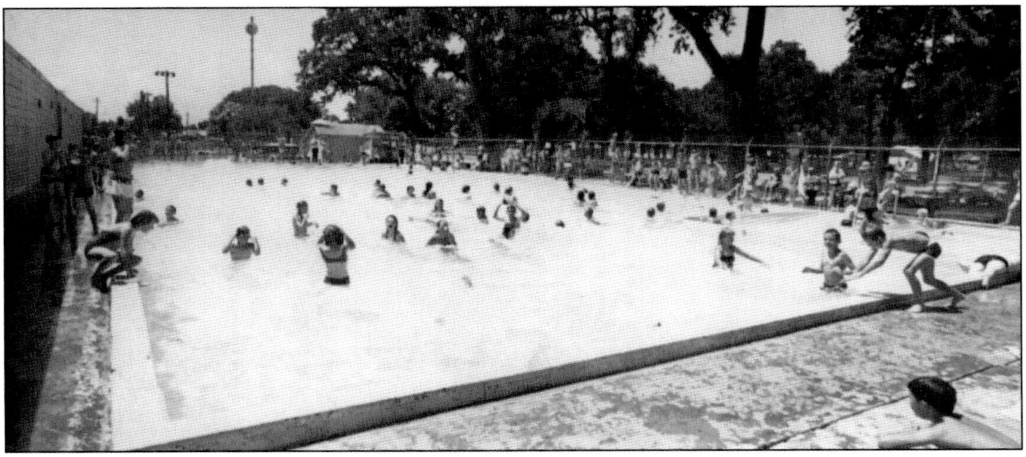

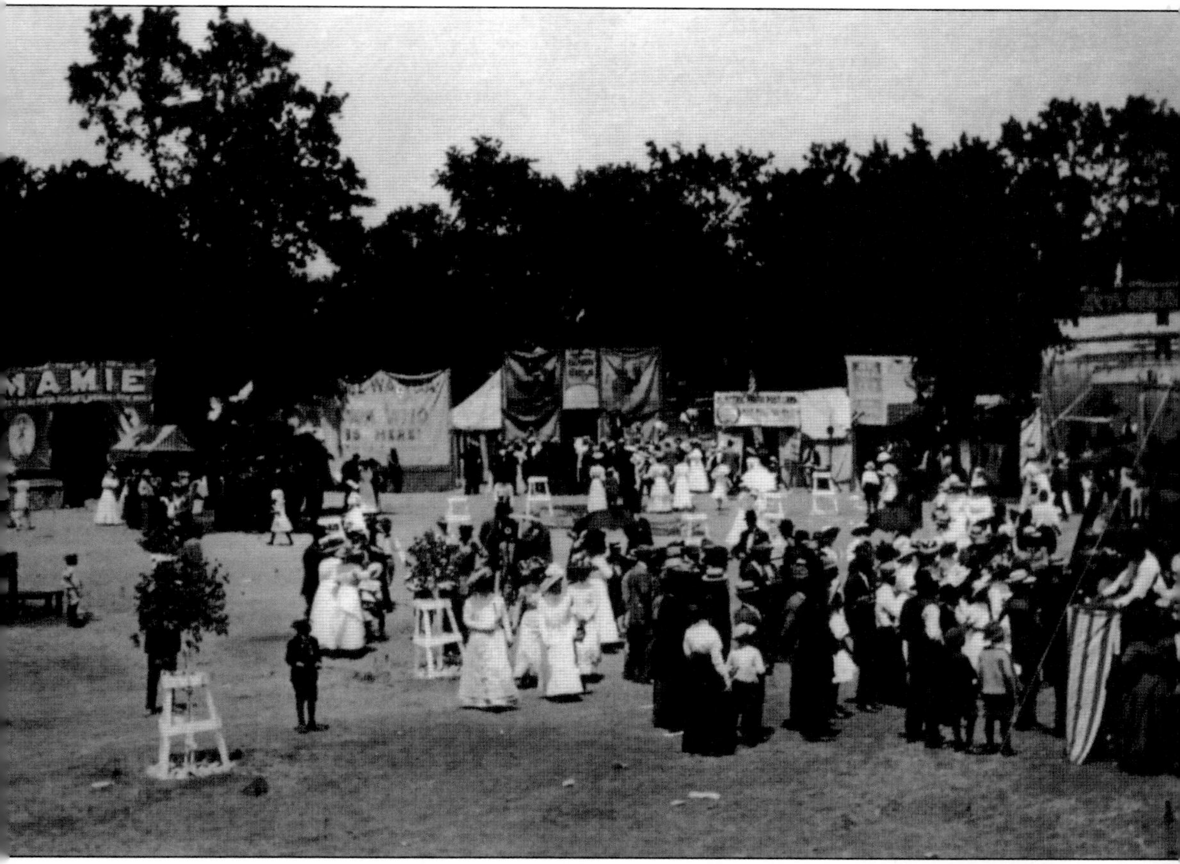

The annual cannery picnic, a local celebration that drew residents of the county and valley from far and near, began at Gridley at the time its first cannery was completed. This annual affair, held in the municipal park south of town near the cannery, was an occasion looked forward to for weeks by the young people of the area. Carnivals, circuses, dancing, barbecues, and a good baseball game were important features. Here, a large crowd is enjoying a fair atmosphere. (Courtesy of Butte County Historical Society.)

Discover Thousands of Local History Books Featuring Millions of Vintage Images

Arcadia Publishing, the leading local history publisher in the United States, is committed to making history accessible and meaningful through publishing books that celebrate and preserve the heritage of America's people and places.

Find more books like this at
www.arcadiapublishing.com

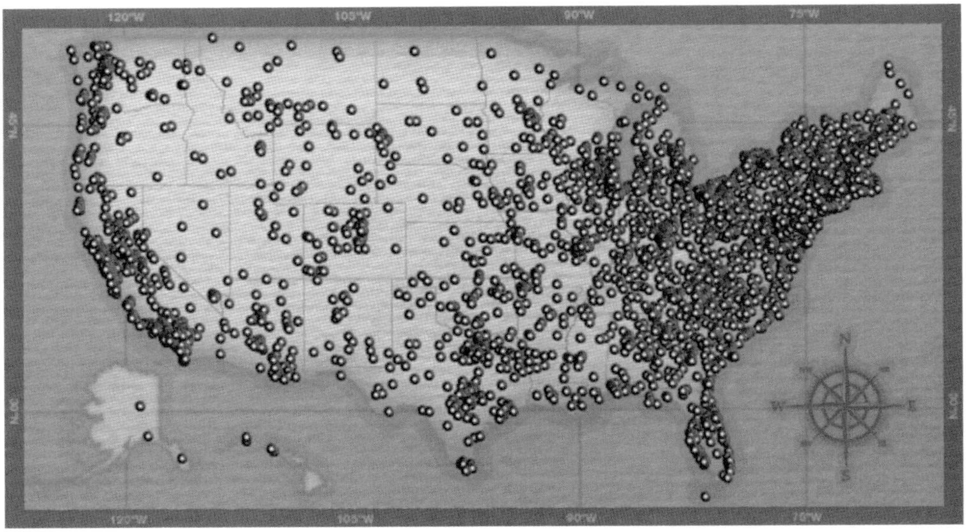

Search for your hometown history, your old stomping grounds, and even your favorite sports team.

Consistent with our mission to preserve history on a local level, this book was printed in South Carolina on American-made paper and manufactured entirely in the United States. Products carrying the accredited Forest Stewardship Council (FSC) label are printed on 100 percent FSC-certified paper.

MADE IN THE USA